Contents

Ireland the magazine 5

Finding Your Feet 33

Dublin 45

Eastern Ireland 71

Southwest Ireland 93

Written by Christopher Somerville
Where to sections by local contributors

Copy edited by Audrey Ho
Page layout by Barfoot Design
Verified by Letitia Pollard and Des Caulfield
Indexed by Marie Lorimer

Verified and updated by Penny Phenix

Edited, designed and produced by AA Publishing
© Automobile Association Developments Limited 2000, 2002, 2005
Third edition
Reprinted July 2005

Northern Ireland mapping reproduced by permission
of the Ordnance Survey of Northern Ireland on behalf
of the Controller of Her Majesty's Stationery Office ©
Crown copyright 2005. Permit No. 50113.

Republic of Ireland mapping based on Ordnance Survey Ireland.
Permit No. 7954.
© Ordnance Survey Ireland and Government of Ireland.

Mapping produced by the Cartographic Department of the Automobile
Association Developments Limited.

Published in the United States by AAA Publishing,
1000 AAA Drive, Heathrow, Florida 32746
Published in the United Kingdom by AA Publishing

ISBN-10: 1-59508-0376
ISBN-13: 978-1-59508-037-0

Cover design and binding style by permission of AA Publishing

Colour separation by Keenes, Andover
Printed and bound in China by Leo Paper Products

10 9 8 7 6 5 4 3 2

A02734

Ireland

the magazine

Ireland leaves memories, warm and indelible, with everyone who visits her. Living here in County Mayo, on the west coast, I am fortunate to be able to share those memories and search out new experiences with visiting musicians and others who pass by and often stay. Mayo has a magical quality. As a traditional Irish musician and visitors' guide, I meet many people – walkers, artists, photographers – who come here to experience that magic.

My Ireland

OLCAN MASTERSON, traditional musician

Cultural vistas and timescapes tell their own story. Ancient hazel woods hide the remains of habitations built 7,000 years ago. Pilgrim feet still tread pathways that pass megalithic standing stones and early Christian oratories. Famine potato ridges stripe the land. All this is a lasting testament of the Celtic heritage that surrounds me.

The rhythms of Celtic culture inspire Ireland's musicians and artists

Gigantic upheavals have moulded the landscape. Some of the tallest cliffs in Europe rise from bays and inlets carved by glaciation. Croagh Patrick, Ireland's Holy Mountain, sweeps down to Clew Bay – a wonderful place to meander the channels, cruising past islands,

beaches, sheltered harbours and clear waters. Visitors often comment on the purity and clarity of the light out here and sunset on Clew Bay, whether gazed at by a walker from the top of Croagh Patrick or framed by a photographer in a camera lens, is, I think, the most beautiful sight you can see.

Over 200 islands stud the waters of Clew Bay; hump-backed Clare Island stands as sentinel of them all. They hold many secrets. I know an island where a 7th-century stone-carved oil lamp lies on an altar built by early Irish Christian monks.

The castles and fortresses of Grace O'Malley, one of Ireland's greatest clan chieftains, guard the inlets of

> **"My Irish music has taken me to play in different parts of the world, but it is Ireland, and especially the music and landscape of County Mayo, that nurtures my art."**

Achill and Newport Bay. Westport House, in my home town of Westport, was built on the foundations of an O'Malley castle, overlooking the harbour and bay against a backdrop of sweeping mountains and valleys.

Westport, one of the few architecturally planned towns in Ireland, is a welcoming and friendly place. Fishing boats tie up at the quay, the anglers beaming with pride over their day's catch. The restaurants and small bars hum with activity. In the evenings music flows from nimble-fingered musicians sharing the rhythm with dancing feet. A singer commands all ears with renditions of local songs and humorous tales.

Over the years, my Irish music has taken me to play in different parts of the world, but it is Ireland, and especially the music and landscape of County Mayo, that nurtures my art. I can but only try to interpret what it gives back to me, and hope I do it justice.

I am, indeed, fortunate to be able to share my Ireland.

Music and landscape, meditation and conversation: Olcan Masterson's Ireland

SPEAKING OF IRELAND...

For the great Gaels of Ireland
  Are the men that God made mad,
For all their wars are merry,
  And all their songs are sad.
G K Chesterton,
Ballad of the White Horse

"Ireland is an infernal country
to manage...the graveyard of
every reputation."
**Benjamin Disraeli,
19th-century British politician**

Connemara – the name drifts
across the mind like cloud shadows on a mountainside, or
expands and fades like circles on
a lake after a trout has
risen...How can I indicate this
Connemara, but as the edge of
brightness that follows a cloud
shadow across the mountainside,
or the stillness of a lake before
the trout rises?
Tim Robinson,
Connemara

**"The Irish are a fair
people; they never
speak well of one
another."
Dr Samuel Johnson,
18th-century essayist,
journalist and
lexicographer**

I am short-sighted; I am
also of Irish extraction;
both facts that make for
toleration...
Somerville & Ross,
Experiences of an Irish RM

*Nelson's Pillar in Dublin, once
a city landmark, was
demolished as a symbol of
British Imperialism*

Before Nelson's Pillar
trams slowed, shunted,
changed trolley, started for
Blackrock, Kingstown and
Dalkey, Clonskea, Rathgar
and Terenure, Palmerston park and upper Rathmines,
Sandymount Green, Rathmines, Ringsend and Sandymount
Tower, Harold's Cross. The hoarse Dublin United Tramway
Company's timekeeper bawled them off:
– Rathgar and Terenure!
– Come on, Sandymount Green!
James Joyce, *Ulysses*

Falls Road mural, Belfast

I particularly remember those stark murals, colourful and grotesque, which have come to be part of Belfast, and part of the historic expression of the people and their city.
Brian Keenan,
An Evil Cradling

You can't get into the soup in Ireland, do what you like.
Evelyn Waugh,
Decline and Fall

Spirit of freedom at Belfast's carnival

THE CRAIC

You'll hear about it everywhere you go in Ireland. The word sounds like "crack", and the English write it like that – short, sharp and brusque, a shape entirely at odds with the word's true meaning. The Irish do it better: they write it as *craic*, a gentler idea altogether. It means, simply, a good time.

As much as the Book of Kells or the Blarney Stone, the Giant's Causeway or the Cliffs of Moher, people come to Ireland in search of the *craic*. You might discover it while lazing under a hedge in County Kerry in the company of travellers. You could stumble across it bubbling away in the kitchen

> **"The craic is a mood, something in the air that can blow in out of nowhere."**

The *Craic* Excited

"...So then the door flies open and in comes a man fit for dancing and he gets up on the floor there and starts into the jig. By this time there's a fiddle going and the whole room dancing...Fierce nice! Ah, the craic was mighty, all right..."
Kerry musician in conversation

Dublin musicians let fly, fuelling the craic

of some anonymous bungalow in a suburb of Belfast or Dublin. It's more than likely to come your way among the horse-racing gamblers at The Curragh of Kildare, or the yelling fans at a hurling match, or Trinity College students celebrating just about anything. And it's a guaranteed certainty that you'll find the *craic* wherever musicians or storytellers, country farmers or city youngsters form a circle round a few pints of stout.

The *craic* is a mood, something in the air that can blow in out of nowhere. It is a bottomless pot into which anyone may throw anything. But the rich stew of the *craic* generally contains one or more of the following ingredients: music, lively chat, a spice of argument, a pinch of nonsense, a drop of strong drink or a sup of tea, a bite of food, and laughter – a gallon of laughter. The *craic* wears

different guises, according to what's going on and who's taking part. It could be great *craic* just sitting and listening in a remote country pub where locals have gathered to sift through their well-worn stock of jokes, songs and tall tales; or huddled out of the rain in a tin hut with two blarneying roadmen; or being whirled round by a total stranger in some unfamiliar dance at a village céilidh. Or the *craic* might be mightier still in an overcrowded bar in city-centre Belfast where the jokes fly black and strong, or among a clutch of elegant girls with their heads together round a table in Dublin's trendy Temple Bar district.

Sometimes you pass it by, grin and keep on going; sometimes it reaches out and sucks you in.

This has to do with the Irish way of viewing the stranger as a bundle of possibilities, the chance provider of a story, song or bit of chat, rather than as a potential threat or source of embarrassment. When you enter a bar or a shop, you can expect to be sized up, questioned and drawn into conversation. There's nothing rude or sinister in this; it's just a very friendly nosiness, a hospitable opening of the door.

People can get all snobbish about the *craic*, holding that it cannot possibly rear its head around manufactured tourist events such as medieval banquets at Bunratty Castle, or busloads of visitors kissing the Blarney Stone. But it can, and does. The *craic* operates its own set of checks and balances,

"Sometimes you pass it by, grin and keep on going; sometimes it reaches out and sucks you in."

You may find the craic in the crowd at The Curragh...

The *Craic* Exalted

Now when the voyage is over
And we are safe and well,
We will go into a public house
And there we'll drink like hell;
We will drink strong ale and
    porter
And make the rafters roar,
And when our money is all
    spent
We will go to sea once more.

from the song "The Holy Ground"

teasing a song out of the woman who swears she can't sing a note to save her life, curbing an aggressive drunk by its good humour, putting wind under the wings of a yarn spinner.

Essentially the craic is about good manners, and having a decent regard for your neighbour, however wild the company and copious the flow of drink.

So don't be scared to join in the *craic*. Put a song or a story into the pot, and you'll give pleasure, and receive it, too. And though everyone hopes that you will contribute, no one expects or demands it. Just relax, hang loose, enjoy the moment... that's exactly what the *craic* is all about.

...over a pint of porter in a pub...

...or dancing to the beat at a city celebration

The *Craic* Exported

The craic was good in Cricklewood,
So they wouldn't leave the Crown;
With glasses flyin' and biddies cryin'
The Paddies was going to town...
Oh Mother dear, I'm over here,
And I never will go back;
What keeps me here? The rake of beer,
The women – and the craic!

from the popular song "McAlpine's Fusiliers"

Movers and Shakers

St Patrick

The patron saint of Ireland was a lad of 16 when Irish pirates lifted him from his native Wales, around the time the Romans were beginning to leave Britain. After six years' enslavement as a shepherd, he escaped from Ireland, getting away to Britain on a ship loaded with a cargo of wolfhounds. Few details are known of the time Patrick spent wandering and studying in Gaul, on the Continent. He became a priest and was consecrated bishop in 432 in order to lead a mission to Ireland. Landing in County Down, he set about converting the island to Christianity.

By the time he died, around 461, the Welsh-born missionary had seen his message take root all across Ireland. A confrontational approach with the local chieftains and druid-priests would have achieved little except his own summary execution. But Patrick, subtle man, preferred to work with existing sacred places and established customs, not abolishing them but changing their focus from pagan to Christian. The Irish responded by grafting the new religion onto their old beliefs, and Patrick had the satisfaction of watching it flourish.

Shepherd on Slemish

It was on the slopes of Slemish Mountain, the cone of an extinct volcano just east of Ballymena in Country Antrim, that St Patrick herded sheep as teenage captive of the local chieftain, Miluic.

St Patrick, the shepherd slave who became Ireland's first and greatest saint

Fionn MacCumhaill (Finn McCool)

Who dares say that Fionn MacCumhaill never existed? Evidence of the Irish hero's mighty deeds is littered all over Ireland, from the rock near Sligo that he split with an angry sword-stroke to the quoit (the massive flat stone from a dolmen tomb) that he threw 100km (62 miles) from the Bog of Allen to Howth Head. Every one of his warrior band, the Fianna Éireann, could write a poem, catch a wild boar, fend off nine spears in one instant, and pick a thorn out of his foot while running at full speed. How many Irish youngsters have been inspired by these tales of the inextinguishable Fionn MacCumhaill, a very literal mover and shaker?

Dervorgilla O'Rourke

The course of Irish history was shaken forever by Dervorgilla, wife of Sligo chieftain Tiernán O'Rourke of Breifne. In 1152, at the age of 44, she had a year-long affair with rival lord Dermot MacMurrough, king of Leinster. Banished several years later for his misconduct, MacMurrough appealed to the Norman Earl of Pembroke, Richard de Clare, aptly nicknamed Strongbow, and in 1169 Strongbow and his men came over to Ireland. This was followed soon afterwards by a full-scale invasion by Norman knights, the start of centuries of Anglo-Irish friction and bloodshed.

Oliver Cromwell

Oliver Cromwell crushed 17th-century Catholic resistance with brutal authority

The Lord Protector of England made it his business to come over to Ireland in 1649, when it looked as if Roman Catholic rebels were getting the upper hand over the Protestant incomers who had been granted Irish land since Tudor times. Cromwell landed in Dublin with his own trained, dedicated army of 20,000 tough, battle-hardened Ironsides. Within three years of merciless campaigning the rebels had been crushed, and hundreds of thousands lay dead. The Catholic landed gentry of Ireland had been forced west into the wastes of Connacht and stripped of their civil rights, while Cromwell's middle-class Protestant backers took over their property.

This was a brutal slam of the door on Ireland's Catholic and Celtic heritage – but, as things turned out, not a final one.

GUINNESS AS USUAL

THERE'S NOTHING LIKE A GUINNESS

Arthur Guinness

Ireland's international image owes much to Arthur Guinness, who in 1759 bought up little Rainsford's Brewery at St James's Gate in Dublin and started black-roasting his malt. His legacy persists in the heady malt and hop smells that waft across Dublin, and in 2.5 million white-froth moustaches gladly worn in over 120 countries worldwide every day.

Daniel O'Connell

"The Liberator", Daniel O'Connell earned his title through the work he did in the 1820s in giving Ireland's Catholic poor a voice in Parliament. O'Connell organised them, won their backing, and was swept in as their representative in Westminster in a landslide election victory in 1828. However, as a Catholic O'Connell was not permitted to take his seat until 1829. In that year the Catholic Emancipation Act became law thanks to O'Connell's involvement in organising enormous, non-violent mass meetings across Ireland in support of the country's right to run its own affairs. Sadly, he was to die at Genoa in 1847 a sick and sidelined man, his peaceful methods having failed to win Home Rule for the Irish.

Dan's Duel

O'Connell had a hectic private life and a past that cast shadows of remorse over his life – in particular a duel he fought in 1815, in which he killed his opponent. The fatal pistol is preserved, along with other O'Connell memorabilia, in his house at Derrynane, County Kerry (▶ 103).

Michael Collins and Éamon de Valera

Michael Collins and Éamon de Valera, who between them oversaw the birth of an independent Ireland, were magnets for polarised opinions, icons at whose shrines bitterly divided opponents still worship. Collins led the British by the nose throughout the War of Independence, but came to see how the cause of Irish nationalism could only move forward on the back of a compromise settlement with the old enemy. The foundations for an independent Ireland were dug just as much by Collins as they were by Éamon de Valera, motivator of the hardline Irish Republican Army (IRA). De Valera had to endure a period in the wilderness after

Top left: "Swaggering Dan" O'Connell in 1830, at the height of his personal influence and popularity

Above: Éamon de Valera rallied republican support at passionate public meetings

Right: Mary Robinson, Ireland's first woman president

the IRA's defeat in the Civil War 1922–23, but he came back to lead his country through its final severance with Britain.

Mary Robinson

Mary Robinson's election as president of the Republic of Ireland in 1990 was a potent symbol of the social change that was sweeping the country. She was the first woman president, a constitutional lawyer known to have strong left-wing political views and to be a champion of human rights and minority causes. During her seven years in office she captured the high ground, going out to meet the people, saying yes to interviews, listening sympathetically to the views of northern Unionists, and throwing her personal and official weight behind Ireland's drive to modernise and develop.

When Mary Robinson took office, the presidency had little more than a ceremonial function. By the time she relinquished it in 1997, to take on an international role as United Nations High Commissioner for Human Rights, it had been reinvented as a dynamic focus for change.

Hunger and Home Rule...these two issues long dominated Irish history. Hunger blighted the middle decades of the 19th century, while Home Rule grew into the principal agenda as that century drew to its close.

FAMINE

Hunger had always been a fact of life among Ireland's Roman Catholic poor. During the 18th century the population had quadrupled, and by the 1840s had reached 9 million – most of

education perfunctory or non-existent. In retrospect, it was a disaster waiting to happen – and it did. In 1845 the *Phytophthora infestans* fungus arrived in Ireland, and potato blight spread rapidly through the country.

At first the British government provided assistance directly, through food depots; then changed their policy, organising relief work projects on which men, women and children laboured at often futile tasks – building unwanted roads, for example – to earn money to pay for corn

Hunger and Home Rule

them living chiefly on potatoes. The potato was nutritious and easy to tend, ideal staple food for a peasant population rapidly increasing on ever-smaller, subdivided parcels of land. Theirs was a precarious existence, subject to the need to pay rent to an all-too-often absentee English landlord. For the peasant millions there was no security of tenure, no social security structure, no hope of betterment. Roads were few and poor, hospitals scarce,

❝And the potato fungus disease kept returning, in 1845, 1846, 1848, 1849, reducing the tubers to stinking black slime.❞

meal. Poor Law Unions set up workhouses and fever hospitals. But such relief was never enough, and never sufficiently widespread or well organised. People died of starvation and disease – cholera, typhus, relapsing fever, infantile diarrhoea. And the potato fungus disease kept returning, in 1845, 1846, 1848, 1849, reducing the tubers to stinking black slime.

Milk, beef and corn continued to be produced in Ireland, but had to be sold to pay the landlords' rents. And many of the landlords themselves were too poor to fund relief, which after June 1847 became their legal, and sole, responsibility. The Great Famine of 1845–50 was an unmitigated catastrophe. Perhaps a million people died. Another 1.5 million emigrated to the USA, Canada and the UK, the start of a mass exodus from under-funded rural areas which continues today. The famine changed the face of Ireland; the country, particularly out west, is still feeling the impact. The Great Hunger had another effect, too: it heightened anti-English sentiments in Ireland and fanned anew the flames of nationalism.

not till then let my epitaph be written."

Through the 19th century the uprisings went on: Young Ireland in 1848, the Irish Republican Brotherhood (IRB) – formed simultaneously in Dublin and New York in 1858 and also known as the Fenians – in 1865 and 1867. But it wasn't until Charles Stewart Parnell rose to prominence as a reforming Irish Member of Parliament at Westminster in the 1870s and 1880s that the Home Rule movement, which called for the establishment of an Irish Parliament in Dublin,

REBELLION

Through the centuries there had been active attempts to win independence from the English, not all of them initiated by southern Catholics. Wolfe Tone, who attempted a French-assisted landing and uprising in 1798, was an Ulster (Northern Irish) Protestant. Robert Emmet, whose 1803 rebellion ended in failure, was also Protestant. The speech he made before being hanged contained a sentence that inspired several generations of nationalists: "When my country takes her place among the nations of the earth, then and

took top place on the political agenda. The Home Rule Act was passed in 1914 and promptly suspended for the duration of World War I.

THE EASTER RISING

This suspension was too much for the Irish Republican Brotherhood, which initiated the Easter Rising of 1916. Led by labour union organiser James Connolly and school-teacher-poet Pádraic Pearse, the rebels (numbering less than 2,000) took over a number of public buildings in Dublin and from the steps of the General Post Office proclaimed Ireland's

British Army soldiers soon put down the Easter Rising of 1916

independence from Britain and the birth of the Republic. Within a week the Rising had been crushed. The rebels were largely ignored by the Irish public at first, but opinion began to turn against the English as, one by one, 15 leaders of the rising were shot in Dublin's Kilmainham Gaol (► 58–9) the following month. It sowed the seed for success at the ballot box in 1918 for the republican Sinn Féin political party, and brought about demands for withdrawal of British troops – something the British government could not countenance. The new Sinn Féin MPs refused to take their seats at Westminster, meeting in Dublin to declare independence for Ireland. The former Irish Republican Brotherhood, renamed the Irish Republican Army (IRA), became Sinn Féin's military wing and began to mobilise for war with Britain.

THE WAR OF INDEPENDENCE

In 1919 the savage War of Independence began. For two years ambushes, bombings and guerrilla raids on the part of

the IRA were matched by counter-raids and arrests on the part of the British – not to mention undisciplined burning, ransacking and killing by the special recruits (known as the Black and Tans because of the colour of their uniform), sent in by the British to control the situation. The dust settled in 1921, when a truce was followed by the signing of the Anglo-Irish Treaty. This effectively allowed for partition of the Six Counties of Ulster (where there was a Protestant majority wishing to maintain the Union with Britain) from the 26 counties of the newly born Irish Free State.

Above: barricades and rubble littered the streets of Dublin during Easter Week 1916

Above right: Protestant landowner Charles Stewart Parnell championed the cause of Home Rule in the 1870s and 1880s

Radical elements in the IRA could not accept the terms of the treaty, and a bloody civil war followed. The charismatic ex-IRA organiser Michael Collins, a key player in the creation of the Irish Free State and Commander-in-Chief of its army, was shot dead by extremists in an ambush in 1922. The next year the IRA accepted defeat and the guns fell silent. The ascetic President of Sinn Féin, Éamon de Valera, did a stretch in Kilmainham Gaol (he was to go on to become both prime minister and twice president of his country), and Ireland settled down to govern herself as a modern independent state.

Today the island is still partitioned: south of the Border is the Republic of Ireland; north, the six counties of Northern Ireland (Down, Derry, Armagh, Antrim, Tyrone and Fermanagh), which remain part of the United Kingdom.

I have met them at close of day
Coming with vivid faces
From counter or desk among grey
Eighteenth-century houses...
All changed, changed utterly:
A terrible beauty is born.
W B Yeats, "Easter 1916"

Flower-rich limestone pavements of the Burren Hills in County Clare

Only the Very Best, Now...

"Undiscovered" places, well away from it all

- **The great Bog of Bellacorick** in northwest County Mayo is lonely, silent and unfrequented country – 260sq km (100sq miles) of blanket bog (sodden peat moss, laid down thousands of years ago), hemmed in by the Nephin Beg Mountains. Both can be stark, dour places in rain and low cloud; both sparkle magically when the sun shines. On such a day, walk out for ten minutes on any track across the bog and savour the smell, the colours – and the silence.
- **The Inishowen Peninsula** in northern Donegal – sternly beautiful, windswept coasts and hills; too far out for all but the most intrepid visitors.
- **The Sperrin Mountains**, County Tyrone – high and wild (but not too high and wild for the average walker) with beautiful valleys between the ridges.

- **The Slieve Bloom Mountains** in County Laois – a perfect ring of lonely hills in the centre of Ireland, with a signed walking trail encircling their heights.
- **Gorumna, Lettermore and Lettermullan**, County Galway – granite-scabbed islands connected by causeways, with thatched houses among tiny, stony fields; an Irish-speaking corner of Galway Bay overlooked by most visitors.
- **Sheep's Head Peninsula**, County Cork – the narrowest and least known of the five southwestern peninsulas; glorious coast, and sheep tracks through the hills.

Top buzzes

- **Inishmaan**, the middle of the three Aran Islands, in a full Atlantic gale – shuddering stone and giant waterspouts.
- **Sunset over two island-studded bays**: Clew Bay, County Mayo, and Roaringwater Bay, County Cork.

- **Sunrise on 21 December** in the inner chamber of the ancient Newgrange passage grave, County Meath (► 81–4) – but you'll have to reserve your place ten years ahead!
- **The view** from the Round Tower at Clonmacnoise monastic site, County Offaly.
- **The first sup** of the first pint of Guinness of your first trip to Ireland.
- **An Ulster Fry** – a hearty breakfast with the black and the white pudding.
- **Reaching the chapel** at the summit of Croagh Patrick, County Mayo.
- **Midnight in McGann's** in Doolin, County Clare (tel: 065 7074133), with a new fiddler just walked in.
- **Watching brent geese** in midwinter on Strangford Lough, County Down.

Three great islands

- **Clare Island**, County Mayo, where the pub opens at midnight...
- **Clear Island**, County Cork, where rare birds make landfall and the islanders treat their guests like friends.
- **Inishmaan**, County Galway, where they still speak Irish and weave their own clothes.

Four memorable views

- **Macgillycuddy's Reeks** seen across Dingle Bay at low tide.
- **Bogland of southern Connemara**, framed by the Maumturk Mountains and the Twelve Bens.
- **The great cliff of Slieve League**, southwest Donegal, from Carrigan Head.
- **The limestone domes** of the Burren, County Clare, in full flower on a May morning.

Serene Connemara countryside, County Galway

The Slieve Bloom Mountains, County Laois

Mist-covered Croagh Patrick, County Mayo

Two brilliant traditional pubs

There's no music, but they are wonderful places to gossip in.
- **Hargadon's**, Sligo (► 141).
- **McGing's**, Westport (► 133).

Fun, Frolics and Festivals

Leopardstown Races with top riders, top runners.
Connemara Four Seasons Walking Festival, based in Clifden, County Galway: experience the interior of Ireland's most romantic landscape as few visitors do.

of *Riverdance*-style jigs and reels from all over the world.
Irish Grand National Steeplechase, held on Easter Monday at Fairyhouse in County Meath.

Belfast Civic Festival and Lord Mayor's Show – street

Pony fair in full swing in Connemara

Jameson Dublin International Film Festival – showcases the best of Irish and international films.

St Patrick's Festival (17 March) parades, music, fun all over the Irish world.

World Championships in Irish Dancing – the very best

shows, entertainments, parades.
Bantry Mussel Fair, County Cork.
Irish 2,000 and 1,000 Guineas races at The Curragh, County Kildare.
Guinness Classic Fishing Festival – fishing and frolicking on and around Lough Erne, County Fermanagh.

Music in Great Irish Houses – superb mix of music

and mansions countrywide.

Bloomsday (16 June):
the classic Dublin pub crawl/
re-enactment/celebration of
events in James Joyce's *Ulysses*,
attended by fans of the author
from Japan to New Mexico.

Irish Derby at The Curragh –
everyone turns up, from dukes
to dustmen. Wear your best
frock and hat.

JUNE / JULY

**Castlebar International
Walks**, County Mayo – a four-
day festival. Walking the Mayo
hills by day, and dedicated
partying in local bars by night.

JULY

**Ballybunion International
Bachelor Festival**, County
Kerry – join the fun, and the
poseurs!

Willie Clancy Week,
Milltown Malbay, County Clare
– piping festival that turns into
a good-time week.

Orangeman's Day (12 July)
in Northern Ireland – parades
and music, Battle of the Boyne
commemorations.

**Ballyshannon Folk and
Traditional Music Festival**
– a long-running event with
big-name performers and a
varied programme.

JULY / AUGUST

Galway Races – attendance
at horse-related events is
optional...linked to:

Galway Arts Festival –
books, music, films, plays.

AUGUST

**Kinsale Regatta and
Homecoming Festival**,
County Cork – expatriates
return. Sailing, walking,
seafood-gourmandising, all in
beautiful Cork coastal location.

Connemara Pony Show,
Clifden, County Galway – sales
of "wild" ponies. An authentic,
local West of Ireland occasion.

**Yeats International
Summer School**, Sligo.

Puck Fair, Killorglin, County
Kerry – crown and enthrone a
goat, then let things develop
from there...

**Sperrins Hillwalking
Festival**, County Tyrone.

**Rose of Tralee
International Festival**,
County Kerry – hyped and
much televised, but still fun.

**Dingle Regatta and Dingle
Show**, Dingle, County Kerry.

All Ireland Fleadh Cheoil –
mighty traditional music
festival.

Oul' Lammas Fair,
Ballycastle, County Antrim (last
Monday/Tuesday) – seafood
and merrymaking.

SEPTEMBER

Matchmaking, Lisdoonvarna,
County Clare – fix yourself up
with a partner, more in fun
than earnest these days.

**All-Ireland Finals of
Hurling and Gaelic
Football**, Croke Park, Dublin –
fiercely contested by players
and fans.

SEPTEMBER / OCTOBER

Dublin Theatre Festival –
the best of Irish and international drama.

OCTOBER

Gourmet Festival, Kinsale,
County Cork. Sample superb
seafood, music and hospitality.

NOVEMBER

Belfast Festival, Queen's
University – arts and pints.

NOVEMBER / DECEMBER

**Dublin Grand Opera's
Winter Season**, Gaiety
Theatre.

DECEMBER

Dingle Wren, County Kerry
(26 December): midwinter
madness, dressing up and dirty
tricks played on friends and
foe alike. Don't attend this
festival without your sense of
humour!

The Pen and the Flute

The Pen...

Even if you have never visited Ireland before, Ireland has almost certainly visited you – through her music, and through the written word. For such a small country, Ireland has produced an enormous number of wonderful writers and musicians, something that strikes everyone who loves a good tune or a well-turned phrase marinated in wit – or both, brought together in a song. And the cliché that every Dublin taxi-driver has his great unfinished novel on the back seat of his cab is truer than you might think, too. Just ask the next one you meet...

To draw up a shortlist of Great Irish Writers would surely start a heated discussion in many a bar. All visitors to Ireland should pack at least a couple of samples in their overnight bag. A selection is suggested (see panel opposite); you'll probably have a few of your own ideas.

King of the walk is James Joyce (► 65), whose *Ulysses* (1922) is certainly one of the greatest novels – many say the greatest – ever written. It's huge, heavy (over 700 pages) and rambling; reading it is like swimming in a salty sea of words and ideas. "The book to which we are all indebted," said T S Eliot, "and from which none of us can escape."

Poetic expressions flow through Irish writing and talk, and poets abound. Famous for polemic and satire was Jonathan Swift (1667–1745), Dean of St Patrick's Cathedral in Dublin and author of such works as *Gulliver's Travels* and *A Tale of a Tub* (► 57). W B Yeats (► 178) is still the best-known "old school" Irish poet, his work rooted in the folklore and landscape of Sligo. County Monaghan's Patrick Kavanagh is another renowned poet, with a fluid and beautiful touch. Derry-born Seamus Heaney, whose deceptively uncomplicated style has a penetrating and innovative quality, wears the crown today, and was awarded the Nobel Prize for Literature in 1995. And the short story – in the hands of masters such as Kerry's humorous celebrant of local heroes, the publican and author John B Keane, Cork's Frank O'Connor with his poignant fables of the War of Independence and Sean O'Faolain, or Clare's Edna O'Brien (also a celebrated novelist) – seems the ideal medium for that very Irish gift of telling a good story grippingly.

Of course the Irish have always been master storytellers. Their bards were spinning tales of the heroes Fionn MacCumhaill and Cuchulainn, and of scheming Queen Mebh and her lust for power that led to the epic Cattle Raid of Cooley, long before anyone in Ireland had learned to put pen to paper. Given this rich heritage of fireside storytelling, with its inherent demand for expressive gesture and drama, perhaps it's not surprising that so many great playwrights originated here: think of Oscar Wilde and Richard Sheridan, J M Synge and Sean O'Casey, George Bernard Shaw and Samuel Beckett. The Abbey Theatre

James Joyce, doyen of Irish writers

Ten Great Irish Reads

- *The Bodhrán Makers* by John B Keane. Funny, touching tale by County Kerry's master storyteller.
- *Experiences of an Irish RM* by Somerville & Ross. Turn-of-the-century high jinks, fizzing with wit and humour.
- *Ulysses* by James Joyce. Weighty, dense, complex, funny and captivatingly full of insight about Dublin, Ireland and the Irish.
- *Resurrection Man* by Eoin McNamee. Dark deeds in Belfast of the recent Troubles, sparsely and poetically told.
- *Twenty Years A-Growing* by Maurice O'Sullivan. Definitive account of growing up on County Kerry's remote Blasket Islands in the early 20th century.
- *The Country Girls*, *Girl with Green Eyes*, *Girls in their Married Bliss* by Edna O'Brien. Rites of passage for girls from the rural west in this celebrated 1960s trilogy.
- *Best of Myles* by Myles na Gopaleen and *At Swim-Two-Birds* by Flann O'Brien (both *noms de plume* of Brian O'Nolan). The first is a collection of the writer's hilarious pieces in *The Irish Times*, the second a unique fantasy that spills over with inventive wit and mad humour.
- *Amongst Women* by John McGahern. Masterfully unadorned language to shade the subtlest of tales about an old IRA man in despair and the iron grip in which he holds his family.
- *Guests of the Nation* by Frank O'Connor. Beautifully observed stories of the War of Independence.
- *The Snapper*, *The Van*, *The Commitments* by Roddy Doyle. Sharp, funny modern trilogy about working-class life in "Barrytown" (Dublin).

founded in Dublin by Synge, Yeats and Lady Gregory is still active, and dozens of other venues over Ireland showcase established and up-and-coming Irish playwrights (▶ 30).

...The Flute

Irish traditional music is essentially music to accompany rural dancing. Jigs and reels predominate, along with the slower airs that were made to float a song on. A round goatskin drum called a *bodhrán* provides the engine

A solo fiddler may carry the tune...

of beat and rhythm, along with guitar, bouzouki or banjo; accordion, melodeon, penny whistle and flute carry the melody, while on top skate the fiddle or uillean pipes. The Irish respect and cherish this music as vibrantly alive; but they are not afraid to experiment, even to the point of translating it altogether to jazz or rock genres, or to neoclassical arrangements for piano and orchestra. The music is tough enough to withstand these wrenchings, and versatile enough to flourish within them. Irish music enjoyed a tremendous vogue in the 1990s, promulgated by stage shows such as *Riverdance*, and by the rediscovery of their traditional

On Disc
- Dervish, *Playing With Fire* (Whirling Discs). Sligo band doing just what the title says.
- Noel Hill, *The Irish Concertina* (Claddagh Records). Beautiful tunes, beautifully played by a master musician.

Live Music

If you're in the vicinity, try these noted session pubs.

- Furey's, Sligo, owned by traditional band Dervish.
- Matt Molloy's, Westport, County Mayo, owned by old Chieftains flute-player Molloy, who often plays.
- O'Connor's, Doolin, County Clare. All the greats have played here...
- O'Donoghue's, Dublin... and here (➤ 70).

Drink with the Greats

Joining one of the numerous "Dublin Literary Pub Crawls" can be good fun, if you're in a convivial and none-too-critical mood. You visit one nice old Dublin pub after another, enjoying a drink while actors re-create the scamps, geniuses and literary topers who haunted them. Details from the Dublin Tourism Centre in Suffolk Street.

Two singers, two styles – Shane McGowan, erstwhile lead singer of The Pogues (right), and Bono of U2 (far right)

...or it may be a friendly ensemble, like this one at Greystones (above left) in County Wicklow

musical roots by rock acts such as U2 and Van Morrison, along with shock artists like The Pogues. In fact the music had never been away, but had always been played with love and respect by local musicians all over Ireland.

Irish music is timeless, which is not to say it is stuck in a time warp. Turlough O'Carolan, the 18th-century blind harpist, is well respected; so are fiddler Michael Coleman and the melodeon player Joe Cooley,

musicians of the early and middle 20th century who directly influenced today's generation of players. The tunes they handed down, many very old, receive new life each time they are played; each rendition is unique. And new tunes are constantly being made. As you listen – or maybe pluck up enough courage to join in – you will be launching yourself on a wonderful voyage of discovery which, if you are lucky, will go on for ever.

Abbey Theatre in Dublin, opened in 1904 by Lady Augusta Gregory and her protégé, the poet W B Yeats. Relocated after a fire, it is still in use as Ireland's national theatre.

Bodhrán, a goatskin drum beaten with hellish enthusiasm by session musicians in pubs and clubs throughout Ireland.

Croagh Patrick, County Mayo's Holy Mountain and a long-time pilgrimage destination (➤ 176–7). When gold prospectors wanted to mine here in 1990, worldwide protests stopped them in their tracks.

Drumcree, Northern Irish town and symbol of Ulster intransigence. This is where Protestant Orangemen insist they have a right to march and Catholic nationalists insist they do not.

Emigration, curse and bugbear of rural Ireland. The population today is one-third of what it was before the Great Famine of 1845–50.

Famine, the most disastrous event in Irish history. It emptied the west, and scarred the national psyche.

General Post Office (GPO) on O'Connell Street in Dublin. It was the scene at Easter 1916 of the rebels' proclamation of the Republic of Ireland, and has acquired the status of a national monument.

Hill of Tara, the great mound rising out of the Meath Plain, from which the ancient High Kings of Ireland ruled for a thousand years (➤ 88).

Irish language, taught in schools, spoken in the Gaeltacht of the west (where Gaelic is in everyday

An ABC of Icons and Touchstone

The Hill of Tara, seat of the ancient High Kings of Ireland

use), and heard around the world in the lyrics of traditional Irish songs.

July 12, Orangeman's Day in Northern Ireland, celebrating William of Orange's victory over James II at the Battle of the Boyne. Orangemen parade to martial music, and tensions rise.

Knock, a pilgrimage centre in County Mayo, and other places in Ireland where ordinary people have seen miraculous visions.

Lazybeds, cultivation ridges that define the former potato fields. Scars on the rural landscape, they are poignant reminders of hard times past.

Music, wild, sweet, infectious, angry, played and sung all over Ireland.

National anthem, "Amhrán na bhFíann" (The Soldier's Song), often sung in Irish at the end of a music session. Everyone stands up for it, so don't be caught napping!

Orange, William of. He's "King Billy", victor of the Battle of the Boyne in 1690, who can be seen riding his white horse on Unionist banners and gable ends.

Poteen, "mountain dew", "the pure drop", "the crater" – a colourless, illicitly distilled spirit, usually made from potatoes.

Queenstown, now called Cobh, the ferry port south of Cork, from which countless thousands of poor Irish families sailed on their emigration journeys to America (▶ 98).

Reels, the unforgettable leaping dance tunes that lie at the heart of Ireland's traditional music.

Stout, a strong beer as black as night, as smooth as velvet. No visit to Ireland is complete without at least a sip. Or to quote author Myles na Gopaleen: "A pint of porter is your only man."

Turf, not as sliced wholesale by Bord na Móna (the Irish Peat Board), but as cut with the special turf spade called a slane, and burned on a hearth for its slow heat and sweet smell.

U2, Dublin's mega-successful rock-band-with-a-conscience, closely followed by...

Van Morrison, east Belfast singer of bluesy soul and soulful blues, one of contemporary music's most enduringly popular figures.

Wells – holy ones, blessed by saints, scattered over the land, whose water can cure your cough, sore back, impotence, weak eyesight, infertility...

Xavier, Brigid, Patrick, Aloysius and dozens of other Christian names from the calendar of saints. There's plenty to choose from.

Yeats brothers, the poet William Butler and the painter Jack, whose love of County Sligo's flat-topped mountains and rugged shores is celebrated in their work.

Zip codes, absence of: a testament to Ireland's small population, and the in-depth local knowledge of Irish postmen.

Shrine at Knock, Ireland's pilgrimage centre

Two modern Irish icons: Bob Geldof (left), who organised LiveAid, and blues soulster Van Morrison

Bet You Didn't Know...

Above: Dublin's trendy Temple Bar – migrants often return to a modern Ireland

Opposite: some things don't change, though – like children's love of Irish dancing

- that over 380 species of wild birds have been recorded in Ireland
- that up to a million people turned up on the Hill of Tara in 1843 to hear Daniel O'Connell castigate the Corn Laws, which protected farmers' interests by keeping the price of corn artificially high
- that there are nearly 5,000 Irish missionaries working in 85 countries worldwide
- that when someone in the Gaeltacht greets you with "Dia dhuit" (God be with you), you should respond "Dia agus Mhuire dhuit!" (God and Mary be with you!)
- that the blood-red fuchsia growing all over the south-west of Ireland was brought in from Chile in the 19th century
- that Erskine Childers, author of the 1903 spy thriller *The Riddle of the Sands*, was shot for treason as an IRA activist in 1922. Or that his son (also named Erskine Childers) was president of Ireland 1973–74
- that up to a million people born in Ireland are living "across the water" in mainland Britain today
- that when the sun warms bogland after rain it smells like fruitcake
- that Aillwee Caves in the Burren, County Clare, were discovered by a local farmer who was looking for his dog (▶ 127)
- that the Irish sport of hurling, a rough-and-tumble version of hockey, has been played since prehistoric times
- that poteen, a spirit made from potatoes, should be run through the still three times to remove the poisons and make it just right for drinking
- that many United States presidents had Irish roots – Messrs Jackson, Polk, Johnson, Buchanan, Grant, Arthur, Cleveland, Harrison, McKinley, Theodore Roosevelt, Wilson, Kennedy and Reagan.

Finding
Your Feet

First Two Hours

Arriving: Republic of Ireland

Dublin and Shannon airports are the main points of entry for visitors arriving by air. Most arrivals by sea come through Dublin Port or Dun Laoghaire south of Dublin; Rosslare, County Wexford, has ferry links with the UK and France. All ports and airports have currency exchange bureaux, the major car-rental firms, and taxi ranks (fares are about five times the bus fare). Most journey times to city centres are between 30 and 60 minutes, depending on traffic.

Dublin Airport ➕ 201 D5
- To get to Dublin city centre from the airport by **car**, take M1 south.
- An **Airlink bus** leaves the airport every 20 minutes (moderate fare, under-16s free) taking passengers to the city centre via the central bus station (Busarus) and Connolly and Heuston railway stations.
- **Taxis** line up outside the Arrivals area. Fares can be expensive.

Dun Laoghaire ➕ 201 E5
- If travelling by **car** to Dublin, simply follow signs for the city centre.
- There is a frequent **Dublin Bus** service to Dublin city centre.
- **Taxi fares** range from moderate to expensive (depending on traffic).
- An inexpensive **DART** service (➤ 35) from Dun Laoghaire to Dublin runs every half-hour (sometimes more frequently).

Shannon Airport ➕ 199 D4
- To get to Limerick from Shannon Airport by **car,** take N18 east.
- **Bus Éireann** runs a frequent, inexpensive airport-to-Limerick/Ennis service.
- **Taxis** from Shannon Airport to Limerick are moderate to expensive.

Arriving: Northern Ireland

Visitors arriving by air will probably fly to either Belfast International or Belfast City airport. Belfast and Larne ferryports are the main points of entry for arrivals by sea. All ports and airports have currency exchange bureaux, the major car-rental firms, and taxi ranks (fares are about five times the bus fare).

Belfast International Airport ➕ 197 E4
- The journey to central Belfast takes 30 to 60 minutes, depending on traffic.
- To get to Belfast city centre from the airport by **car**, follow A52 east.
- **Airbus service** (moderate fare, children free) runs from the airport to Belfast city centre every 30 minutes (sometimes hourly on Sundays).
- **Taxi fares** from the airport to central Belfast tend to be expensive.

Belfast City Airport and Belfast Ferryport ➕ 197 E4
- The journey to Belfast takes 10 to 15 minutes, depending on traffic.
- **Taxi fares** to Belfast city centre are moderate.

Larne Ferryport ➕ 197 E4
- The journey to central Belfast takes 30 to 60 minutes, depending on traffic.
- To get to Belfast city centre from the ferryport by **car**, take A8 south.
- An **Ulsterbus** service runs frequently to the city centre.
- **Taxi fares** to central Belfast tend to be expensive.
- There is a frequent **rail service** to Belfast Central railway station.

Tourist Information Offices

The central Dublin and Belfast tourist offices provide an excellent service, giving assistance with reservations and information on what's on in each city.

- **Dublin Tourism** Suffolk Street, tel: 1850 230330 or 01 605 7700 (within Ireland); 0800 039 7000 (UK); 353 66 979083 (from all other countries); email: information@dublintourism.ie; www.visitdublin.com.
- **Belfast Welcome Centre** 47 Donegall Place, Belfast, tel: 028 9024 6609; fax: 028 9031 2424; email: info@belfastvisitor.com; www.discovernorthernireland.com or www.gotobelfast.com.

Admission Charges

Admission charges for museums and places of interest are indicated by price categories: pounds for Northern Ireland, Euros for the Republic (➤ 189).

inexpensive: up to £3/€4 **moderate**: £3–£6/€4–€8 **expensive**: over £6/€8

Getting Around: Republic of Ireland

CIE runs bus and train services in the Republic of Ireland through its subsidiaries Irish Rail (Iarnród Éireann; www.irishrail.ie), Irish Bus (Bus Éireann; www.buseirann.ie) and Dublin Bus (Bus Átha Cliath; www.dublinbus.ie).

Dublin

The **DART**, an efficient and moderately priced rail service, connects outer Dublin, north and south, with the city centre. **Dublin Bus** (tel: 01 873 4222) runs services in Greater Dublin, as far as the outskirts of counties Meath, Kildare and Wicklow.

Bus Services

- Tickets can be bought on the buses, but it is cheaper to buy them *en bloc* in advance from the CIE information desk in Dublin Airport, Dublin Bus (59 Upper O'Connell Street), or from one of the many ticket outlets in the city.

DART (Dublin Area Rapid Transit)

- There are 25 DART stations altogether; the three most central are **Connolly** (north of the river, a ten-minute walk from O'Connell Street), **Tara Street**, and **Pearse Street** (both south of the river and five minutes from Trinity College).
- **Trains** run every 5 minutes in rush hours, every 10 to 15 minutes at other times of the day.
- **Tickets** are available singly from any DART station, but it is cheaper to buy them *en bloc* from Dublin Bus (59 Upper O'Connell Street), from some newsstands around the city or at the stations.

Taxis

- You cannot hail or stop Dublin taxis in the street: call them by telephone (numbers in the *Golden Pages*), or find a taxi rank.
- The main city centre **taxi ranks** are at St Stephen's Green, College Green, O'Connell Street, and Westland Row to the east of Trinity College grounds.
- Dublin taxis are mostly metered; agree fares in advance with drivers of those that are not. Expect delays at busy times of the year.

Public Transport

All the major towns and cities in the Republic are connected by rail. Bus services run to all towns and cities, and to many rural villages. Public transport in the Republic is more efficient than folklore would have you believe. Timetables, however, particularly on the railways, become subject to creative interpretation the further from Dublin that you travel.

Railway Services
- **Irish Rail** (tel: 01 836 6222) runs the Republic's railway services. These are efficient north and south of Dublin, but in need of investment further west.
- The **Dublin–Belfast express** (eight trains per day) takes two hours: book ahead in the high season, and for crowded last trains on Friday and Sunday evenings.

Bus Services
- **Irish Bus** (tel: 01 836 6111), with its distinctive red-setter logo, runs services to all towns and cities, and to many rural villages.
- The daily **express coaches** between Dublin and Belfast are good value, and can beat the train for time if traffic conditions permit.

Tickets
- Tickets are available from any train or bus station or online at www.buseireann.ie.
- Under-16s and other concessionary fares can be as little as half-price.
- There are good ticket deals, changing from year to year. Examples include **Irish Explorer** (eight-day), valid on bus or train; **Emerald Card**, valid on Irish Rail, Irish Bus, Dublin Bus, Northern Irish Railways and Ulsterbus; **Irish Rover** and **Irish Rambler** (bus only), valid in both the Republic and Northern Ireland.

Student Discounts
- The **International Student Identity Card** gives good discounts on mainline rail, long-distance bus and ferry tickets for the price of a paperback novel. It's available from **USIT** (19–21 Aston Quay, O'Connell Bridge, Dublin 2, tel: 01 602 1600). You will need proof of your student status.

Internal Air Travel
Aer Lingus, the national airline (tel: UK 0845 084 4444; US 1-800 474 7424; Ireland 0818 365000; www.aerlingus.ie), flies from Dublin to Shannon. **Aer Arann** (tel: 01 814 1058) flies from Dublin to Donegal, Sligo, Knock, Galway, Kerry and Cork.

Car Ferries
Two short car ferry trips that save hours on the road are:
- Across the Shannon (20-minute crossing, every hour every day except 25 Dec) between Killimer, County Clare, and Tarbert, County Kerry (tel: 065 9053124).
- Across Waterford Harbour (10-minute crossing, continuous operation) between Ballyhack, County Wexford, and Passage East, County Waterford (tel: 051 382480).

Driving

Driving in the Republic, generally speaking, is still a pleasure. Out of the big towns the roads are uncrowded and most drivers courteous. The further west you go, the more patience you need: roads are narrower, steeper and more twisty. Signposts take some getting used to, with distances shown in kilometres on green-and-white signs and in miles on black-and-white signs.

Driving Essentials
- Drive on the **left-hand side** of the road.
- Drivers and front seat passengers must wear **seat belts**.
- The **speed limit** in the Republic is 48kph (30mph) in towns, 96kph (60mph) on other roads and 112kph (70mph) on motorways. The **legal alcohol limit** for motorists is 0.08 per cent (80mg) alcohol per 100ml blood.

Renting a Car
- **Fly-drive** or **rail/sail-drive** packages offer the best deals. Book ahead, mid-July to mid-August, or you may not get a car.
- **Prices** are half as much again during high season; they usually include Third Party, fire, theft and passenger indemnity insurance, as well as unlimited mileage and VAT (value added tax). You will have to pay a deposit.
- You will need a **full valid driving licence** of your country of residence, held for two years without endorsement. The age limit is generally 25–70.

Bringing Your Own Car
- You will need a **motor registration book** (with letter of authority if car is not registered in your name), a **full driving licence** or international permit and a Green Card or **insurance certificate**, valid for the Republic of Ireland.
- No Irish resident is allowed to drive your car, apart from a garage employee.

Leaving Dublin
- M1/N1 to Dublin Airport, Drogheda, Dundalk and Belfast
- N2 to Ashbourne, Slane and Derry
- N3 to Navan, Cavan and Enniskillen and Sligo
- N4 to Kinnegad (where N6 leaves for Galway), to Longford (where N5 leaves for Westport), and on to Sligo
- N7 towards Cork, Limerick and Killarney
- N81 to Blessington and West Wicklow
- N11 to Bray, Wicklow, Wexford and Rosslare car ferry

Getting Around: Northern Ireland

Belfast

Bus Services
- **Citybus** (tel: 028 9066 6630; www.translink.co.uk) operates buses within the city of Belfast.
- Buy tickets in **Europa Bus Centre** (Glengall Street) or **Laganside Bus Centre**, near Central railway station (Oxford Street) or on board buses. Multiple tickets/concessions are available.
- A **free bus** connects Central railway station with the two main bus stations and the International Youth Hostel (you must have a valid bus or train ticket to travel free); **Rail-link bus** connects Central and Yorkgate railway stations.

Taxis
Find taxi firm numbers in *Yellow Pages*. Black "London" cabs with yellow identifying discs are metered; others may not be. City-centre taxi ranks are at Yorkgate and Central railway stations, at both bus stations and at City Hall.

Public Transport

Public transport in Northern Ireland is reasonably priced and well run. For information on ticket deals and student discounts ➤ 36.

Railway Services

■ **Northern Ireland Railways** (tel: 028 9066 6630; www.translink.co.uk) runs an efficient service from Belfast to Larne (Yorkgate Station, tel: 028 9074 1700), and to Derry, Bangor and Dublin (Central Station, tel: 028 9089 9411).

■ Buy **tickets** at stations. For **discounts**, contact Northern Ireland Railways.

Bus Services

■ **Ulsterbus** (tel: 028 9066 6630; www.translink.co.uk) runs services to all towns and most villages across Northern Ireland.

■ Buy **tickets** at bus stations or on board buses. For cheap round-trip fares, unlimited travel tickets, bus/rail options, and concessionary fares, contact Ulsterbus.

Driving

Road surfaces tend to be better than in the Republic and signpost distances are given in miles only. The same rules and laws apply as in the Republic, with the legal alcohol limit at 80mg alcohol per 100ml blood.

Renting a Car

■ **Requirements** as for the Republic (➤ 37), except that you need only have held a driving licence for one year. If you plan to drive in both the Republic and Northern Ireland, check that your insurance covers you.

Bringing Your Own Car

■ No documents are needed, apart from a **driving licence**, by those arriving with a car by ferry from the UK or by road from the Republic of Ireland.

Leaving Belfast

■ A2 north up the coast to Antrim and the Giant's Causeway, east through Bangor and round the Ards Peninsula
■ M2/A6 to Derry
■ M1 to Dungannon/A4 to Enniskillen
■ M1 to Junction 7/A1 to Dundalk and Dublin

Accommodation

This guide recommends a carefully selected cross-section of places to stay, ranging from luxury hotels to farmhouses. Standards of accommodation are generally high in both the Republic and Northern Ireland and prices are similar. That said, the choice of well-run, interesting places to stay is more limited in Northern Ireland.

Guest-House and Bed-and-Breakfast Accommodation

Even inexpensive **bed and breakfasts** (B&Bs) usually have simple private bathroom facilities and, if you want to meet Irish people and go to the places the locals like, this can be the best option. Most (but not all) B&B and **guest-house** accommodation is in the **family home**, and hosts are usually pleased to help you plan itineraries in the locality and recommend places to go for food, shopping and entertainment.

Many **specially built guest houses**, with a standard of accommodation similar to a small hotel, have been built in the last few years. The level of comfort is high, but, as the **hosts usually live elsewhere**, visitors who had hoped to stay in a family home (and sample traditional Irish hospitality) can sometimes be disappointed. It's useful to know that **food** in smaller establishments is usually limited to **breakfast** and, in country areas, sometimes **high tea** is served in the evening instead of dinner. Many hosts take pride in breakfast, and the best B&B, guest house or farmhouse breakfasts can beat any hotel's. As well as the traditional **Irish breakfast** (bacon, egg, sausages, tomato, often black or white pudding, possibly also mushrooms and potato bread, served with soda bread), many places now offer a wider choice including **fresh fruits, fish,** and **farmhouse cheeses.** **Freshly baked bread** or scones (biscuits) and specialities like potato bread are often served at breakfast and at high tea.

Hotels

As the best guest houses provide standards of comfort that compete with hotels', the cost of some hotels can seem hard to justify, until the **location**, the **facilities** and, particularly, the **service** are taken into consideration. Hotel amenities have improved dramatically and many now have excellent **leisure facilities**, often including fitness centres and golf. It's always worth asking at hotels about **special offers** or short breaks, especially off-season. If the price quoted is beyond your budget, never be afraid to see if the hotelier will bargain.

Booking Accommodation

Booking ahead is always wise. The **cities**, especially Dublin, are busy all year. Except for the very remote scenic holiday areas, where most (but not all) accommodation closes for the winter, the **season** starts earlier and ends later than used to be the case. Summer does attract bumper crowds to seaside resorts, especially West Cork, Kerry and Galway, so an **off-season** visit can be more enjoyable. The weather is notoriously unreliable in Ireland at any time of year. All-year pressure on accommodation in **Dublin** has made it very **expensive** and it's hard to find bargains. One solution is to use hotels such as the **Jurys Inns** (found both in the Republic and the North), which provide comfort without service and charge a **flat rate** for a room without breakfast. Further information on accommodation is available from tourist information offices everywhere or you can refer to these sources:

■ The **AA Hotel Booking Service** is a free and fast way to find a place for a short break, holiday or business trip (tel: 0870 505 0505). Full listings of the Irish hotels and B&Bs available can be found and booked at the **AA's internet site**: www.theaa.com

■ The **Irish Hotels Federation** (13 Northbrook Road, Dublin 6, tel: 01 497 6459; email: info@ihf.ie; www.ihf.ie) publication *Be Our Guest* (€6) lists hotel and guest-house accommodation (including Northern Ireland).

■ **Town & Country Homes Association** (Belleek Road, Ballyshannon, Co Donegal, tel: 071 9822222; email: admin@townandcountry.ie; www.townandcountry.ie) produces a B&B directory (€5).

■ **Tourist offices** also have a range of other specialised directories, including ones that cover self-catering and farmhouse accommodation.

■ The **Northern Ireland Tourist Board** (www.discovernorthernireland.com) publishes a series of free accommodation guides, including hotels and guest houses, bed and breakfasts, budget accommodation and self-catering.

Food and Drink

Eating well can be a highlight of a visit to Ireland. Good-quality local ingredients, such as Galway oysters, Dublin Bay prawns, Atlantic salmon, Connemara lamb and organically grown vegetables and herbs have become a point of pride, and there's no shortage of talent among Irish chefs. At its best, whether it's a special meal or simple pub food, eating out in Ireland is a satis-fying combination of genuine hospitality, high standards and value for money.

International Cooking

International cooking styles tend to predominate over local tradition in a way that many visitors find disappointing, and you are far more likely to find world cuisine than traditional Irish food. When well produced this cos-mopolitan food is fun, vibrant and tasty, but often it's just a muddle.

- **Hotel dining-rooms** are emerging as serious contenders in the restaurant stakes as they have taken on top-class chefs. The accommodation recom-mendations reflect this, including the Clarence and Shelbourne hotels in Dublin (➤ 68–9), and many examples around the country.

- There is a shift towards buzzy, informal **cafés and bars** serving colourful, cosmopolitan fare. Lively, efficiently run bistros and brasseries such as Isaacs in Cork (➤ 113) and Roly's in Dublin (➤ 67) provide value for money, as do café-bars like Dublin's Café en Seine, where drink (often coffee rather than alcohol) is the main attraction and food is the accompaniment.

Irish Cooking

Until the 1990s Irish dishes such as colcannon (mashed potatoes and green cabbage, seasoned with chives), boxty (filled potato pancakes), Dublin cod-dle (a stew made with sausages, bacon, onions and potato), Irish stew and corned beef with dumplings and cabbage were most likely to be found only in pubs. With a few notable exceptions, restaurant chefs felt that traditional Irish dishes were too plain, but this is changing. With the active support of the **Restaurant Association of Ireland** (11 Bridge Court, City Gate, St Augustine Street, Dublin 8, tel: 01 677 9901; email: info@rai.ie; www.rai.ie) and **Bord Bia** (the Irish Food Board), many of Ireland's top chefs are now working on the concept of a **New Irish Cuisine**. Though light and modern, it is based on traditional ingredients, including many **artisan Irish food products**, such as farmhouse cheeses and smoked Atlantic salmon.

- **Bord Bia** has produced a New Irish Cuisine **recipe booklet** (tel: 01 668 5155 for details).

- Much of the country's best food is produced by owner-chefs in **family-run restaurants** and country houses.

- **Kinsale** in County Cork started the first Good Food Circle in the early 1970s and, since then, many others have flourished. There is also an annual themed Kinsale Gourmet Festival.

- **Kenmare** (County Kerry) has two of the country's finest hotels – Sheen Falls Lodge (tel: 064 41600) and Park Hotel Kenmare (tel: 064 41200) – and the most concentrated collection of fine restaurants, quality accommodation and good pubs.

■ Other culinary hotspots around the country include **Dingle** (County Kerry), **Clifden** (on the Connemara coast), **Carlingford** (at the foot of the Mountains of Mourne), **Athlone** (right in the centre of the Republic) and **Moycullen** (just outside Galway), all of which have something exciting to offer.

A Practical Guide to Eating Out

The following tips give practical information to make eating out in Ireland an enjoyable and carefree experience.

■ **Eating hours** are: breakfast from about 7:30 or 8 am to 10 or 10:30 am; lunch from noon or 12:30 to 2:15 pm or 2:30 pm; early dinner (often especially good value) from 5:30 or 6 pm and main dinner from about 7:30 to 9:30 pm or 10:30 pm.

■ There is no specific **service charge** – it can be anything from 10 to 15 per cent, or discretionary.

■ Many restaurants offer **early evening menus** (usually up to 7:30 pm) which are very good value. Where lunch is available at leading restaurants, it's usually a bargain.

■ **Dress codes** are increasingly relaxed and very few restaurants will insist on jacket and tie, although many people like to create a sense of occasion when dining out and feel more comfortable with a little formality.

■ The key **language** on menus throughout the country is English, although some will include an Irish version. A few enterprising restaurants (especially near the Shannon, which attracts holidaymakers and fisherfolk from Europe) offer menus in several European languages.

■ For further reference, the Restaurants Association of Ireland and Bord Fáilte produce a **restaurant directory**, *Restaurant and Events Guide* (€6). In Northern Ireland you can pick up the free *Taste of Ulster* guide. Both are available from tourist information offices.

Shopping

It would be hard to imagine a visit to Ireland that didn't include at least a little light shopping. The traditional goods for which the country is famous are in the main high-quality classics that will give years of pleasure. Much to the surprise of those who have been making and selling them for generations, many have recently become fashionable too.

Irish Classics

As natural fabrics and country looks become more desirable, Irish **tweeds**, **linen** and **hand-knitted sweaters** are suddenly "must-haves" for discerning shoppers from all over the world. This turn of events has resulted in a new generation of all kinds of goods with verve and style: for example, Irish **crystal** manufacturers have commissioned designers such as John Rocha to create high-fashion contemporary designs that appeal to a younger, more design-conscious shopper. The same applies in other areas: Louise Kennedy, for example, designs **clothes** for the international market but the roots of her inspiration are firmly Irish.

Where to Buy Irish Classics

Dublin has the biggest selection of shopping options anywhere in the country; notably, Irish fashions, antiques, books, handicrafts, food and drink. **Cork** is smaller and more selective, but is particularly enjoyable for shopping, or just browsing, and has outstanding food. **Galway** has a good range of small galleries, boutiques and specialist shops, and is renowned for books.

■ **Crafts** of a high standard are widely available across the country and you can often find something special at one of the many craft workshops – a beautiful turned wooden bowl or one-of-a-kind item of jewellery perhaps.

■ **Antiques** can still be a good buy in Ireland, although the days of easy-to-find bargains have gone. Belfast, Dublin, Cork, Galway and Limerick are all good browsing grounds, and it's worth checking the newspapers for auctions, which are often held outside the cities.

■ **Jewellery** is worth considering. Check out the antiques shops, but also look at modern designer jewellery (see Kilkenny ► 92 and Belfast ► 170) and the traditional Irish wedding rings called Claddagh rings (see Galway ► 143).

■ Irish cut **lead crystal** has been produced since the 18th century and is world famous. The best known, Waterford Crystal, is available in department stores and gift shops all over the country as well as from the factory itself (► 79). Other hand-cut crystals, from Dublin, Cork, Kinsale, Tipperary, Galway and Tyrone, are less expensive, and there is also interesting contemporary uncut crystal, such as Jerpoint (► 92).

■ **Traditional Irish foods** are much sought after. Foods that travel well include smoked salmon; make sure it's wild **Atlantic salmon**, not farmed, and buy it vacuum packed. The firmer, milder, whole hand-made **farmhouse cheeses** such as Gubbeen, Durrus and Cashel Blue are also a good buy; they are widely available in delicatessens, specialist cheese shops and supermarkets, and at airports (where you pay much more).

■ **Irish whiskey** has great cachet. A tour of one of the distilleries – Old Jameson Distillery, Dublin; Old Midleton Distillery, County Cork (► 108); and Old Bushmills Distillery, County Antrim (► 163) – will include a whiskey tasting, and you can buy some unusual blends on site. The well-known brands, like Jameson, Paddy, Powers and Bushmills, are widely available. **Baileys**, now one of the world's top-selling drinks, was created to make the best possible use of ingredients plentiful in Ireland – cream and whiskey. Along with **Irish Mist**, a sweetish liqueur made from whiskey and honey, it is widely available.

■ **Knitwear** is highly popular and everything from chunky Aran sweaters to sophisticated fashion knits are on offer. Every craft shop in the country has something of interest.

■ **Linen** is a great luxury, but worth the price, being wonderfully hardwearing. Most linen is made in Northern Ireland (► 170). As well as the classic table- and bed-linen, linen can also be high fashion, as reflected in designer clothes in shops such as Kilkenny in Dublin (► 69).

■ **Tweeds**, too, never date. The best buys are classics such as men's jackets, although more contemporary-styled clothing is becoming increasingly popular. Many craft shops stock tweeds, and there are specialist shops around the country (see Magee's ► 144), as well as in the major cities.

Opening Times

Opening hours are usually 9 am or 10 am until 5 pm or 6:30 pm Monday to Saturday for mainstream shopping, with limited Sunday hours and, in cities, late-night shopping until 8:30 pm or 9 pm on Thursday. In country areas, some shops still close for a half day (Wednesday and Saturday are most likely), and craft shops in holiday areas have variable hours. Browsing is quite acceptable: although assistance will usually be offered, pressure to buy is the exception.

Payment

Credit cards are widely accepted, except in small craft shops.

Entertainment

Irish entertainment most often takes the form of festivals (devoted to just about everything, ➤ 24–5), sporting events and music. Bord Fáilte (the Irish Tourist Board) and the Northern Ireland Tourist Board jointly produce a calendar of events, which is worth having if you're spending some time in Ireland. Bord Fáilte also produces booklets on golf, cycling, walking, hiking, fishing, sailing, tracing your ancestors, literary Ireland, wildlife and many more. These are available from larger tourist offices. There are similar publications relating to Northern Ireland. Detailed information on all aspects of Irish sport and entertainment is available daily in the local press and, for advance information, the Internet becomes more comprehensive all the time.

Spectator Sports

- **Horse racing** is central to Irish sporting life. There are 25 racecourses and races are held virtually every day. Major events are widely publicised; for information contact **Horse Racing Ireland** (tel: 045 842800; email: info@hri.ie; www.hri.ie).

- **Greyhound racing**, held at night, is enjoying a revival, and Irish dogs are highly regarded internationally; ask locally about events.

- Ask about venues for **Gaelic football** and **hurling**, both fast, exciting games.

Outdoor Activities

- **Golf** brings many visitors to Ireland. There are over 360 golf courses in the country, including many world-class championship courses and new ones opened in the late 1990s. The Republic of Ireland's golfing association, the **Golfing Union of Ireland** (81 Eglinton Road, Donnybrook, Dublin 4, tel: 01 269 4111; email: gui@aol.ie; www.gui.ie) can supply information.

- **Hiking** is increasingly popular; long-distance paths are indicated by trail markers and signposts. The longest in the south is the Kerry Way (214km/133 miles); Northern Ireland's 800-km (497-mile) Ulster Way, a circuit round Northern Ireland and County Donegal, is an even greater challenge, but splits into a number of shorter Waymarked Ways, ranging from 32km (20 miles) to 52km (32 miles).

Pubs and Clubs

- Increasingly strict drink-driving laws have forced pubs to diversify, and many now serve **food**, at least at lunch-time.
- **Music in pubs** is usually free if it's in the main bar, but amplified music and/or dancing in a separate room has an entrance fee.

- Impromptu sessions are still common around the country, but music is increasingly organised and, to the chagrin of many enthusiasts, even small pubs are introducing amplification.

Festivals

Consult newspapers and check your hotel room and the Tourist Information Offices for local guides to what's on (► 24–5).

Dublin

- Dublin's festival season begins with the **Jameson Dublin International Film Festival** (mid-February) and the **St Patrick's Day Festival and Parade** (around 17 March), followed by **Bloomsday** (mid-June), **Kerrygold Dublin Horse Show** (early August), **Dublin Theatre Festival** (early October) and **Dublin City Marathon** (mid-October).

Cork

- The **Cork Film Festival** (mid-October) and the **Cork Jazz Festival** (late October) are major events.

Galway

- Kinvarra holds a traditional boat gathering, **Cruinniu na mBad** (tel: 091 637579), in early August, and also in Kinvarra you can attend **literary banquets** themed on local writers, including W B Yeats and Sean O'Casey, in the medieval Dunguaire Castle (tel: 061 360788; www.shannonheritage.com).
- Galway's festivals include **Galway Arts Festival** (tel: 091 509700) in mid- to late July, followed by **Galway Races** (Ballybrit, tel: 091 753870), then several September **oyster festivals**. August brings Clifden's **Connemara Pony Show.**

Belfast

- Belfast is really buzzing all the time these days, with events at the Waterfront Hall, the Grand Opera House, King's Hall, Ulster Hall and numerous theatres, as well as the Odyssey science centre and entertainment complex.
- The **Belfast Folk Festival** in late July to early August is a great weekend of traditional music in city-centre venues.
- Northern Ireland's cultural highlight is the **Belfast Festival** at Queen's University, a mixture of film, theatre, music and dance in late October to early November.

Gay Scene

Outhouse is Dublin's resource centre for gay issues (105 Capel Street, tel: 01 873 4932; email info@outhouse.ie; www.outhouse.ie). **Queerspace** (www.queerspace.org.uk) has information for Northern Ireland.

Pronunciation Guide

á is an "aw" sound. So *bodhrán* is pronounced bow-r*aw*n
ane is a short "an" sound. So Cloghane is pronounced Clogh-*an*
bh is a "v" sound. So Cobh is pronounced Co*v*e
ch is pronounced in the same way as "ch" in the Scottish word loch
dh is silent in the middle of a word. See *bodhrán* above
eagh or **eigh** is an "ay" sound. So Glenveagh is pronounced Glen-*vay*
gh is silent at the end of a word and slightly softer than the "ch" sound in loch in the middle of a word
h is slightly throatier than "h", slightly less throaty than loch

Dublin

Getting Your Bearings

"In Dublin's fair city, where the girls are so pretty..."
Is it that snatch of an old romantic song that attracts so many
people to Dublin? Or is it Dublin's fast-growing reputation as
the most enjoyable capital city in Europe, a 24-hour party
town where people still have time for the stranger? Whatever
the cause, the effect has been spectacular. During the last
couple of decades of the 20th century, Dublin broke free of a
clinging image of shabbiness and quaintness, of being far
behind the times, and emerged as a go-ahead modern
city – loud, joyful, affluent, with a brashness that
attracted more than it repelled.

Dublin lies low and beautiful. There are few high-rise blocks
to overshadow the historic buildings – Trinity College, the
Custom House, St Patrick's Cathedral. And this is a
compact city, easy to walk around in a day, with the
admirable Dublin Area Rapid Transit railway
(DART) to get you out along the shores
of Dublin Bay.

South of the river you'll
find the chic pavement
cafés and fashionable
watering holes of Temple
Bar, once a run-down area
but now Dublin's snappiest
spot. Only a stone's throw
away is Ireland's best
Georgian architecture in
the streets and squares
around St Stephen's Green.
North of Dublin's river, the
Liffey, the 1960s and 1970s
developers had far too free
a hand, but wide
O'Connell Street, with the
General Post Office jutting out,
is getting a major facelift. To the west
there are street-market quarters and hidden
pubs to discover. The further north and east you
go, preferably by DART, the greener, quieter and
more respectable grow the neighbourhoods.

Dublin has so much going for it. There are literary
connections in abundance – from old masters James Joyce and
Sean O'Casey to irreverent young lions such as Roddy Doyle. Music
flows through the heart of the city, from the stadium rock of U2 to
the cheery good-time pub folk of bands such as The Dubliners.

This is a friendly city. And the friendliness is genuine, not part of
some PR campaign. Enjoy it to the hilt, and then some...

An elegant, Georgian door in Fitzwilliam Square

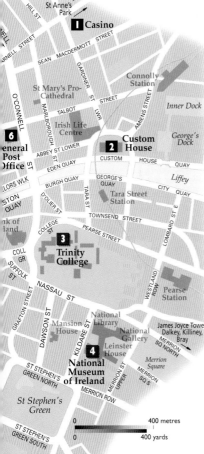

Above: the Ha'penny Bridge

Previous page: an eternal image of Dublin, a welcoming face in a friendly bar

See the priceless Book of Kells at Trinity College and the treasures of the National Museum of Ireland, wander the grim corridors of Kilmainham Gaol and relax in Phoenix Park.

Dublin in a Day

9:30 am

Be at **3** **Trinity College** (➤ 50–3) bright and early, to avoid the crush in the "Picturing the Word" exhibition and so get an uncluttered look at the glorious Book of Kells (right). Leave Trinity by the Nassau Street exit, and make your way down Kildare Street.

10:30 am

Pop into the **4** **National Museum of Ireland** (➤ 54–6) to view the dazzling gold and jewels of ancient Ireland. Turn down Molesworth Street and cut through to reach Grafton Street, Dublin's shop-till-you-drop thoroughfare. Relax with a coffee and a sticky bun in Bewley's Oriental Café (left), and watch the buyers go by.

12:00 noon

Stroll down the west side of St Stephen's Green and take a look at Harcourt Street to see superb Georgian houses with their characteristic rounded doorways. Then follow Cuffe Street and Kevin Street to **11** **St Patrick's Cathedral** (detail of a gilt coat of arms on the railings outside the cathedral, right, ➤ 57), to pay your respects at the grave of Jonathan Swift, writer and dean of the cathedral. From here it's a 10-minute walk via Golden Lane to South Great George's Street.

1:30 pm

Take the weight off your feet and enjoy the excellent soup and sandwiches in **The Globe** on South Great George's Street. After lunch, walk on north through trendy **7 Temple Bar** (➤ 61) until you meet the River Liffey, and turn right for Aston Quay.

3:00 pm

Hop on a 51 or 79 bus at Aston Quay for the 10- to 15-minute ride out to **12 Kilmainham Gaol** (➤ 58–9), an icon of Irish history. After the tour of the gaol, make your way up the South Circular Road to the Islandbridge Gate into **14 Phoenix Park**.

5:00 pm

Blow away the cobwebs with an hour's saunter through the wide open spaces of Phoenix Park (➤ 64–5). You might see anything from a herd of deer to a hurling match (above left). Then catch the 10 bus back to Aston Quay.

6:30 pm

The night is yours! Start in Temple Bar (right), maybe, with a drink in the St John Gogarty, followed by dinner at the lively Elephant and Castle, perhaps, or **The Mermaid Café** in Dame Street (➤ 67). Then on to the Brazen Head or the Long Hall or Doheny & Nesbitt's or…

3 Trinity College and the Book of Kells

Renowned as the most beautiful book in the world, the glorious and priceless Book of Kells is the unchallenged star of the show at Trinity College. These 680 pages of monkish Latin script and painting present a virtuoso display of richness of imagination, breadth of humour and wit, and faithful observation of the world of nature, all executed with a breathtaking delicacy of touch. The monks who copied out and illustrated the four Gospels at the Monastery of Kells in County Meath around the year 800 may have learned their skill in St Columba's celebrated monastery on the Scottish island of Iona; they were certainly among the best illuminators at work in that area.

Trinity College

The Book of Kells is on display at Trinity College, an iconic Irish institution in itself. As you turn off College Street and pass through the low, unobtrusive doorway under the blue clock face, the roar of traffic fades and is overlain by the chatter of young voices and the clop and scuffle of shoes on the cobbled courtyards of Trinity College. In these peaceful quadrangles, surrounded by the mellow architecture of four centuries, you catch a sense of how Dublin must have been in a quieter age.

Not that Trinity, Ireland's premier university, is a stuffy or hidebound place these days. The college was founded in 1592 by Queen Elizabeth I "to civilise Ireland with both learning and

The magnificently illustrated Greek letters Chi-Rho, formed from the first two letters of the Greek word for Christ, beginning a verse in Matthew's Gospel. The microscopic detail is characteristic of the Book of Kells

✚ 202 C3 ✉ College Street, Dublin 2
☎ 01 608 2320/608 2308; www.tcd.ie/library/
🕐 Old Library and Book of Kells Exhibition: Mon–Sat 9:30–5, Sun 12:30–4:30, Oct–May; Sun 9:30–4:30, rest of year. Closed 10 days over Christmas and New Year. The Dublin Experience: daily 10–5, mid-May to late Sep
🚌 All cross-city buses 💲 Moderate

the Protestant religion…for the reformation of the barbarism of this rude people." Up until 1966 Catholics were admitted only under special dispensation; today Trinity is completely mixed by both religion and sex (women were admitted to degrees as long ago as 1903).

Emerging from the tunnel-like entrance into the cobbled enclosure of Parliament Square, you will find to your left the **university chapel**, built in 1798 to an elegant oval design. Inside, its walls are lined with rich dark wood, its ceiling stuccoed green, grey and peach. Ahead stands a tall Victorian **campanile**. In front of this bear right around the end of the **Old Library** (1733) to reach its entrance. Inside, the excellent **"Picturing the Word" exhibition** leads you unfussily through an account of religious illustration and manuscript, helpfully preparing you for your encounter with the Book of Kells.

The Book of Kells

The book lies under glass and the pages on show are changed every three to four months. The monkish illustrators used chalk for white colour, lead for red, lapis lazuli for blue. Blue also came from woad, black from carbon and green from copper verdigris. Over the centuries, the colours on the much-admired principal pictorial pages have faded; the pages of less highly decorated script are remarkably white and well preserved. The more you look, the more you see: sinners misbehaving, angels, ravening beasts and demons, floral tendrils, scenes wildly fantastic and touchingly domestic, conundrums of geometry that resolve, as you stare at them, into initial letters.

Georgian grandeur in the peaceful heart of Trinity College

Trinity literary son, Oscar Wilde

Significant Students

Illustrious Trinity alumni include: Jonathan Swift, Dean of St Patrick's Cathedral and author of *Gulliver's Travels* and *Tale of a Tub*; playwrights Oliver Goldsmith, William Congreve, Oscar Wilde and Samuel Beckett; patriots and politicians Wolfe Tone, Robert Emmet, Edward Carson and Henry Grattan…

Alert Attendants

Make time to chat to the attendants posted around the "Picturing the Word" exhibition. Not only are they polite and friendly, they are also extremely knowledgeable, and will enthusiastically point out and explain tiny details tucked away in the intricate illustrations.

TAKING A BREAK

Meander from Trinity College into Temple Bar, a district packed with lively cafés and bars. The exuberant café-restaurant **Elephant and Castle** (► 66) is a good choice for a light lunch.

High book stacks and a vaulted roof give a tunnel effect to the Long Room

Other precious manuscript gospels are displayed in rotation alongside the Book of Kells: the 8th-century **Book of Mulling** and **Book of Dimma**, the **Book of Armagh** from about 807, and the **Book of Durrow**, which probably dates back to around 675 and is the oldest surviving decorated gospel book.

The Long Room

From the Book of Kells display room, climb the stairs to reach the cathedral-like Long Room. Well over 60m (200 feet) long, this superb old library room contains nearly a quarter of a million vintage books under its wooden barrel-vaulted roof. On display here is one of the precious dozen surviving copies of the original **Proclamation of the Republic of Ireland**, whose rolling phrases were read out by Pádraic Pearse from the steps of the General Post Office on Easter Monday 1916: "…we hereby proclaim the Irish Republic as a Sovereign Independent State, and we pledge our lives and the lives of our comrades-in-arms to the cause of its freedom, of its welfare, and of its exaltation among the nations."

Nearby, on the right as you walk through the Long Room, stands a **harp**, gnarled and shiny with age, beautifully carved out of dark willow wood. It can be hard to spot, its ancient brown wood camouflaged against the brown hues of the surrounding books. Un-romantic carbon dating says the harp was made around 1400. But legend tells a better tale, insisting that it was once owned by Brian Boru, mightiest of the High Kings of Ireland, who fell on Good Friday 1014 at the moment of victory over the Danes at the Battle of Clontarf.

THE BOOK OF KELLS: INSIDE INFO

Top tips On a summer holiday weekend it can get very crowded around the case containing the Book of Kells, and you may end up with a frustratingly brief glimpse before being ushered onwards. If possible, visit on an out-of-season weekday, when you will have time to let your eyes adjust and there will be plenty of space to stand and stare.

4 National Museum of Ireland

The National Museum of Ireland encompasses four museums, three in Dublin and one in County Mayo (▶ 133), but for many visitors the name is synonymous with the central Dublin branch, which houses the main historical collections. Officially the Museum of Archaeology and History, it preserves the historic heart and spirit of Ireland. This superb collection includes Europe's finest ancient gold items; richly ornamented early Christian crosses and cups; and Viking bows.

The 8th-century Tara Brooch has provided inspiration for countless pieces of Irish jewellery

Most of this treasure – much of it dug up by chance from peat bog or potato field – is displayed in the **Treasury** in the museum's Great Hall. There is far too much fine artistry to take in during one visit, but try at least to see the Ardagh Chalice, the Cross of Cong and the "Ireland's Gold" exhibits.

The **Ardagh Chalice,** a heavily decorated two-handled 8th-century silver cup, was discovered by a labourer named Quinn while digging up potatoes he had planted in the ring fort of Reerasta, near Ardagh in County Limerick. Quinn, unaware of its true value, was delighted to sell his treasure trove – the chalice, some brooches, a cup and other items – for a few pounds to a local doctor. The **Cross of Cong** is a processional cross made in 1123 for Turlough O'Conor, King of Connacht, with decorative animal heads, beaded gold wire and inlaid enamel. The magnificent 8th-century **Tara Brooch,** gleaming with amber and coloured glass and covered in intricate interlacing patterns, is the finest piece of Irish jewellery in existence, and certainly the most copied by modern jewellers.

The **Broighter Hoard,** unearthed in County Derry in the 1890s, is the Treasury's biggest collection of gold objects. Made in the 1st century BC of sheet

Victorian iron-work frames the roof of the National Museum of Ireland

The glorious craftsmanship of the 8th-century Ardagh Chalice makes it one of Ireland's finest pieces of silver-ware

gold beaten to paper thinness, it includes a wonderful miniature boat, elaborate collars, and a string of hollow gold balls forming a necklace. Remarkable, too, are the shrines made of worked metal and wood to hold sacred objects. Among them is the 12th-century shrine of **St Patrick's Bell**, complete with the big, iron bell itself, which is early 5th century and contemporary with the saint. Legend has it that St Patrick's Bell was used to good effect when its owner climbed the holy mountain of Croagh Patrick. Attacked by a black cloud of demons, St Patrick hurled his bell at them, and they promptly disappeared.

Other major attractions are the enormous **Lurgan log boat**, made around 2400 BC, which is long enough to transport the population of an entire village; the **Viking Gallery** with its swords, pins, brooches and splendid 10th-century yew longbow; and the three galleries of the **Medieval Ireland** exhibit, documenting rural life, the nobility and religious practise from 1150 to 1550.

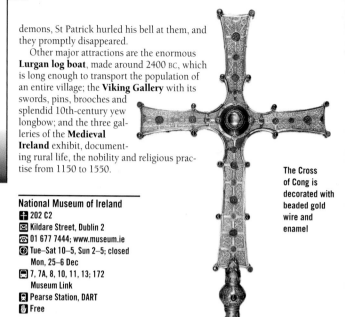

The Cross of Cong is decorated with beaded gold wire and enamel

National Museum of Ireland
- 202 C2
- Kildare Street, Dublin 2
- 01 677 7444; www.museum.ie
- Tue–Sat 10–5, Sun 2–5; closed Mon, 25–6 Dec
- 7, 7A, 8, 10, 11, 13; 172 Museum Link
- Pearse Station, DART
- Free

Museum of Decorative Arts and History
- 202, off A3
- Benburb Street, Dublin 7
- 01 677 7444; www.museum.ie
- Tue–Sat 10–5, Sun 2–5; closed Mon, 25–6 Dec
- 25, 25A, 66, 67, 90
- Heuston Station (main line)
- Free

TAKING A BREAK

Hang out with the fashionable crowd at nearby **Café en Seine**, a great place for coffee and cakes on warm summer days. Alternatively, stop for a relaxed cup of coffee at a Dublin favourite, **Bewley's Oriental Café** (78 Grafton Street) and watch the shoppers as they pass by on the busy street outside.

NATIONAL MUSEUM OF IRELAND: INSIDE INFO

Top tips If you have time, make the 2-km (1-mile) trip from the city centre to Collins Barracks, a handsome, early 18th-century building that was once used as a barracks but now houses the **Museum of Decorative Arts and History**. The collection here, varied and often bizarre, details Ireland's social history with exhibits ranging from domestic furnishings and dress to relics of Ireland's many political martyrs, as well as paintings and sculpture.

Hidden gem Tucked away in the National Museum of Ireland is a collection of *sheela-na-gigs*, stone carvings of women uninhibitedly displaying their charms. To inspect them, you have to apply in advance to the curator.

One to miss You could afford to miss the **Egyptian exhibition** on the National Museum's upper floor; there is plenty in the Irish exhibits to keep you fascinated for hours on end.

11 St Patrick's Cathedral

St Patrick's Cathedral is a dignified church, large and handsome, dating back to 1190, with its tower and spire soaring to 68m (223 feet).

Inside you'll find the **memorials** to **Dean Jonathan Swift** (1667–1745), passionate social reformer and author of *Gulliver's Travels* (▶ 26), and his companion "Stella", whose real name was Esther Johnson (1681–1728), with whom he had a long relationship. They lie side by side under brass plaques set into the nave floor, beside the second pillar just beyond the entrance desk. On the aisle wall nearby is Swift's self-penned memorial: "Laid where fierce indignation can no longer rend the heart. Go travellers, and imitate, if you can, this earnest and dedicated Champion of Liberty".

The cathedral also contains some splendid tombs, notably the 17th-century monument to the Boyle family (of which the scientist Robert Boyle was a member), and a collection of memorials to Irish soldiers killed in British Empire wars. Often overlooked, in the aisle wall south of the choir, are four superb 16th-century brass memorial tablets, very rare in Ireland. In the north aisle is a rather uninspiring memorial to the revered blind harpist Turlough O'Carolan (1670–1738); he deserves something bigger and better.

St Patrick's is at its peaceful best early in the morning or late in the afternoon.

Above: memorial to Archbishop Jones. Below: the high altar

TAKING A BREAK

The Globe on South Great George's Street, a 10-minute walk from the cathedral, is a great place for a light snack.

➕ 202 A2
✉ St Patrick's Close, Dublin 8
☎ 01 475 4817
🕐 Mon–Fri 9–6, Sat 9–6 (9–5, Nov–Feb), Sun 9–11, noon–6, 4:15–6 (10–11 Nov–Feb); visitors are welcome to attend services
🚌 50, 54A, 56A (Eden Quay)
🚉 Pearse Station 💷 Moderate

Swift's Skull

One item in the little Swift exhibition in the north transept is a plaster cast of the great man's skull, a reminder of 19th-century fascination with the macabre. The skull was dug up in the 1830s and "passed around the drawing rooms of Dublin". It was reburied in 1920.

12 Kilmainham Gaol

The grim but atmospheric old prison of Kilmainham is a national monument that holds within its walls the key to much of Ireland's turbulent history. Here Home Rule rebels – Wolfe Tone's 1798 supporters, "Young Irishmen" of 50 years later, Fenians, and leaders of the Easter Rising – suffered imprisonment, punishment and death.

Kilmainham's entrance sets the tone, a thick door with a spyhatch in a massive stonework frame. The **guided tour** (which is obligatory) starts in the museum, introducing you to bygone Dublin and the slum conditions that bred the debt and petty crime for which most prisoners were incarcerated here. As the guide will tell you as you are taken into the great four-storey hall with its multiple floors of tiny, cold, stone cells, Kilmainham Gaol was considered a model prison when it opened in 1796. Dark corridors lead to granite stairs worn hollow by the tread of feet. Debtors, murderers, sheep stealers, rapists, prostitutes, all ended up here. Famine victims, too – during the 1840s and 1850s the gaol became overcrowded with people who had committed petty crimes in order to qualify for the thin but regularly served prison gruel.

- ✚ 202, off A3
- ✉ Inchicore Road, Dublin 8
- ☎ 01 453 5984;
  www.heritageireland.ie
- 🕐 Daily 9:30–5, Apr–Sep;
  Mon–Sat 9:30–4, Sun 10–5,
  rest of year
- 🚌 51 (Aston Quay), 51B, 78A, 79
  (Aston Quay)
- 🚉 Heuston Station
- 💷 Moderate

You'll be shown the cells that held Pádraic Pearse, Thomas Clarke, Joseph Plunkett, James Connolly and the other leaders of the 1916 Easter Rising (► 19); the chapel where Plunkett and his fiancée, Grace Gifford, were married; and the high-walled yard where the leaders were shot for treason. The last prisoner to be released before Kilmainham closed in 1924 was the

Above left: the Five Devils of Kilmainham, symbolising the containment of evil

Above: the landings and cells in the gaol's grim interior

Republican leader Éamon de Valera – later to become both head of government and president of Ireland.

Whatever your views, you can't fail to be moved by the stories you'll hear, or by the atmosphere in this cold, echoing, haunted place. It's essential viewing for any visitor who wants to understand Ireland's recent history.

At Your Leisure

Dubliners opposed the construction of the 18th-century Custom House, fearing that it would be an eyesore

❶ Casino at Marino

You can take a guided tour around Dublin's strangest building, a well-kept secret tucked away off a suburban road. Built between 1758 and 1776 by the Earl of Charlemont, it is a three-storey pleasure palace of cleverly designed, ingeniously lit rooms, all concealed in what looks from the outside to be a simple one-roomed temple. Despite its name, the Casino houses no roulette or blackjack tables, just some contemporary furniture. Bizarre!

🚹 202, off C5 ✉ Off Casino Park, Malahide Road ☎ 01 833 1618; www.heritageireland.ie 🕙 Mon–Fri 10–6, Sat–Sun noon–4, Jun–Sep; Mon–Fri 10–5, Sat–Sun noon–4, Oct and May; rest of year tel: 01 647 2461 🚌 20A, 20B, 27, 27A, 42, 42C, 123 🚆 Clontarf, DART 🎫 Moderate

❷ Custom House

This is Dublin's grandest building, a great domed Georgian masterpiece started in 1781 by English architect James Gandon (1743–1823) to replace the old customs point further up the River Liffey. It stretches its portico and long arcaded wings along the north bank of the river, just east of O'Connell Bridge. Republicans torched it in 1921; restored, it houses a visitor centre. Much the best view of the Custom House is from George's Quay across the river.

🚹 202 C4 ✉ Custom House Quay, Dublin 2 ☎ 01 878 7660 🕙 Mon–Fri 10–5, Sat–Sun 2–5, mid-Mar to Oct; Wed–Fri 10–5, Sun 2–5, rest of year 🚌 Cross-city buses 🚆 Tara Street Station, DART 🎫 Inexpensive

❺ Dublin Writers' Museum

A beautifully restored and refurbished house, 10-minutes' walk north of O'Connell Bridge, contains this excellent museum dedicated to some of Ireland's greatest writers. There are photographs, first editions, personal belongings, letters, rare books, and masses of memorabilia to satisfy your curiosity about Swift, Sheridan, Joyce, Shaw, Wilde, Yeats, Beckett, Brendan Behan and many others.

🚹 202 B5 ✉ 18 Parnell Square North, Dublin 1 ☎ 01 872 2077; www.visitdublin.com 🕙 Mon–Sat 10–5 (also Mon–Fri 10–6, Jun–Aug), Sun, public hols 11–5 🚌 10, 11, 11A, 11B, 13, 16, 16A, 19, 19A, 22, 22A, 36 🚆 Connolly Station, DART 🎫 Moderate

❻ General Post Office (GPO)

This splendid Palladian building (1814–18) is almost all that was left of Dublin's late Georgian architecture after the developers got their hands on the city centre in the 1960s and 1970s. The GPO was the headquarters of the Irish Volunteers during the Easter Rising of 1916 (➤ 19) and it was from its steps that Pádraic Pearse read out the Proclamation of the Irish Republic. In the intense shelling that followed (you can still see shrapnel scars on the columns), the GPO was gutted by fire. Reopened in 1929 after rebuilding, it became a potent symbol of Irish independence. Inside is a plaque recording the Proclamation, and a sculpture of the mythical hero Cuchulainn, a symbol of Irish heroism.

🔳 202 B4 ✉ O'Connell Street, Dublin 1 ☎ 01 705 7000 🕐 Mon–Sat 8–8 🚌 Cross-city buses 🚉 Tara Street Station, DART 💷 Free

🔟 Temple Bar

In the 1980s Temple Bar was a run-down area, due for demolition to make way for a bus station. These days it's Dublin's trendiest, liveliest and most innovative quarter.

This is definitely a place to stroll the cobbled streets without a time limit. Young Dublin architects have twisted roof levels, inserted metal panels, and used glass and ceramics freely as they have renovated the old buildings. Street eateries and serious restaurants rub shoulders; so do street musicians and artists.

The heart of Temple Bar is Meeting House Square, often the venue for open-air performances. Around the square cluster the **Irish Film Institute** (tel: 01 679 3477; www.fii.ie) and **Film Archive**, an arts centre, the **Gallery of Photography** (tel: 01 671 4654; www.irish-photography.com), and the **Ark,** with children's workshops and activities (tel: 01 670 7788; www.ark.ie; advance booking advisable). Wander around the Saturday morning food market here while Dubliners breakfast in the open air.

One word of caution: the atmosphere late at night can be a bit intimidating; this is when youngsters with rather too much alcohol aboard come raucously out of the pubs and clubs. And lively stag and hen nights celebrate in noisy style…

🔳 202 B3 ✉ Just south of Wellington and Aston Quays, on the south bank of the Liffey. Temple Bar Audio-Visual Centre (information centre) is at 18 Eustace Street, Dublin 2 ☎ 01 677 2255; www.temple-bar.ie 🕐 Mon–Fri 9–5:30 🚌 All city centre buses 🚉 Tara Street Station, DART

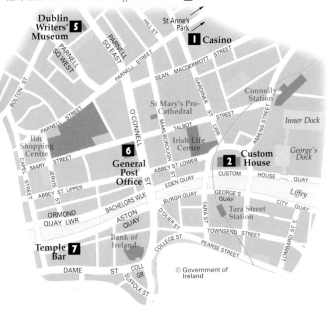

© Government of Ireland

The sumptuously furnished State Drawing Room at Dublin Castle

8 Dublin Castle

Grand occasions such as the inauguration of the president and European summit meetings take place in Dublin Castle's splendid State Apartments. Some of the original Norman castle still exists, but much is very fine 18th-century rebuilding. You can examine all this, along with the restored 19th-century Chapel Royal with its carved stone likenesses of British royalty outside and its elaborate woodwork and plasterwork within.

🏛 202 A3 ✉ Dame Street, Dublin 2
☎ 01 677 7129 🕐 Mon–Fri 10–5, Sat–Sun, public hols 2–5 🚌 50, 50A, 54, 56A, 77, 77A, 77B 🚆 Tara Street, DART 🎟 Moderate

9 Chester Beatty Library and Gallery

This is one of the world's great private art collections, notable not for its size (though it contains more than 22,000 manuscripts, rare books and miniature paintings), but for its quality. Sir Alfred Chester Beatty (1875–1968), a Canadian millionaire who made his fortune through mining and came to live in Dublin in 1953, put together his collection over most of his long lifetime. The Japanese scrolls are particularly fine, dating from the early 17th to the late 19th centuries. Religious legends, tales of romance and scenes of battle are painted in meticulous detail across rolls of paper or silk up to 25m (82 feet) long. There are Japanese prints of actors and tea drinkers and courtesans with oblique gazes and tiny mouths, and a whole clutch of delicately carved *netsuke*, or cord toggles. Other exotic curiosities include tiny snuff bottles in mother-of-pearl, jade and porcelain from China, and an Egyptian love poem written in 1160 BC, the world's most important surviving example of ancient Egyptian poetry.

Pride of place goes to the library's collection of manuscripts. Some of these are astonishingly old and rare,

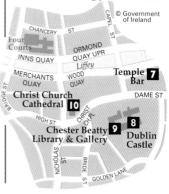

including ancient copies of the Koran, richly gilded and tooled, and a medieval Iraqi treatise on engineering, artillery and astronomy. There are also some very early biblical fragments, such as a Gospel of St Luke and a Book of Revelations, both dating from the 3rd century, and the Epistles of St Paul, written out in the 2nd century, as well as portions of the Books of Numbers and Deuteronomy that date back to about AD 150.

➕ 202 A3 ✉ The Clock Tower, Dublin Castle, Dublin 2 ☎ 01 407 0750; www.cbl.ie
🕐 Mon–Fri 10–5, May–Sep; Tue–Fri 10–5, Oct–Apr; Sat 11–5, Sun 1–5, all year 🚌 50, 50A, 54, 56A, 77, 77A, 77B 🚆 Tara Street, DART
🎟 Free

The original crypt runs the full length of the church; don't miss the gloomy statues, monarchical relics, and a celebrated showpiece, "the cat and the rat", whose mummified remains were found in an organ pipe.

➕ 202 A3 ✉ Christ Church Place, Dublin 8 ☎ 01 677 8099; www.cccdub.ie 🕐 Daily 9:45–5 or 5:30 🚌 50 (Eden Quay); 78A (Aston Quay) 🚆 Tara Street, DART 🎟 Moderate

Left: part of the Oriental collection at the Chester Beatty Library and Gallery

Below: the interior of Christ Church Cathedral

⑩ Christ Church Cathedral

The 11th-century Norse king Sigtryggr Silkenbeard founded it in wood, then around 150 years later the Norman Earl Strongbow rebuilt it in stone: splendid names, and a splendid early Norman cathedral, the oldest stone building in Dublin. Despite an over-thorough restoration in the 19th century, plenty of that Norman stonework remains inside. "Strongbow's tomb" lies in the south aisle, but the Norman earl himself is probably buried elsewhere.

Off the Beaten Track

St Stephen's Green, just south of Trinity College, is a popular place to hang out in the sunshine. If you walk on south down Harcourt Street, however, and turn left into Clonmel Street, you will discover the much more private, tranquil and uncrowded **Iveagh Gardens**. A beautiful green retreat among fountains and mature trees, the little-known gardens are a great place to escape from the rigours of city life.

For Kids

Dublin Zoo (tel: 01 677 1425; www.dublinzoo.ie, open: Mon–Sat 9:30–6, Sun 10:30–6, in summer; Mon–Fri 9:30–4, Sat 9:30–5, Sun 10:30–5, in winter; admission: expensive), surrounded by the wide open spaces of Phoenix Park, is good of its kind. **National Wax Museum** (tel: 01 872 6340, open: Mon–Sat 10–5:30, Sun noon–5:30, admission: moderate), in Granby Row, off Parnell Square, is great fun.

13 Guinness Storehouse

Ireland's favourite brew has travelled to more corners of the world than the Irish themselves, which is saying something, and the first thing many visitors to Ireland want to do is to taste it on its home soil. The next step is to visit this exhibition at the brewery itself, to discover just why the "black stuff" has such appeal. Housed in a former fermentation plant, the Storehouse tells the story of Arthur Guinness and his brewery, with displays about how Guinness is made, how it is transported worldwide, and its hugely popular and entertaining advertising campaigns. At the end of the tour you get a complimentary pint in the circular roof-top Gravity Bar, with floor-to-ceiling windows and spectacular views over Dublin.

🔢 202, off A3 ✉ St James's Gate, Dublin 8 ☎ 01 408 4800; www.guinnessstorehouse.com ⏰ Daily 9:30–5 (till 9 pm Jul–Aug); closed Good Fri and 24–6 Dec 🚌 51B, 78A (Aston Quay), 90 (Connolly Station), 123 (O'Connell and Dame streets) 🚉 Heuston 💶 Expensive

Phoenix Park, west of central Dublin, is the perfect place to escape frenetic city life

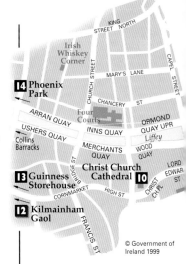

© Government of Ireland 1999

14 Phoenix Park

Phoenix Park (main entrance about 1.5km (1 mile) west of the city centre) is the largest walled city park in Europe, covering nearly 800 hectares (2,000 acres). This huge expanse of land, laid out in the mid-18th century, contains woods, lakes, hillocks, streams and gardens, set against the backdrop of the Wicklow Mountains. The Irish president lives here in a mansion, Áras an Uachtaráin. Here, too, are 17th-century Ashtown Castle, housing

North of the Liffey
It's less fashionable than south of the river, but check out trendy Smithfield; try the markets in Moore Street (fruit, vegetables and backchat) and Mary's Lane (Saturday mornings; horses and hoarse traders); Blessington Street Basin Gardens in an old canal bed; and for a freaky thrill, a peek at the mummified bodies in the crypt of St Michan's Church on Church Street.

the Phoenix Park Visitor Centre (tel: 01 677 0095); the American ambassador's residence; St Mary's Hospital; and Dublin Zoo – all swallowed up in the vastness of the park.

➕ 202, off A3 ✉ Main entrance on Parkgate Street, opposite Heuston Station; www.heritageireland.ie
🕐 Visitor centre: daily 10–6, Apr–Sep; 10–5:30, mid-Mar to end Mar; 10–5, Oct; Sat–Sun 10–5, rest of year. Last admission 45 minutes before closing
🚌 25, 25A, 26, 51, 51B, 66, 66A, 67, 67A from city centre 🎟 Park: free. Visitor centre: inexpensive

Outer Dublin
Riding the DART (➤ 35) is by far the best way to taste the many delights of outer Dublin, and gain enjoyable views along the waterfronts, the Liffey and the city centre.

St Anne's Park
This quiet park, 8km (5 miles) from the centre, is little visited by non-Dubliners. It is crossed by a number of footpaths; the best runs down through the park's extensive woodland, past follies and temples hidden among the trees, to emerge beside the coast road with wide views out over North Bull Island to Howth Head.

➕ 201 E5 🚉 Killester or Harmonstown, DART

James Joyce Tower
The Martello Tower that overlooks the sea at Sandycove was featured by James Joyce in the opening sequence of *Ulysses*. Joyce lived in the tower for a month in 1904. Today it houses a collection of Joyce curios and memorabilia, along with photographs, books and a selection of letters. The oval tower itself, built early in the 19th century against the threat of a Napoleonic invasion, makes an atmospheric place to visit, and from the roof you can enjoy the same fine view as Buck Mulligan did in *Ulysses*.

➕ 201 E5 ✉ Sandycove Point, Sandycove ☎ 01 280 9265; www.visitdublin.com 🕐 Mon–Sat 10–1, 2–5, Sun 2–6, Apr–Oct 🚉 Sandycove, DART 🎟 Moderate

Dalkey
This quiet little seaside town 14.5km (9 miles) from central Dublin, immortalised with mordant humour by Flann O'Brien in *The Dalkey Archive*, is not so much a resort as a well-heeled commuter haven with a tangle of narrow lanes and a pleasant "out-of-it-all" feel.

➕ 201 E5 🚉 Dalkey, DART

Killiney
Killiney is a very exclusive place these days, the seaside refuge of rock stars, artists and other fashionable Dublin escapees. The best thing to do once you are tired of celebrity-spotting is to climb Killiney Hill and enjoy the splendid view out over Dublin Bay.

➕ 201 E5 🚉 Killiney, DART

Bray
Bray is a jaded seaside resort, 24km (15 miles) from the centre, with good sands and a plethora of cheap and cheerful amusements. You might prefer a windswept walk around Bray Head.

➕ 201 E5 🚉 Bray, DART

St Valentine's Shrine
Ever wondered if St Valentine really existed? He did, and was martyred in Rome on 14 February, 269, for performing outlawed marriage ceremonies for young lovers. Strange to say, his remains are in Dublin, and can be viewed in a beautiful black and gold chest under an altar in Whitefriar Street Church at 56 Aungier Street.

Where to...
Eat and Drink

Prices
Expect to pay per person for a meal, excluding drinks and service

€ up to €20   €€ up to €32   €€€ over €32

Café Boulevard €

As Continental as its name implies, the Café Boulevard serves up cosmopolitan cuisine in a very relaxing atmosphere. The menu, ranging from smoked crespolini to Cajun prawn tagliatelle to Irish lamb cutlets, is strong on Italian dishes, but incorporates interesting oriental influences. The pizzas, made to order using fresh mozzarella and a special recipe sauce, have some interesting topping choices.

🛨 202 B3 ⊠ 27 Exchequer Street, Dublin 2 ☎ 01 679 2131; fax: 01 670 4940 🕙 Mon–Sat from 9 am, last dinner order approx 9 pm; closed Good Fri and 25–6 Dec

Chapter One Restaurant and Café €€€

Good food, using first-class seasonal ingredients in a blend of modern Irish and international cuisines, is served in this arched basement beneath the Dublin Writers' Museum. Pre-theatre dinner is served between 6 pm and 7 pm, and it is possible to return after the theatre for dessert and coffee.

🛨 202 B5 ⊠ 18/19 Parnell Square, Dublin 1 ☎ 01 873 2266/873 2281 🕙 Restaurant: lunch Tue–Fri, dinner Tue–Sat; closed public hols, 2 weeks Christmas. Museum coffee shop: Mon–Sat 10–5; closed 1–15 Aug and 25–6 Dec

Cornucopia €

This long-established vegetarian restaurant off Grafton Street continues to be a favourite for its nice atmosphere and its excellent choice of delicious and imaginative dishes, such as African sweet potato and chick pea curry, Moroccan Pie (lentil with couscous) and roasted Mediterranean vegetable filo parcels. Breads and cakes are all home-baked too. The menu changes daily, and caters to special diets.

🛨 202 B3 ⊠ 19 Wicklow Street, Dublin 2 ☎ 01 677 7583; fax: 01 671 9449; email: cornucopia@tinet.ie 🕙 Mon–Sat 8.30–8 (till 9 Thu), Sun noon–8

L'Ecrivain €€€

Named after its collection of Irish writers' portraits, this stylish modern restaurant is now twice its previous size after a major rebuild – there's a 110-seater restaurant, private dining-room for 20 people, bar and baby grand. Expect a welcoming atmosphere, seriously good cooking in atmosphere, and delightful unique combination of new Irish and Mediterranean influences, and delightful

service. Unusually, service charge applies to food only, excluding drinks.

🛨 202 C2 ⊠ 109 Lower Baggot Street, Dublin 2 ☎ 01 661 1919 🕙 Mon–Fri 12:30–2, 7–10, Sat 7–10; closed public hols, Christmas week

Elephant and Castle €

Buzzy and youthful, this exuberant, noisy café-restaurant was one of Temple Bar's first new-wave places and is still one of the best. Ingredients are carefully selected and served in a range of generous and wholesome salads (their special Caesar salad is legendary), pasta dishes, freshly made burgers and huge baskets of chicken wings. On the down side, service can be slow, although friendly, and the bill can climb unexpectedly quickly. Book ahead.

🛨 202 B3 ⊠ 18 Temple Bar, Dublin 2 ☎ 01 679 3121 🕙 Mon–Fri 8 am–11:30 pm, Sat 10:30 am–11:30 pm, Sun noon–11:30 pm; closed 3 days Christmas

Jacobs Ladder €€€

Overlooking the playing fields of Trinity College, this cool, modern first-floor restaurant provides a lovely setting for the fine cooking. Well-balanced, hearty seasonal menus always include several imaginative vegetarian dishes. There's a good selection of local fish, shellfish and speciality Irish produce such as carrageen (edible seaweed) and farmhouse cheeses.

➕ 202 C2 ⊠ 4 Nassau Street, Dublin 2 ☎ 01 670 3865 🅶 Lunch and dinner: Tue–Fri. Dinner: Sat; closed 3 weeks Christmas

Kilkenny €

With its relaxed atmosphere and agreeable first-floor outlook, Kilkenny is one of Dublin's most pleasant restaurants. Wholesomeness is its great strength: all the ingredients – and products on sale in the Food Hall – are fresh and additive free. Salads, quiches, casseroles, homebaked breads and cakes are the specialities. For quicker bites, try the shop's second eating place, the popular Kilkenny Café, where the same principles apply.

➕ 202 C2 ⊠ 6 Nassau Street, Dublin 2 ☎ 01 677 7075 🅶 Mon–Fri 8:30–5 (7 pm on Thu), Sat 9–5, Sun 11–5

The Mermaid Café €–€€

In this welcoming restaurant on the edge of Temple Bar the mood is modern, and the attention to detail touches everything. Imaginative American-inspired cooking is the hallmark; a speciality is the Atlantic seafood casserole. Interestingly served Irish cheeses, excellent coffees and unusual wines add to the appeal.

➕ 202 A3 ⊠ 69/70 Dame Street, Dublin 2 ☎ 01 670 8236 🅶 Lunch and dinner: Mon–Sat; Sun brunch noon–3:30; closed Christmas week

Old Jameson Distillery €

The restored Old Jameson Distillery is a great spot for a bite to eat. In the attractively bright, contemporary café-style Still Room Restaurant the combination of self-service and table service hits just the right tone. Light food is available all day and locals eagerly join the line for lunch, which features such well-made Irish specialities as bacon and cabbage soup and John Jameson casserole.

➕ 202, off A3 ⊠ Smithfield, Dublin 8 ☎ 01 872 5566 🅶 Daily 9–5:30; closed Good Fri and 25 Dec

The Porterhouse €

This genuinely contemporary pub was Ireland's first microbrewery; here, connoisseurs can sample excellent beers brewed on the site. The Porterhouse is innovative yet sympathetic to tradition: brewing-related displays entertain and inform. The food is well above average and, like the pub, it blends tradition with originality.

➕ 202 A3 ⊠ 16 Parliament Street, Dublin 2 ☎ 01 679 8847 🅶 Daily noon–9:30; closed Good Fri and 25 Dec

Romanza €€

Morels is in a semi-basement adjoining Stephen's Hall, Dublin's first "all-suite" hotel. The restaurant has a patio area, accessible in fine weather. Sunny decor and a zesty style of cooking underline the Mediterranean theme. It's a good spot for a meal before a performance at The National Concert Hall.

➕ 202 C1 ⊠ 14–17 Lower Leeson Street, Dublin 2 ☎ 01 662 2480 🅶 Lunch: Mon–Fri. Dinner: Mon–Sat; closed public hols

101 Talbot Restaurant €€

This cheerful first-floor restaurant is an oasis in the inner city culinary desert north of the Liffey. A constantly changing exhibition decorates the walls, and you'll often find a lively crowd, drawn by the reasonably priced, creative food with Mediterranean and Middle Eastern influences. The selection of vegetarian dishes is particularly tempting.

➕ 202 C4 ⊠ 101 Talbot Street, Dublin 1 ☎ 01 874 5011 🅶 Dinner: Tue–Sat 5–11; closed public hols, 1 week Christmas

Roly's Bistro €€–€€€

Dublin's first big contemporary café-restaurant is a bustling two-storey bistro offering a warm welcome, with irresistible breads and imaginative menus that reveal influences from classical French, Irish and world cuisines. The standard of cooking is high, yet the prices are low, and there is good service, unlimited coffee and keenly priced wine.

➕ 202, off C2 ⊠ 7 Ballsbridge Terrace, Dublin 4 ☎ 01 668 2611 🅶 Lunch: daily noon–2:45. Dinner: 6–9:45 pm; closed Good Fri, 3 days Christmas

Where to... Stay

Prices

Expect to pay per person staying
€ up to €40 €€ up to €77 €€€ over €77

Aberdeen Lodge €€€

This restored Edwardian house is a charming private hotel. Accommodation is charged by the room, with breakfast, providing good value for the location and high standard. Comfortably furnished rooms include two with four-poster beds; two suites have whirlpool spa baths. Dinner is available and facilities include parking, a garden and a gym close by.

🚇 202, off C3 🏠 53–55 Park Avenue, Ballsbridge, Dublin 4 🕿 01 283 8155; email: aberdeen@iol.ie; www.halpinsprivatehotels.com
🕲 Open all year

The Clarence €€€

The rock group U2 bought this mid-19th-century Liffey-side hotel in the early 1990s and refurbished it in a contemporary style that is in sympathy with its Arts and Crafts origins. It offers the luxury and amenities expected by the many stars who stay here. The hotel's fashionable restaurant, **The Tea Room**, is one of Dublin's favourite dining-rooms, and Temple Bar's top meeting place is the oak-panelled Octagon Bar.

🚇 202 A3 🏠 6–8 Wellington Quay, Dublin 2 🕿 01 407 0800; fax: 01 407 0820; email: reservations@theclarence.ie; www.theclarence.ie 🕲 Open all year

Jurys Inn Christchurch €€€

This modern hotel, in a central position near Temple Bar, offers a good standard of accommodation for a fixed room rate. You'll be pleasantly surprised by spacious, well-furnished rooms sleeping up to three adults (or two adults and two children), with well-lit desktops, tea/coffee facilities, TV, direct-dial phone and small, simple bathrooms with bath and shower. No room service, but there's a pub and restaurant on site. There's direct access from an adjoining car park.

🚇 202 A3 🏠 Christchurch Place, Dublin 8 🕿 01 454 0000; email: jurysinnchristchurch@jurysdoyle.com; www.jurys.com 🕲 Closed 24–6 Dec

Jurys Inn Custom House €€€

Overlooking the Liffey, this sister hotel to Jurys Inn Christchurch has the same large bedrooms, but also fax/modem lines, a higher standard of finish, and slightly better bathrooms. No room service, but there's a bar and restaurant, as well as conference facilities, a staffed business centre and even a mini-gym. A parking garage adjoins the hotel.

🚇 202 C4 🏠 Custom House Quay, Dublin 1 🕿 01 607 5000; email: bookings@jurysdoyle.com; www.jurys.com 🕲 Closed 24–6 Dec

Kilronan House €€–€€€

This Georgian house is in a peaceful setting, within walking distance of St Stephen's Green and The National Concert Hall. It's stylish throughout, with original features and Waterford Crystal chandeliers. You'll find crisp linens and orthopaedic beds in the bedrooms, plus TV, beverages and baskets of quality toiletries. Breakfasts are a highlight, with smoked salmon, pancakes, fresh fruit and the traditional Irish breakfast on the menu. This is a no-nonsense establishment.

🚇 202, B1 🏠 70 Adelaide Road, Dublin 2 🕿 01 475 5266; email: info@dublin.com 🕲 Open all year

Le Meridien Shelbourne €€€

The 1922 Irish Constitution was drafted at this opulent 18th-century hotel; today it is ranked among the world's greatest hotels. The Horseshoe Bar is renowned as a meeting place for the famous, and The Shelbourne Bar on Kildare Street serves bar food; other amenities include an impressive Health and Fitness Club. The 24 luxurious suites are seriously grand, with separate sitting rooms and dressing rooms. There's a choice of restaurants: the elegant **No 27 The Green** for fine dining, or a striking minimalist café-restaurant, **The Side Door At The Shelbourne**, entered from Kildare Street. Afternoon tea taken in the Lord Mayor's Lounge is a traditional treat.

🔢 202 C2 ⌧ 27 St Stephen's Green, Dublin 2 ☎ 01 663 4500; fax: 01 661 6006; email: rooms@shelbourne.ie; www.shelbourne.ie ⊙ Open all year

Raglan Lodge €€

In a peaceful position, yet only a short walk from the city centre, this elegant Victorian residence has exceptionally comfortable bedrooms with private bathrooms and all the necessary amenities. Restored in 1987, it is now one of the city's most desirable guest houses, for the high level of comfort and service provided and also for outstanding breakfasts. Theatre reservations can be arranged and there's private parking.

🔢 202, off C1 ⌧ 10 Raglan Road, Dublin 4 ☎ 01 660 6697; fax: 01 660 6781 ⊙ Closed 2 weeks Christmas

Where to... Shop

Shopping Hours

Usual shopping hours are 9:30–5:30; late opening to 8 pm on Thursday. Some shops open on Sunday, usually from noon until 5 or 6 pm.

Central Dublin's main shopping areas span the Liffey from the rejuvenated Henry Street and O'Connell Street area (on the north bank) to the more exclusive Grafton Street area (south bank), with a pedestrian link through Temple Bar and across the Ha'penny Bridge. Some of the top shops are unique to Dublin, including department stores such as Arnotts (Henry Street), Clery's (O'Connell Street) and the ultrachic Brown Thomas (Grafton Street), and there are many specialist shops. International brands are everywhere, particularly in big shopping malls (such as St Stephen's Green Centre at the top of Grafton Street and the Jervis Centre on Mary Street, north of the Liffey), but it is owner-managed shops and boutiques that really make shopping here an enjoyable experience.

THINGS IRISH

South of the river, you'll find classy little cosmopolitan shops in the Grafton Street area, notably on Hibernian Way, off Dawson Street. And there are outlets for quality Irish goods such as tweeds, woollens, pottery and crystal along **Nassau Street**. **Kilkenny** is the most interesting and stylish shop to browse, with a time range of contemporary Irish fashions in natural fabrics (for both men and women), silver jewellery and pottery and crafts. Kilkenny is also a good choice for a meal (▶ 67), featuring its own specialist food products. Nearby, **Blarney Woollen Mills** specialises in tweeds and sweaters, **Kevin & Howlin** is the place to go for men's traditional handwoven tweed jackets, suits and hats, while **House of Ireland** is an upmarket gift shop carrying a wide selection of typically Irish goods, including crystal, tweeds and woollens.

BOOKS AND ANTIQUES

Greene's (Clare Street) and **Cathach Books** (Duke Street) are the specialists for second-hand books, while **Hodges Figgis**, the city's biggest bookshop, faces a large **Waterstones** across Dawson Street. Waterstones also has an outlet in the Jervis Centre.

Dublin's long tradition of craftsmanship makes it a good browsing ground for antiques. Bargains are rare nowadays, but you'll have plenty of fun looking.

The trade is centred in Dublin's oldest district, The Liberties. Francis Street especially is renowned. **The Powerscourt Townhouse Centre** (South William Street) has an antiques gallery selling mainly silver and china. Here, too, is the Crafts Council of Ireland's HQ Gallery. There are many antiques and jewellery shops in the same neighbourhood, and antiques and collectables fairs are held twice a month on Sundays throughout the year at **Newman House** (St Stephen's Green, tel: 01 670 8295).

MARKETS

At **Temple Bar Market** (Meeting House Square), the best of artisan foods are sold every Saturday. **Mother Redcap's**, a covered market on Back Lane (Christchurch, open: Fri–Sun 11–6) has all sorts for sale, much of it second hand. At the **Tower Design Centre** (Pearse Street, tel: 01 677 5655) you can watch craftspeople at work and buy silk painting, jewellery, designer knitwear, pewter, woodwork and such like.

Where to...
Be Entertained

Detailed listings covering theatre, cinema, live music, sporting events and festivals are carried in daily papers, *In Dublin* magazine (published every two weeks) and *Events of the Week*, a free sheet available from pubs and guest houses. The *Irish Times* website (www.ireland.com) is a valuable source of information. Dublin Tourism Centre at St Andrew's Church, Suffolk Street, Dublin 2 (tel: 01 605 7700) can also help.

FAMOUS PUBS

Spontaneous entertainment is provided by Dublin pubs: **Doheny and Nesbitt** (5 Lower Baggot Street, tel: 01 660 2945) and **The Horseshoe Bar** (Le Meridien Shelbourne Hotel, St Stephen's Green) are both renowned for politician spotting, while **Toner's** (139 Lower Baggot Street) is a delight and said to be the only pub W B Yeats ever entered. There's even a Dublin Literary Pub Crawl (▶ 29). More sober affairs include a Georgian Literary Walking Tour and a Medieval Walking Tour; details available from tourist information offices.

NIGHT-LIFE

Pub music O'Donoghue's (15 Merrion Row, tel: 01 676 2807) is renowned, and there's traditional music and good food in Dublin's oldest pub, **The Brazen Head** (20 Lower Bridge Street, tel: 01 679 5186). **Jurys** (Ballsbridge, tel: 01 660 5000) hotels offer regular cabaret. Outside the city, **Johnnie Fox's** (Glencullen, tel: 01 295 5647) is equally famous for its seafood menus and Irish "Hooley Nights", while **Howth's Abbey Tavern** (tel: 01 839 0307) offers staged traditional Irish music. **Taylors Three Rock Bar** in Rathfarnham (tel: 01 494 2999) has music and dancing in three bars. A young crowd heads for Temple Bar and other venues regularly featuring Irish and international artists, such as **The Village Bar** (26 Wexford Street, tel: 01 475 8555) and **Whelan's** (25 Wexford Street, tel: 01 478 0766).

Night-clubs **P.O.D.** (Harcourt Street, tel: 01 478 0225) is an established favourite. **Club M** (Blooms Hotel, Temple Bar, tel: 01 671 5622) is popular with younger clubbers. The **Gaiety** (South King Street, tel: 01 677 1717) and **Olympia** (Dame Street) theatres stage late-night music. For details of shows and events at **The National Concert Hall** (Earlsfort Terrace) and **The Point**, consult newspapers and events listings. The **Comedy Cellar** (International Bar, Wicklow Street, tel: 01 677 9250) has Irish and international stand-up comedy every Mon, Wed, Thu, and Sat.

Eastern Ireland

Getting Your Bearings

Eastern Ireland has subtle charms that well repay your time. The steep Wicklow Mountains – Dublin's own mini-mountains – rise right on the city's southern doorstep, and extend southwards with a fine coast of cliffs and long sandy beaches. South from here, big river estuaries (paradise for birdwatchers) cut into Ireland's southeastern foot around Wexford and Waterford. West of Dublin lie the great open spaces of The Curragh in County Kildare (prime horse country), while out to the north of the city the land smooths into green farming country.

Dotted throughout are the slow-paced small towns and villages so characteristic of rural Ireland. Life runs as easy here as it does in the west, and with half the tourist crowds, even though the chief attractions of eastern Ireland are among the best known in the country. Dubliners may venture south from the city to take a stroll in the Wicklow Hills or buy some knitwear from the weaving shops at Avoca, but many visitors look further west for their pleasures, hurrying through towards the dramatic scenery of Galway and Clare. All the more elbow room for those who allow themselves a few days to sample this overlooked corner of Ireland.

The hills of Wicklow offer superb walking and even better sightseeing, especially the monastic remains at Glendalough. Down in Waterford you can watch Waterford crystal being made, then buy a piece of this world-renowned glassware. Kilkenny is the most appealing medieval town in Ireland.

Previous page: the ancient church and graveyard at Glendalough

There are equine eccentricities at the National Stud and Horse Museum near Kildare, and a chance to see thoroughbreds at full gallop on The Curragh. Relics of a glorious ecclesiastical past vary from the ancient churches and round towers of Monasterboice and the Rock of Cashel to the richly carved high crosses at Moone and Castledermot.

Pride of place, though, has to be given to the remarkable Stone Age passage grave north of Dublin at Newgrange, heavily decorated with enigmatic swirls of stone carving. One of Ireland's most memorable experiences is to creep along the ancient stone corridor to the chamber at the heart of the burial mound, where the sun still enters at the winter solstice to celebrate death and rebirth, as it has for 5,000 years.

Enjoy the wild beauty of the Wicklow Mountains, the craftsmanship of the glass-blowers and engravers at Waterford Crystal, and the unforgettable atmosphere in the ancient tombs at Newgrange.

Eastern Ireland in Three Days

Day One

Morning Leave Dublin (N81 or N11) in plenty of time to allow a morning's idling south through the **❶ Wicklow Mountains** (right, ➤ 76–7), leaving at least an hour to explore **Glendalough** (above). Aim to reach Avoca in time for lunch in The Fountain (aka Fitzgerald's Pub).

Afternoon Continue south via Arklow to Enniscorthy. If you have some time to spare, turn south here for half an hour to reach **❸ Wexford** and the **wildfowl reserve** on the mudflats of the North Slob (➤ 85). Otherwise, continue south-west to a night's stop in Waterford.

Day Two

Morning Spend an hour or so in the **5 Waterford Crystal** factory (right, ➤ 79), then it's a 50-km (30-mile) drive north to **8 Kilkenny** (High Street above, ➤ 80), another place that's worth at least two hours' exploration and is a good place to stop for lunch.

Afternoon Head north from Kilkenny to Portlaoise; then northeast via Portarlington and Edenderry across the Bog of Allen, one of Ireland's most extensive and evocative peat bogs. It's a vast expanse of wild country whose flatness either repels or fascinates, depending on your mood. Continue to Trim, beautifully placed with its Norman castle beside the River Boyne; then on via the splendid ruins of Bective Abbey towards Navan.

Day Three

Morning Continue northeast to **13 Brú na Bóinne** and **Newgrange** passage grave (➤ 81–4) – the site deserves at least a morning's exploration.

Afternoon Enjoy lunch in historic Drogheda. Afterwards follow N1, which saunters to the coast at Balbriggan before setting its sights south for the capital; or if you are in no hurry, idle back via the rural and delightful R108 through Naul and Ballyboghil.

❶ The Wicklow Mountains

The Wicklow Mountains beckon irresistibly on the Dublin skyline, enticing city-dwellers out at weekends in their thousands to enjoy the fresh air and freedom of the "Garden of Ireland".

Roads from Dublin into the Wicklow Mountains are all beautiful. You can ease yourself in from Bray on the northeast coast, ride in grandly from the west via the Sally Gap or the Wicklow Gap, or wriggle down from the north over Powerscourt Mountain. The real pleasure of these mountains is in taking a side turning and discovering the beautiful gorges, glens and remote pieces of wild country for yourself. But the main attraction is undoubtedly Glendalough, a scatter of monastic remains along an exceptionally lovely lake valley in the heart of the mountains.

Filling the country south of the capital, the Wicklow Mountains rise in peaks that are small

✚ 201 D4

✉ Immediately south of Dublin, via N81, then R759 or R756. Alternatively, N11, then R755; or R115. Tourist information: County Wicklow Tourism, Rialto House, Fitzwilliam Square, Wicklow

☎ 0404 69117; email: wicklowtouristoffice@eircom. net

in comparison to the world's great mountain ranges; the highest, Lugnaquilla, rises to just 925m (3,035 feet), and most of the other summits struggle to make 850m (2,790 feet). But they provide wonderful walking, through a network of local footpaths and along the long-distance Wicklow Way footpath, which traverses the range from north to south. Wicklow is the most thickly forested county in Ireland. There are excellent forest trails in the Devil's Glen on the east of the mountains, at Djouce Woods near Powerscourt, at Ballinafunshoge in Glenmalure south of Glendalough, and around Glendalough itself.

High open country of the Wicklow Mountains, a favourite fresh-air retreat for Dubliners

Glendalough

The monastic site of Glendalough incorporates a 12th-century **Round Tower** (33m/108 feet high), the 11th-century **St Kevin's Kitchen** (a beautiful stone-built oratory), and a number of glorious views of the lake and its mountain backdrop. Founded possibly as early as the 6th century, the monastery gained a Europe-wide reputation for learning. Its most illustrious member (some say its founder) was St Kevin, who was of the royal house of Leinster in the 6th century.

It is best to avoid Glendalough in high season: on sunny summer holiday weekends, it becomes something less than the tranquil paradise it can seem on a quiet spring or autumn evening.

Reservoir Road

A fine scenic road curves around the shores of Poulaphouca Reservoir between Blessington and Hollywood – a good introduction or farewell to the Wicklow Mountains.

Avoca

The village of Avoca, in the southern part of the Wicklow Mountains region, has Ireland's oldest hand-weaving mill and quality handloom weaving for sale. To get there, go 21km (13 miles) south from Glendalough (R755 to Rathdrum; R752 to Avoca).

TAKING A BREAK

Stop in the Wicklow Mountains at the renowned **Roundwood Inn** (➤ 89), where excellent bar food is served in an informal environment. In Avoca, try **The Fountain** or the **Avoca Handweavers** (➤ 89).

THE WICKLOW MOUNTAINS: INSIDE INFO

Top tips To get from **Dublin to Glendalough's** monuments and lakes, take the N81 Wexford road south from Dublin; at Hollywood (40km/25 miles) a left turn on to R756 takes you through the Wicklow Gap and on to Glendalough.
• If you intend to go **walking in the Wicklow Mountains**, take a good map. The Irish OS 1:50,000 Sheets 56 and 62 maps cover the area in detail.

Hidden gem The **side road** that (almost) circumnavigates Trooperstown Hill, just east of Laragh and Glendalough, is a beautiful 14.5-km (9-mile) meander, usually ignored by tourists in a hurry.

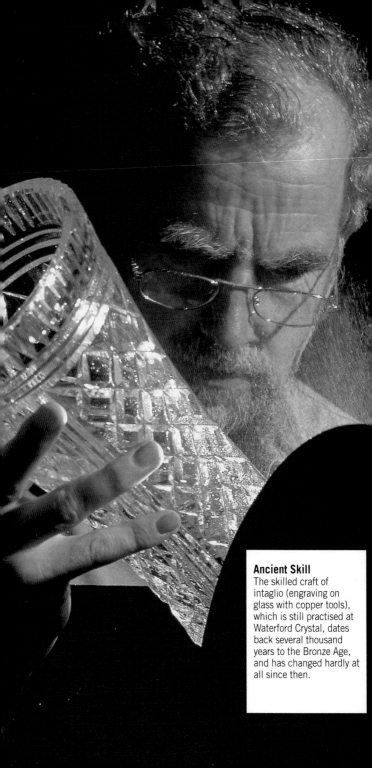

Ancient Skill
The skilled craft of intaglio (engraving on glass with copper tools), which is still practised at Waterford Crystal, dates back several thousand years to the Bronze Age, and has changed hardly at all since then.

5 Waterford Crystal

Watching a piece of Waterford Crystal slowly taking shape is like watching an expert magic trick: you can see every stage as it happens, but the end result still amazes.

Waterford Crystal is a commercial operation, well aware of its glamorous international reputation, and touring the glassworks, you can feel a bit like a sheep being herded along in a flock. But don't miss it.

The celebrated glassware is made in the same town on the south coast of Ireland, and by much the same method, as it was when the business was started up in 1783 by English brothers William and George Penrose. The expertise required, the instinct that tells a craftsperson when something is exactly right, and the long hours of practice that eventually make perfect – these remain timeless.

On your tour through the process you see how silica sand, litharge (lead monoxide) and potash – unprepossessing in themselves – are mixed in furnaces, then drawn out to be blown into glowing balls of molten crystal. Skilfully patted and smoothed in wooden and iron moulds, the crystal fades to pale yellow, then to a smoky transparency as it is shaped.

The next stage is the cutting, each craftsperson at a wheel carving the characteristic deep patterns of wedges and swirls into the cooled crystal. Then comes the engraving and sculpting workshop where master craftspeople cut delicate designs of faces, foliage, animals and birds. At all stages of the process the workers are happy to explain what they are doing and to answer questions.

Afterwards, you can buy some crystal from the showroom. However, bargain-hunters looking for a cheap "second" with some trifling flaw are wasting their time. To preserve the crystal's reputation, any imperfect glass is smashed at the factory.

🔡 200 C3
✉ Kilbarry, Cork Road, Waterford
☎ 051 373311/358397;
  www.waterford-usa.com
🕐 Tours daily 9–6 (last tour 4:15),
  Mar–Oct; 9–5 (last tour 3:15),
  rest of year. Showroom daily 9–6,
  Mar–Oct; 9–5, rest of year
💲 Moderate

TAKING A BREAK

Enjoy an informal meal at **The Wine Vault** (▶ 89), a lively wine bar in the oldest part of Waterford.

WATERFORD CRYSTAL: INSIDE INFO

Top tips If you want to avoid uncomfortably crowded tours (and Waterford Crystal is one of Ireland's most popular tourist attractions), take the **early morning tour**. In the high holiday season, book ahead to make sure of a place.

• Try the **quieter R733** as an alternative to the main N25 Wexford to Waterford road. It leads you into the Hook Head peninsula on the east side of Waterford Harbour. There are old castles here at Ballyhack and Slade, and coastal views.

Hidden gem Friday visitors, if lucky, get to enjoy a dramatic sight – workers in sinister face masks wilting as they withdraw **molten crystal** from the glare of a white-hot furnace at 1,400°C (2,552°F).

⑧ Kilkenny

Kilkenny is a medieval gem, ideal for a leisurely exploration on foot. War and wild times have swept regularly through the little town, leaving it with an impressive castle, a fortress of a cathedral, and a maze of sloping side streets packed with ancient buildings. Ask at the tourist office about Pat Tynan's one-hour walking tours, a quick and amusing introduction to the historic town.

Kilkenny Castle is a fine Victorian remodelling of a 12th-century Norman fortress, superbly sited on a bend of the River Nore, with wide wooded parklands to stroll in. At the other end of the straggling High Street is **St Canice's Cathedral,** a squat 13th-century stronghold with a stubby tower like a head hunched between the high shoulders of the roofs. The nave is filled with beautifully carved old monuments and tomb slabs – a treasury of the stone-carver's art that shouldn't be missed.

Climb the cathedral's round tower for the best view over Kilkenny; then make for the little well house on Kenny's Well Road, just beyond the cathedral. **St Canice's Holy Well** here dates back to the 6th century AD – and probably much further.

Kilkenny's Witch
The oldest inscribed slab in Kilkenny Cathedral is to Jose de Keteller, who died in 1280. He was probably the father of Dame Alice Kyteler, who was accused in 1324 of being a witch. She escaped, leaving her maid Petronella to be burned at the stake in her place.

The Long Gallery in Kilkenny Castle

Tourist Information
✚ 200 C4
✉ Shee Alms House, Rose Inn Street, Kilkenny
☎ 056 7751500; www.southeastireland.com

St Canice's Cathedral
✉ Dean Street, Kilkenny
☎ 056 7764971
🕐 Mon–Sat 9–1, 2–6, Sun 2–6, Easter–May; daily 9–6, Jun–Aug; Mon–Sat 10–1, 2–4, Sun 2–4, rest of year
🎟 Inexpensive

Kilkenny Castle
✉ The Parade, Kilkenny
☎ 056 7721450
🕐 Daily 9:30–7, Jun–Sep; 10:30–5, Apr–May; Tue–Sat 10:30–12:45, 2–5, rest of year
🎟 Moderate

13 Newgrange and Brú na Bóinne Irish Heritage Site

Brú na Bóinne ("Palace of the Boyne"), a curve of quiet green farmland along a 15-km (9-mile) stretch of the River Boyne, is the site of Europe's richest concentration of ancient monuments – henges, forts, enclosures, standing stones and a superb collection of neolithic passage graves: Dowth, Knowth and Newgrange.

Below left: characteristic whorls of 5,000-year-old stone carving at Newgrange

Detail of the tomb's circular wall

Newgrange had already been standing for 500 years when pyramid-building started in Egypt and had been in use for a thousand years when work began on Stonehenge. As you explore this mighty tomb of beautifully crafted stone slabs incised with mysterious carved patterns and symbols, your imagination cannot fail to be stirred.

The introductory **exhibition** gives a good idea of the little that is known about the period 4000 to 3000 BC, when enormous tombs like these were built all over Europe, and it provides an excellent introduction to the monuments of Brú na Bóinne, in particular the two great passage graves of Newgrange and Knowth.

The Building of Newgrange

Newgrange was built some time between 3300 and 2900 BC, a giant mound 85m (279 feet) across and 15m (49 feet) high, its perimeter defined by nearly a hundred huge kerbstones. At least 200,000 tonnes of stone went into its construction, a mind-numbing amount of material to transport and put into position. A passage 19m (62 feet) long, walled and roofed with more huge slabs, was built into the heart of the mound, opening out there into three chambers, like a shamrock leaf. It is thought to have taken the neolithic farming community between 40 and 80 years to build Newgrange – twice the life-span of an active male in that hard and dangerous era.

The tomb sits high above the road, a great mound bounded by its circular kerbstone wall and topped by a green grassy dome of a roof. Outside the entrance (rebuilt since it was first rediscovered in a collapsed state in 1699) lies the Threshold Stone, a big weathered slab lying on its side, covered in spiral and diamond carvings. Above the doorway is a slit in the stonework like a large letterbox. It is through this roof box that the dawn light enters at the winter solstice.

Right: the mighty, carved Threshold Stone and roof box at the entrance to Newgrange

Far right: a blinding shaft of dawn light enters the passage of Newgrange during the winter solstice

Once inside the tomb, the guide leads you by torchlight along the darkened passageway, sometimes stooping under the low stone slab roof. Spiral patterns are carved into the walls all around, though they can be hard to spot in the gloom. At the end of the passage, you straighten up under a beehive domed roof to find yourself in the central burial chamber. The roof has rainproof qualities of which any modern builder would be proud. Vaulted with cleverly interlocked stone slabs, it has kept the chamber perfectly dry for over 5,000 years. The three recesses which open off this central area contain wide, shallow sandstone bowls, receptacles that once held the cremated remains of the dead.

The circular kerbstone wall and grass-topped roof of Newgrange passage grave

Riddles of the Tomb

If you lie prone on the floor of the furthest recess from the entrance, you can squint along the passage to see the roof box slit outlined in light.

On 21 December, the shortest day of the year – and for a couple of days each side – the dawn light creeps in through the slit and advances along the roof and through the central chamber until it reaches halfway up the back wall. Here it lingers for a few minutes, and then withdraws. There is a ten-year waiting list for people wanting to witness this phenomenon; due to over-subscription, the list is temporarily closed. When Newgrange was excavated, the remains of

only half a dozen bodies were found. Though speculation is rife, it appears that funerary remains must have been regularly removed from the chamber. Why remove them? Why labour so long and hard to build a device for trapping a momentary ray of winter sun? Did the ancients have a yearly midwinter clear-out of cremated remains, in the belief that the retreating ray of light had taken the spirits of the dead with it, perhaps to ensure the return of next year's spring sunshine? Or is there another explanation? Stand at the mysterious heart of Newgrange and your guess is as good as anyone's.

A carved mace head, one of the archaeological finds at Knowth

Knowth

Knowth, Newgrange's neighbouring tomb, lies surrounded by at least 17 smaller passage graves, like a cluster of big green anthills. The tomb has two passages pushing in from east and west, and is rich in spiral and line carvings. Whorls, zigzags and parallel lines decorate the great stones, offering powerful evidence that, like Newgrange, the tomb had a significance beyond that of a simple burial place.

TAKING A BREAK

Daly's of Donore (in the village of Donore, tel: 041 982 3252) is within walking distance of Newgrange and is open for breakfast from 7 am to 10 am, and for lunch from 12:30 pm to 3 pm.

🔹 197 D1
✉ Boyne Valley Archaeological Park, 11km (7 miles) southwest of Drogheda, Co Meath
☎ 041 988 0300;
www.heritageireland.ie
🕓 Daily 9–7, Jun to mid-Sep; 9–6:30, May and mid- to end Sep; 9:30–5:30, Mar–Apr and Oct; 9:30–5, rest of year. Newgrange open all year round; Knowth open May–Oct (exterior only). Last tour of monuments 1 hour 30 minutes before closing; last admission to visitor centre 45 minutes before closing
💶 Moderate

NEWGRANGE AND BRÚ NA BÓINNE: INSIDE INFO

Top tips If you want to bypass the explanatory exhibition at the entrance to the site and **go straight to the passage grave**, go down the stairs and out of the building, and cross the footbridge. The coach to Newgrange tomb waits at the end of this path. If you're visiting between June and September, it's advisable to arrive early in the morning and book your guided tour of Newgrange immediately. Better still, book well in advance. Those who turn up late in the day, unbooked, risk missing the tour.

Hidden gem When you are in the central chamber of Newgrange, inspect the **walls and roofs of the right-hand compartment**. They are richly carved with spirals and other motifs, hard to spot unless a light is held near them.

One to miss If hordes of visitors have descended on Newgrange, opt for the Knowth tomb visit – it's far less crowded, and the passage tomb art is better. But note that the tomb interior remains closed to the public while excavations continue.

At Your Leisure

2 The Wicklow Coast

The Wicklow coast south of Bray and Greystones, the southern terminus of the DART (Dublin Area Rapid Transit) railway, is well worth exploring via R761, R750 and their side roads. Long sandy beaches fringe the coast as it approaches Wicklow on a long estuarine creek. South again are Wicklow Head, great for windy walks, and the Silver Strand around Brittas Bay, a fine strip of pale sand beaches. Sea anglers love this coast, fishing the shallows for cod and bass. Arklow is an attractive little fishing town, noted for boat-building. The coast road makes an enjoyable return route to Dublin after a day in the Wicklow Hills.

✚ 201 E4

3 Wexford Wildfowl Reserve

Wexford is Ireland's prime birdwatching county, and the silted harbour of the North Slob – a tidal wetland just north of the town – is one of the best sites. About 10,000 Greenland white-fronted geese (one-third of the world population) overwinter here, along with many other goose and duck species. Swans, reed warblers, reed buntings, greenshank and redshank can be seen at other times of the year. The reserve offers well-placed hides (blinds) and guided tours.

✚ 201 D3 ✉ North Slob, Wexford
☎ 053 23129 🕐 Daily 9–6, mid-Apr–Sep; 10–5, rest of year (other times by arrangement with the warden)
✋ Free

4 Irish National Heritage Park

Ideally, allow a couple of hours for a stroll through Irish history in this large forest park beside the River Slaney, 5km (3 miles) north of Wexford. Reconstructed buildings range from pre-Christian round houses with thatched, conical roofs to a full-size *crannog* (stone-built defensive tower on a lake island), a Viking shipyard complete with long-boats under construction, and a Norman motte-and-bailey castle.

✚ 201 D3 ✉ Ferrycarrig, Co Wexford
☎ 053 20733; www.inhp.com 🕐 Daily 9:30–6:30 (last admission 5 pm)
✋ Moderate

Tonelagee

The mountain called Tonelagee, one of the highest in the Wicklow Mountains at 818m (2,684 feet), seems to be presenting its posterior to the prevailing wind. Hence its name – which in Irish literally means "arse-to-the-wind".

The Rock of Cashel, perched atop a rocky outcrop, County Tipperary

6 Jerpoint Abbey

The ruins of Jerpoint Abbey are worth the short detour south from Kilkenny. These beautiful buildings show work from several centuries between the abbey's foundation in the late 12th century and its dissolution about 400 years later. Carved figures – one of a woman in a long pleated skirt, another of St Christopher with staff and upraised hand – stand between the double pillars of the fine cloister arches. A handsome pinnacled tower overlooks the roofless nave of the church. In the choir is the carved tomb of Abbot Felix O'Dulany, whose crosier is depicted being swallowed by a snake.

➕ 200 C3 ✉ Thomastown, Co Kilkenny
☎ 056 7724623; www.
southeastireland.ie 🕐 Daily 9:30–6,
Jun–Sep; 9:30–5, Oct; 10–5, mid-Mar to
May; 10–4:30, rest of year
💰 Inexpensive

7 Rock of Cashel

The Rock of Cashel astonishes at first sight. Perched spectacularly on a high rock outcrop is a walled cluster of historic ecclesiastical buildings, one of Ireland's most important centres in medieval times, from which powerful kings and churchmen ruled for nearly a thousand years.

On the rock you'll find an early 12th-century round tower complete with conical cap, the lovely Cormac's Chapel (1127–34), and a lofty, roofless 13th-century cathedral. Take a torch (flashlight) with you so that you can enjoy the remarkable stone carving tucked away in the dark above the north door of Cormac's Chapel – a centaur in a Norman helmet, firing an arrow at a grinning lion which is trampling two smaller animals beneath its feet. This is a windswept, haunting spot in which to linger as you admire the brilliance and humour of the medieval master masons.

➕ 200 A3 ✉ Cashel, Co Tipperary
☎ 062 61437; www.heritageireland.ie
🕐 Daily 9–7, mid-Jun to mid-Sep;
9–5:30, mid-Mar to mid-Jun; 9:30–4:30,
rest of year 💰 Moderate

9 Dunmore Caves

A guided tour takes you along walkways (with 106 steps) through this series of well-lit limestone caves. The caves are of sombre repute: legend says that the Lord of the Mice was slain here, while a more credible story tells of hundreds of locals slaughtered in the caves by Vikings in AD 928; skeletons of women and children have been found (though without signs of violence), along with Viking coins. You can see how the caves got their spooky reputation as you walk from one bizarre and freakish stalactite and stalagmite formation to the next.

➕ 200 C4
✉ Ballyfoyle, near Castlecomer, Co Kilkenny ☎ 056 7767726 🕐 Daily 9:30–6:30, mid-Jun to mid-Sep; 9:30–5, Mar to mid-Jun and mid-Sep to Oct; Fri–Sun and public hols 10–4:30, rest of year. Last admission 1 hour before closing
💶 Inexpensive

⑩ Moone and Castledermot High Crosses

The pre-Norman high crosses in the County Kildare villages of Moone and Castledermot are well worth a detour. The cross at Moone is over 5m (16 feet) tall; the two at Castledermot stand near a beautiful little Romanesque doorway and a ruined round tower. All three crosses are made of granite and are carved with scenes from the Bible.

➕ 200 C4 ✉ Moone and Castledermot are on N9, south of Naas 💶 Free

⑪ Irish National Stud, Irish Horse Museum and Japanese Gardens

In 1902 rich and eccentric Scots brewery heir Colonel William Hall-Walker established the Irish National Stud on the southern outskirts of the town of Kildare. The colonel was fascinated by astrology and exotic religion. Stallions and mares were paired off according to the compatibility of their birth signs, their foals' progress was

Mare and foal at Kildare's National Stud

charted by horoscope, and the boxes in which they were accommodated had lantern skylights to allow entry of the influential rays of moon and stars.

The nearby grounds were laid out in 1906–10 as a Japanese garden, symbolising the life of a man through a journey to the Garden of Peace and Contentment by way of such obstacles and encouragements as the Hill of Learning, the Walk of Wisdom, the Hill of Ambition and the Bridge of Life.

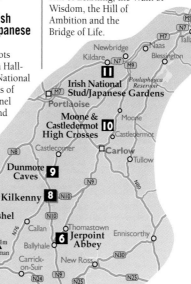

Heavenly verticals – the round tower and high cross at Monasterboice

Allow at least a couple of hours to visit the National Stud's stallions in their stalls and paddocks, view the Irish Horse Museum (which displays the skeleton of champion steeplechaser Arkle) and stroll the subtle pathways of the Japanese Gardens.

✚ 200 C5 ✉ Tully, Co Kildare
☎ 045 522963/521617;
www.irish-national-stud.ie ⊙ Daily
9–6, mid-Feb to mid-Nov 🎟 Expensive

⓬ Hill of Tara

This green hill, surrounded by earthworks, has been an important site since late Stone Age people built a passage tomb here. Its heyday of influence was during the first millennium AD as the main religious and political centre of Ireland, where kings and priests would gather every three years to make laws and settle quarrels. Tara features in many Irish myths and legends – and in more recent history too. Daniel O'Connell chose the Hill of Tara, symbol of Irish nationhood, as the venue for a "monster meeting" in 1843 to oppose the oppressive Corn Laws. And his instinct was justified when more than 100,000 people turned up (or maybe a million – estimates varied). This is a wonderful place to roam and enjoy the superb view.

✚ 197 D1 ✉ Off N3 south of Navan, Co Meath ☎ 046 9025093; www.heritageireland.ie ⊙ Daily 10–6, May–Oct 🎟 Inexpensive

⓮ Monasterboice

An astonishing variety of historic Christian monuments is crammed into this compact monastic site north of Drogheda: a leaning, 33m- (108-foot)-tall 10th-century round tower, ancient grave slabs, the ruined shells of two venerable churches, and – in pride of place – three wonderfully carved high crosses. Best of all is the South Cross or Cross of Muiredach, over 5m (16 feet) tall. Its carved panels include depictions of Eve tempting Adam, Cain murdering Abel, an Adoration of the Magi that seems to feature not three but four Wise Men, and a Judgement Day in which St Michael weighs the souls of the dead while the Devil tugs on the scales to gain more than his rightful share.

✚ 197 D1 ✉ Off N1, north of Drogheda, Co Louth ⊙ Daily
🎟 Free

Off the Beaten Track

Try the strand of Curracloe, not far north of Wexford, for a memorable sunrise walk along miles of empty sands with only seabirds and your own shadow for company.

Where to... Eat and Drink

Prices

Expect to pay per person for a meal, excluding drinks and service

€ up to €20 €€ up to €32 €€€ over €32

WICKLOW MOUNTAINS

Avoca Handweavers €

You'll find delicious home-cooked food here, based on organic and locally produced ingredients. Delicatessen foods include farmhouse cheeses, home-baked breads and preserves, and vegetarians do especially well. There's a sister shop/restaurant at Powerscourt House, Enniskerry (tel: 01 204 6066).

🚪 201 E5 ⊠ Kilmacanoge, Co Wicklow ☎ 01 286 7466; fax: 01 286 2367; email: info@avoca.ie; www.avoca.ie ⏰ Mon–Sat 9:30–5, Sun 10–6; closed 25–6 Dec

Roundwood Inn €–€€€

The perfect place to take a break in the Wicklow Mountains, this renowned inn has everything: roaring log fires, excellent bar food, and a formal restaurant too (requiring reservations), which serves a separate menu. Specialities include substantial soups, Galway oysters, smoked Wicklow trout and hearty hot meals including the house version of Irish stew.

🚪 201 D4 ⊠ Roundwood, Co Wicklow ☎ 01 281 8107 ⏰ Bar meals: daily 12:30–9:30. Restaurant: Lunch: Sun 1 pm. Dinner: Fri–Sun 7:30–midnight. Inn: closed Good Fri and 25 Dec

WATERFORD

Dwyer's Restaurant €€€

Converted Royal Irish Constabulary barracks make an elegant setting for consistently excellent food and service at this centrally located restaurant. The style of cooking is basically classic French, with some country French and New Irish influences, and always based on the best seasonal local produce, including Wexford mussels and strawberries, both great specialities of the area. A keenly priced three-course early dinner (must be ordered before 7 pm and finished by 9 pm) is especially good value.

🚪 200 C3 ⊠ 8 Mary Street, Waterford ☎ 051 877478; fax: 051 877480; email: info@dwyersrestaurant.com; www.dwyersrestaurant.com ⏰ Mon–Sat 6 pm–midnight; closed 1 week Christmas, public hols

The Wine Vault €

Based in a building that dates back to the Elizabethan era, this informal wine bar serves lively, international bistro-style food. The fresh fish and vegetarian dishes tend to be especially good. You'll find a particularly fine selection of wines from far and wide. The daily lunch specials and the early evening menu (5–7:30 pm) are particularly good value.

🚪 200 C3 ⊠ High Street, Waterford ☎ 051 853444; email: info@waterfordwinevault.com; www.waterfordwinevault.com ⏰ Mon–Sat 12:30–2:30, 5:30–10:30; closed 1 Jan, Good Fri and 25 Dec

CASHEL

Cashel Palace Hotel €€

Built in 1730 as a bishop's residence, Cashel Palace is a beautifully proportioned Queen Anne-style house. The informal Bishop's Buttery restaurant in the basement is open all day, and the Guinness Bar serves light snacks from 11 am until late evening. Some of the reception rooms and bedrooms overlook the gardens and the Rock of Cashel.

🚪 200 A3 ⊠ Main Street, Cashel ☎ 062 62707; fax 062 61521; email: reception@cashel-palace.ie ⏰ Closed 24–6 Dec

Chez Hans €€–€€€

This converted Wesleyan chapel under the Rock of Cashel has great atmosphere and food to match: seasonal menus offer a wide choice and put local ingredients to the best use in classic French cooking that is never less than excellent. Specialities include fresh fish and shellfish, roast duckling and rack of Tipperary lamb. There's always a good selection of farmhouse cheeses and an irresistible dessert tasting-plate.

✚ 200 A3 ⊠ Moor Lane, Cashel, Co Tipperary ☎ 062 61177 ⏰ Tue–Sat 6:30–10 pm; closed 3 weeks Jan, Good Fri and 25 Dec

Lacken House €€–€€€

A husband-and-wife team runs the well-appointed cellar restaurant of this Victorian house located on the edge of Kilkenny. You'll get to taste good local produce in a blend of traditional and New Irish recipes, featuring mouth-watering specialities such as baked crab gateau, excellent local steak and a range of farmhouse cheeses served with home-made biscuits (cookies). Overnight guests get delicious breakfasts too.

✚ 200 C4 ⊠ Dublin Road, Kilkenny ☎ 056 7761085; fax: 056 7762435; email: info@lackenhouse.ie ⏰ Tue–Sat 7–10 pm, Sun 7–10, Jun–Sep. Restaurant: closed 2 weeks Christmas

Nicholas Mosse Country Shop Café €

The informal café in the Nicholas Mosse Country Shop at Bennettsbridge is an ideal place to stop for a break. The shop overlooks the river. It's an attractive spot for lunch or afternoon tea. Light, modern dishes include some Irish influences, with an emphasis on wholesome ingredients (tasty traditional farmhouse cheeses accompanied by home-made chutneys). There are also a variety of imaginative pasta dishes and some interesting vegetarian specialities.

✚ 200 C3 ⊠ Bennettsbridge, Co Kilkenny ☎ 056 7727505 ⏰ Shop Mon–Sat 9–6, Sun 1:30–5; closed 1 Jan and 25–6 Dec

Ballymore Inn €€

This country pub has an open fire, unusual furniture, interesting pictures and good food too. Superb pizzas and open sandwiches, salads and pasta dishes are served in the bar/restaurant.

✚ 201 D5 ⊠ Ballymore Eustace, Co Kildare ☎ 045 864585; email: theballymoreinn@hotmail.com ⏰ Restaurant: Tue–Thu 12:30–3, 6–8, Fri–Sat 12:30–9, Sun noon–7, Mon 12:30–3. Pub closed Good Fri and 25 Dec; restaurant closed public hols

Moone High Cross Inn €

This 1870s country pub near Kilkea Castle (▶ 91) has open fires in both bars. The larger bar serves traditional dishes such as Irish stew and bacon and cabbage. There are eight bedrooms with bathrooms upstairs.

✚ 200 C4 ⊠ Bolton Hill, Moone, Co Kildare ☎ 059 8624112 ⏰ Mon–Thu 8 am–11:30 pm, Fri–Sat 8 am–12:30 am, Sun 8 am–11 pm; closed Good Fri and 25 Dec

Forge Gallery Restaurant €€–€€€

This two-storey restaurant is furnished and decorated with flair, making a fine setting for excellent food, hospitality and service. Menus combine country French, New Irish and world (notably Thai) cuisines, using seasonal and largely local ingredients with home-made breads.

✚ 197 D1 ⊠ Collon, Co Louth ☎ 041 982 6272; fax: 041 9826584; email: forgegalleryrestaurant@ eircom.net ⏰ Dinner: Tue–Sat 7–9:30; closed 2 weeks Jan and over Christmas

Tides Bistro €€

This is a classy bistro, upstairs from its cool bar, serving an interesting range of European cuisine with some Oriental touches, and traditional Irish staples smartened up with modern influences. Meat, fish and vegetarian options are available.

✚ 197 D1 ⊠ Wellington Quay, Drogheda, Co Louth ☎ 041 9801942; www.tidesbistro.com ⏰ Tue–Sat 6–late, Sun 5–9

Where to... Stay

Prices
Expect to pay per person staying
€ up to €40 €€ up to €77 €€€ over €77

Tinakilly Country House €€€
Originally built for Captain Halpin, commander of the Great Eastern, which laid the first transatlantic telegraphic cables, the house is in classic Victorian-Italianate style, as are the 3 hectares (7 acres) of gardens. Elegantly furnished with antiques, the hotel has some four-poster beds and some suites, which have wonderful sea views. The food has won a number of awards, including "Top Irish Breakfast" and "Top Wine List."

✝ 201 E4 ✉ Rathnew, Co Wicklow
☎ 0404 69274; fax: 0404 67806;
email: reservations@tinakilly.ie;
www.tinakilly.ie

WATERFORD

Foxmount Country House €€
This 17th-century house on a working dairy farm is just 15 minutes' drive from Waterford city centre. Yet it offers guests tranquillity, comfort and delicious home-cooked food. There's table tennis and a hard tennis court, and the accommodation includes a family room; all bedrooms have private bathrooms.

✝ 200 C3 ✉ Passage East Road,
off Dunmore East Road, Waterford,
Co Waterford ☎ 051 874308; fax:
051 854906; email:
info@foxmountcountryhouse.com;
www.foxmountcountryhouse.com
⊘ Closed Nov–Mar

Granville Hotel €€–€€€
Charles Stuart Parnell made speeches in this large waterfront hotel. The Georgian building has been sensitively improved resulting in elegant public areas and good accommodation. There are 100 comfortably furnished bedrooms with private bathrooms.

✝ 200 C3 ✉ Meagher Quay,
Waterford, Co Waterford ☎ 051
855111; email: stay@granvillehotel.ie;
www.granvillehotel.ie ⊘ Closed
25–7 Dec

Hanora's Cottage €€–€€€
Up in the mountains about an hour's drive from Waterford, this hospitable guest house is a perfect base for walking or horseback riding. There is luxurious accommodation, legendary breakfasts and home-baked bread. The restaurant (open to non-residents for dinner) specialises in local produce.

✝ 200 B3 ✉ Ballymacarbery Nire
Valley, via Clonmel, Co Waterford
☎ 052 36134; email:
hanorascottage@eircom.net
⊘ Restaurant closed Sun

CASTLEDERMOT

Kilkea Castle & Golf Club €€€
This 12th-century castle is now a romantic hotel where many rooms have views over gardens, countryside and an 18-hole championship golf course. The most luxurious bedrooms are in the castle; the rest surround an adjacent courtyard. There are excellent sports facilities.

✝ 200 C4 ✉ Castledermot, Co
Kildare ☎ 059 9145156; fax: 059
9145187; email: kilkea@iol.ie;
www.kilkeacastle.ie ⊘ Closed
23–7 Dec

NEWGRANGE AREA

Conyngham Arms Hotel €
The stylish public areas are welcoming in this attractive stone hotel. The Game Keeper's Lodge restaurant serves traditional Irish and European food from noon to 10 pm. The bedrooms are comfortably furnished, and there's one suite.

✝ 197 D1 ✉ Slane, Co Meath ☎ 041
988444; fax: 041 9824205; email:
reservations@conynghamarms.com

Where to... Shop

See the mill in operation at one of the country's finest craft and gift shops, **Avoca Handweavers** (Kilmacanogue, tel: 01 286 7466). They sell fabrics, clothing, crafts and specialist foods; there's also a branch at Powerscourt House (Enniskerry, tel: 01 204 6066). For country clothing try **Fishers of Newtownmountkennedy** (tel: 01 281 9404). Roundwood village has gift shops and a Sunday afternoon market.

Distinctive pots are hand-thrown at the **Kiltrea Bridge Pottery** (Enniscorthy, County Wexford, tel: 054 35107). At the **Waterford Crystal Visitor Centre** (Waterford City, tel: 051 332500) you can watch craftspeople at work, then buy from the display (▶ 79).

Kilkenny At **Kilkenny Design Centre** (tel: 056 7722441), opposite the castle,

there is a fine range of textiles, ceramics and jewellery. Look for young designers at **Crescent Workshops** (Castle Yard, tel: 056 7727329), the modern jewellery of **Rudolf Heltzel** (10 Patrick Street, tel: 056 7721497) and striking hand-thrown pottery at **Stoneware Jackson** (John's Bridge, tel: 056 7727175).

Bennettsbridge and Thomastown Visit the **Stoneware Jackson Studio** (Ballyreddin, tel: 056 7727175), as well as the **Nicholas Mosse Pottery** (tel: 056 7727105), renowned for traditional spongeware. At nearby Thomastown, watch lead crystal being hand-blown at the **Jerpoint Glass Studio** (tel: 056 7724350), beside the famous Abbey (▶ 86). Also in Thomastown is **Toner Leather** (tel: 056 7724055) for hand-crafted leather.

Timolin Allow time to stop at the **Irish Pewter Mill** (tel: 059 8624164) at Timolin, in County Kildare. It has a museum as well as the factory, and also a shop which sells traditional pewter items.

Where to... Be Entertained

OUTDOOR ACTIVITIES

Activities in the Wicklow Mountains include walking, cycling, horse-riding, angling and golf. Local tourist information offices can provide details. There's an **Adventure Centre** (tel: 045 865092) on the Blessington Lakes.

Horse country County Tipperary is home to three racecourses: Thurles, Clonmel and Tipperary. Riding and lessons are available at Kilcooley **Abbey Equestrian Centre** at Thurles (tel: 056 7734222). Kildare has three racecourses: The Curragh (tel: 045 441205), Punchestown (tel: 045 897704) and Naas (tel: 045 897391).

Golf The Arnold Palmer-designed **K Club** course (Straffan, County

Kildare, tel: 01 6017300) is supremely challenging. There's also **Kilkea Castle** course (Castledermot, County Kildare, tel: 059 9145555), set in rolling parkland beside a 12th-century castle. In County Meath, **Laytown & Bettystown Links** (tel: 041 9827534) are almost on the beach.

MUSIC

For set dancing, try **Bean ALeanna** (Dungarvan, County Waterford, tel: 058 44882). In Waterford, one of Ireland's oldest pubs, **T and H Doolans** (George's Street, tel: 051 872764), has traditional music on summer nights and winter weekends. The **Wexford Opera Festival** (box office tel: 053 22144) from mid-October/early November stages a selection of rarely performed operas.

Southwest Ireland

Getting Your Bearings

The wild Atlantic blows up hundreds of storms a year along the coasts of counties Cork and Kerry, at the southwestern tip of Ireland. Here waves and wind have eaten away at the coast, creating big, ragged-edged peninsulas where the land faces directly into the Atlantic, and sheltered little coves between rocky headlands on the south-facing coast of Cork. You'll find literally hundreds of fine sandy beaches to enjoy along this, the most spectacular coastline in Ireland. But there are also plenty of attractive and enjoyable places inland, especially in the side valleys of the Shehy and Derrynasaggart mountains.

Sailing, diving, sea fishing and water sports of all kinds are big hereabouts. The climate, though often wet and windy, is notably mild and frost free, so there are a number of exotic gardens with plants and trees you would normally expect to find far nearer the equator. The Kerry Way offers superb long-distance walking through the hills, and there's good trout fishing in the lakes of the Iveragh Peninsula (whose circular Ring of Kerry must be Ireland's best-known scenic drive) and Killarney National Park, justly famed for its beauty. Inhabitants of Kerry and Cork are well known for their laid-back approach to life and for their elliptical wit.

Cork is Ireland's "Second City" – even if Cork natives think Dublin should carry that title.

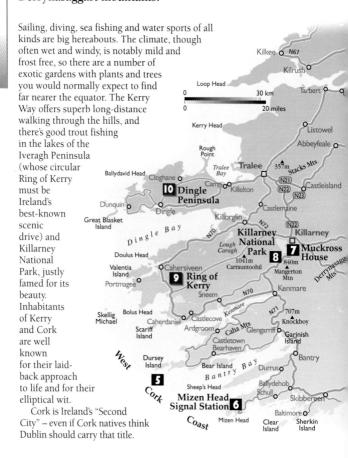

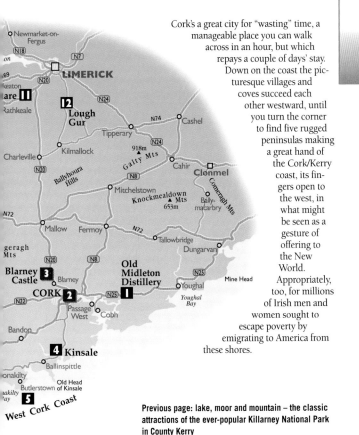

Cork's a great city for "wasting" time, a manageable place you can walk across in an hour, but which repays a couple of days' stay. Down on the coast the picturesque villages and coves succeed each other westward, until you turn the corner to find five rugged peninsulas making a great hand of the Cork/Kerry coast, its fingers open to the west, in what might be seen as a gesture of offering to the New World. Appropriately, too, for millions of Irish men and women sought to escape poverty by emigrating to America from these shores.

Previous page: lake, moor and mountain – the classic attractions of the ever-popular Killarney National Park in County Kerry

Journey far into Ireland's most scenic region, from lively Cork City to the wave-cut peninsulas of the coast. And don't forget to kiss the Blarney Stone...

Southwest Ireland in Four Days

Day One

Morning Make sure to allow at least a morning for wandering around **2 Cork City** (city-centre street musician right, ➤ 98–9), looking in at the art gallery, having a chat and a snack lunch in the English Market, maybe climbing the hill to ring the Bells of Shandon.

Afternoon Go on, you have to do it...make the short trip out north to **3 Blarney Castle** (➤ 100), and kiss the Blarney Stone. Then it's back into Cork to try out your new gift of the gab in the **Hi-B** (➤ 99).

Day Two

Morning Make an early start south to **4 Kinsale** (➤ 108–9) for breakfast or coffee. Then follow the rural road west to Clonakilty (R600). Continue to Rosscarbery, sidetracking from here via beautiful Glandore, Unionhall and Rineen to steep and attractive little Castletownshend. Then head west via Skibbereen to reach the one-time hippy hangout of **Ballydehob** (old-fashioned butcher's shop, left) in time for lunch.

Afternoon Cruise two of the **5 Five Fingers** (➤ 109): go out to the cliffs of Mizen Head to visit the **6 Signal Station** (➤ 109–10) and back, then round the mountains and drink in the wonderful island views of the Beara Peninsula. You'll be tired, and satiated with beautiful landscapes, by the time you reach **Kenmare** for an overnight stop (➤ 115).

Day Three

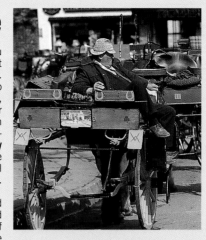

Morning From Kenmare you can enjoy a fairly late start to make up for yesterday. Drive at your ease over to **8 Killarney** (jaunting-car, right, ➤ 111), and stop for a quick cup of coffee; then set out on the wonderful circuit of the **9 Ring of Kerry** (➤ 101–3). Lunch in the Blind Piper at Caherdaniel (tel: 066 9475346).

Afternoon Look around **Derrynane House** and grounds (➤ 103) – home of Daniel O'Connell, "The Liberator" – then complete your leisurely tour of the Ring of Kerry before pushing on from Killarney to stay overnight in Tralee.

Day Four

Morning Take the whole day to explore the **10 Dingle Peninsula** (Dingle Bay below, ➤ 104–7). A ten o'clock start would put you in Dingle Town in time for a stroll before lunch.

Afternoon Carry on around the peninsula via Dunquin and Cloghane (don't forget a windy saunter on the Magharees sandspit!); then return from Tralee to Cork.

2 Cork City

Ireland's "second city" is a charming place that quickly slows you down to its easy pace. The River Lee divides into two channels as it flows through, forming an island of the city centre. Bridges are numerous, each with a fine riverfront view making Cork an excellent place for a town stroll.

South of the South Channel, **St Fin Barre's Cathedral** on Bishop Street is worth a visit for its exterior statues, its fine collection of 19th-century stained glass, and the delicately coloured mosaic floor of the choir. Lift the choir seats to enjoy the handsome carvings of insects that decorate the misericords (and spare a thought for the weary choristers who perched on these ledges during long services).

In the city centre the covered **English Market** off Grand Parade is a lively mix of food, drink, book and craft stalls. Nearby in the Huguenot Quarter, an area of the city inhabited in the 18th century by French Protestant craftsmen fleeing religious persecution, you can stroll narrow pedestrian streets between small-scale old houses, shops, cafés and pubs, all chic and sleek. Head north

towards the river to visit the excellent **Crawford Municipal Gallery** (tel: 021 4273377, open: Mon–Sat 10 am–5 pm) on Paul Street.

North of the river, climb the steep streets of Shandon to reach **St Anne's Church** (▶ Top Tips) and take time to look around the craft workshops in the adjacent **Butter Exchange**. Half an hour's stroll west brings you to the Sunday's Well area, where you can learn all about the misery of 19th-century prison conditions at the old **Cork City Gaol** (tel: 021 4305022, open: daily 9:30–6, Mar–Oct; 10–5, rest of year; admission moderate). Housed in the old railway station at Cobh, southeast of Cork, is **The Queenstown Story** (tel: 021 4813591, open: daily 10–6,

Above: Georgian-style St Patrick's Bridge, spanning the River Lee

Left: St Patrick's Street, one of Cork's principal shopping thoroughfares

May–Oct; 10–5, rest of year; admission moderate; www.cobhheritage.com). Cobh, formerly known as Queenstown, was once a port of embarkation for the United States. This exhibition explores the pain of separation, hardship and danger suffered by the hundreds of thousands who, over the past two centuries, emigrated to America on the notorious "coffin ships". It is detailed, moving and inspiring.

If you can't find it in Fitzpatrick's, it probably never existed at all...

✚ 199 E2
✉ Tourist Information Office, Grand Parade
☎ 021 4273251;
www.corkkerry.ie

TAKING A BREAK

Call in to the first-floor **Farmgate Restaurant** (► 114) for good home-baked pastries and a bird's-eye view of the English Market.

Rockin' Rory

In the heart of the Huguenot Quarter is Rory Gallagher Square, named after the late rock musician, a sometime resident of Cork. He has a bold sculpture, a twisted Fender Stratocaster electric guitar entwined in flowing staves of music and lines from his songs.

CORK CITY: INSIDE INFO

Top tips Try ringing the bells at St Anne's Church on the Shandon side of town. The carillon was popularised in the 19th-century ballad "The Bells of Shandon". You can "read" your tune off a crib card as you ring, or go at it freestyle.
• At the Crawford Art Gallery, make straight for the Gibson Galleries and the Irish Art Collection, which is by far the most enjoyable part.

Hidden gem Tucked away above a chemist's shop opposite the General Post Office on Oliver Plunkett Street, the Hi-B (it stands for Hibernian Bar) is an entirely unspoiled pub, comfortable, a bit shabby and very friendly.

One to miss If you are short of time, give the rather threadbare "Titanic" section at The Queenstown Story a miss.

3 Kissing the Blarney Stone

Blarney Castle is a notably rugged and romantic-looking 15th-century tower in beautiful grounds full of pleasing grottoes and magic Druidic rocks half-hidden in greenery. None of this matters to the majority of visitors, who have come for one thing only: to kiss the Blarney Stone.

One legend says that the Blarney Stone was the pillow used by Jacob when he had his dream of angels in the desert. Another holds that the slab is only half of a much bigger stone, and that the other half is the Stone of Destiny on which Scottish (and then English) monarchs were crowned. The best-known legend, of course, says that anyone who can kiss the Blarney Stone will have the gift of eloquence magically bestowed on them.

The castle is extremely popular: come as early or late in the day as possible to avoid having to wait and head straight up the steps to the roof, where you will find the Blarney Stone built into the outer face of a gap in the battlements. You'll have to bend backwards and hang your head down (over a safety grille, and supported by one of the sturdy custodians) to kiss the stone. One word to the wise…empty your pockets before you kiss the Blarney Stone, or all your money will trickle out as you lean backwards.

Popular legend maintains the gift of the gab will be bestowed on anyone who kisses the Blarney Stone

🕇 199 D2
✉ Blarney Castle, Blarney, Co Cork
☎ 021 4385210 or 4385669; www.blarneycastle.ie
🕐 Daily 9–7, Jun–Aug; 9–6:30, May and Sep; 9–dusk, rest of year; closed 24–5 Dec
💰 Moderate

9 Ring of Kerry

The Ring of Kerry scenic route around the Iveragh Peninsula is the most popular drive in Ireland, and certainly one of the most beautiful, with wild boglands, wonderful coastal views and fine hill scenery.

Upper Lake at Killarney, a mecca for boaters, walkers and holiday idlers

Starting in Killarney, you skirt the north side of mountain-framed Lough Leane on your way west to **Killorglin**. This atmospheric small town is best known for the three-day Puck Fair in August, where there's drinking, dancing, livestock buying and selling – and a goat on a podium presiding over the whole affair. From Killorglin take the side road to Lough Caragh – this route introduces you to the boglands and puts you in the right frame of mind for wilder country ahead.

Back on the main road (N70), Glenbeigh is the first village. Below on the coast lies **Rossbeigh Strand,** a pebbly beach with a 3-km (2-mile) spit of dunes and a wonderful view of the hilly backs of the Iveragh and Dingle peninsulas. A steep hill road brings you circling back to the main road, on which you continue southwest in increasingly hilly and beautiful scenery.

✚ 198 C2
✉ Tourist Information Office, Beech Road, Killarney, Co Kerry
☎ 064 31633

Steep hillsides, patched with small fields and farms, rise through bracken and heather to sharp peaks nearly 800m (2,625 feet) high.

Near **Cahersiveen** you pass the smoking chimney of a peat-fired power station. On your left just before the bridge into the village are the ivy-covered ruins of the house where Daniel O'Connell was born. O'Connell (1775–1847) was one of the most important political figures in 19th-century Ireland: he earned his nickname, "The Liberator", leading impoverished Roman Catholics towards emancipation. In the village a right turn past the eccentric castle-like "Barracks" (the 19th-century Royal Irish Constabulary barracks, now housing a heritage centre) takes you along side roads. Brown "Stone Houses" road signs lead to two remarkable stone forts: first **Cahergall,** then **Leacanabuaile** on its crag, with the remains of 9th-century beehive huts enclosed within an intact circular wall 25m (82 feet) in diameter.

Another worthwhile side-track from Cahersiveen takes you further west to Portmagee

RING OF KERRY: INSIDE INFO

Top tips If you have **limited time** and simply want to enjoy a three-hour drive amid beautiful scenery, stick to the main road circuit: N72 from Killarney to Killorglin, N70 from Killorglin to Kenmare, N71 from Kenmare to Killarney.
• For **the best view of Lough Caragh**, fork left at O'Shea's shop in Caragh village ("Hotel Ard Na Sidhe" sign). In 1.5km (1 mile) turn left up a forestry track (wooden "Loch Cárthaí/Caragh Lake" sign) for 800m (875 yards) to reach a wide parking place with a wonderful high view over lake and mountains.

Hidden gem Anyone with an extra half-day to spare, and steady nerves on narrow hill roads, should try the wild and beautiful **side-road that runs northeast up the Inny Valley** from a turning 3km (2 miles) north of Waterville. It climbs in rare mountain scenery to the Ballaghisheen Pass (304m/997 feet) between the peaks of Knocknagapple and Knocknacusha, then dips over lonely bogland to Bealalaw Bridge, where you turn left for Lough Caragh and Killorglin.

and the causeway to Valentia Island. This is a beautiful, quiet spot, with wonderful subtropical gardens laid out on the north side at Glanleam, and some spectacular cliff views on the north and west. Subject to weather conditions, boats leave **Portmagee** for trips to the **Skelligs**, craggy rocks several miles offshore with remarkable early Christian monastic remains.

There are glimpses of the Skelligs beyond Ballinskelligs Bay as you climb out of Waterville over Coomakista, and breath-taking views forward to the island-studded mouth of the Kenmare River. Down in Caherdaniel a side-road leads to **Derrynane House** (tel: 066 9475113, open: Mon–Sat 9–6, Sun 11–7, May–Sep; Tue–Sun 1–5, Apr, Oct; Sat–Sun 1–5, rest of year; admission inexpensive). The house was inherited by Daniel O'Connell in 1825 and is full of mementoes, from portraits and personal possessions to the bowl in which he was baptised and the bed in which he died. In the grounds are beautiful gardens, an ancient ring fort and a Mass rock, where Catholics would gather to hear Mass said during the 18th century, when the oppressive Penal Laws forbade its observance.

Left: Skellig Michael, a rugged sea rock where early Christians established a lonely hermitage

View across Valentia Harbour

At Castlecove a sidetrack leads north to **Staigue Fort,** Ireland's best-preserved prehistoric fort, a round stone tower in a spectacular location up a lonely valley. After this the road reaches pretty little Sneem, and forks left at R568 for a wild mountain run back to Killarney.

TAKING A BREAK

Two excellent, welcoming places to eat and drink in Caherdaniel are **The Blind Piper** and **Freddie's Bar**. They are just off the main Ring of Kerry road, on the signposted side road to Derrynane.

⑩ Dingle Peninsula

The Dingle Peninsula, a remote finger of unspoilt countryside stretching for some 50km (31 miles) due west of Tralee, is a magical place to explore. It has mountains and a rugged coastline, sandy beaches, small towns of character and a remarkable concentration of prehistoric and early Christian monuments along with the Blasket Islands scattered romantically in the sea.

You leave Tralee along N86, passing the big white sails of the restored Blennerville windmill, and run west to the village of **Camp** with the indented wall of the Slieve Mish mountain range on your left. The waymarked Dingle Way long-distance footpath – a beautiful wild walk – runs on the slopes above the road.

High above Camp stands the 851-m (2,792-foot) mountain of **Caherconree.** From below you can just make out a stone wall near the summit that marks an ancient fort. Legend says that King Cu Roi MacDaire abducted Blathnaid, sweetheart of the hero Cuchulainn, and held her there. But Blathnaid sent a signal to her lover, whitening the waters of the River Finglas by pouring milk into its spring. Cuchulainn attacked the fort, killed the king, and rescued his lady.

At Camp, take the mountain road over to **Inch**, on the peninsula's south coast. The view from here has to be one of Ireland's best; giant sandspits and whorled sandflats in Castlemaine Harbour, with Macgillycuddy's Reeks on the Iveragh Peninsula as a backdrop.

The south coast road goes on west, turning inland through **Anascaul.** The South Pole Inn by the bridge was run during the early 1900s by Thomas Crean, one of Captain Scott's team on the ill-fated 1912 Antarctic expedition.

Next along is **Dingle**, a friendly small town on a circular bay where a playful, semi-tame dolphin is a frequent visitor. There's usually

Top: early mist curls off the Slieve Mish Mountains, backbone of the Dingle Peninsula

Above: the green hump of Great Blasket, largest of the Blasket Islands

excellent traditional music at O'Flaherty's (➤ 118). Don't forget to try Dingle pie, mutton pie with mutton broth poured over it, a local delicacy. Every year on 26 December the town goes mad, as fantastically dressed "Wren Boys" play rowdy tricks on each other and attempt to drink the pubs dry (➤ 25). In the past, participants in this event used to hunt and kill wrens (hence the name), which, custom held, had betrayed Christ.

Hog Hoard
Locals will tell you about the Spanish treasure ship that was wrecked in Tralee Bay. A golden pig was salvaged and buried in a triangular field near by – so they say. It has never been unearthed.

Towards the western end of the peninsula are **Ventry** on its perfect scythe-shaped bay, **Mount Eagle** whose slopes are covered with the *clochans* (beehive huts) of early Christian hermits, and, facing the open Atlantic, little **Dunquin**, where the 1970 film *Ryan's Daughter* was shot.

Out in the sea lie the **Blasket Islands**, Great Blasket, Inishvickillaun, Inishnabro and Inishtooskert. Between 1928 and 1939, islanders Tomás O'Crohan, Peig Sayers and Maurice O'Sullivan produced literary masterpieces about life on Great Blasket, whose population of 120 spoke little or no English and lived simple, remote lives. You can buy copies locally of their books (respectively *The Islandman*, *Peig* and *Twenty Years A-Growing*). A fisherman will probably run you out to Great Blasket if you want to wander through the writers' ruined village; the island was evacuated in 1953 when life became too hard. The sense of place and isolation can be overwhelming; it's an experience not to be missed, if you have the chance. If not, console yourself by reading about it in Dunquin's Blasket Centre on the mainland.

Start your journey back through Ballyferriter, stopping to admire the tiny **Gallarus Oratory**, built in stone over a thousand years ago in the form of an upturned boat.

Local fishermen carry their light, canvas-covered *currach* up from the sea after a day's fishing

The Slow Train

Along the road between Tralee and Dingle you may spot portions of trackbed and rusty old bridges. This is all that's left of the Tralee & Dingle Light Railway, one of the slowest and sleepiest rural branch railways in the world. Its working life lasted from 1891 to 1953. The firemen's duties included throwing coal at stray sheep on the line. A short section between Tralee and Blennerville runs restored steam trains in the summer months.

Sunset strikes a golden pathway across the water of Dingle Harbour

Just 1.5km (1 mile) away is **Kilmalkedar Church,** a very fine 12th-century ruin with some notable stone carving.

Side roads lead to **Ballydavid Head** and some headspinning cliffs. If you have time and a clear day on your side you can walk the waymarked **Saints' Road** over to little Cloghane on the north coast; from here determined walkers can ascend the 953-m (3,127-foot) **Mount Brandon** to St Brendan's Oratory at the peak. Before setting course back to Tralee, do make sure to take a detour up the sandspit of the **Magharees.** The beaches here are just about the best you'll find anywhere.

☒ Tourist Information Offices:
Ashe Memorial Hall, Tralee ✚ 198 C3 ⓐ All year
Main Street, Dingle ✚ 198 A3 ⓐ Apr–Oct
☎ Tralee 066 7121288; Dingle 066 9151188/9151241

TAKING A BREAK

In Dingle, try **Lord Baker's pub** (➤ 115), probably the town's oldest bar. At **The Tankard** (➤ 115), west of Tralee, sample some excellent seafood and enjoy unbeatable sea views.

DINGLE PENINSULA: INSIDE INFO

Top tips If all you are looking for is a wonderful bathing beach and endless clean sand to run or walk on, look no further than the **sandy spit of the Magharees** that separates Brandon Bay and Tralee Bay on the north of the Dingle Peninsula, 24km (15 miles) west of Tralee.

• In spite of the crowds, **August is a great month to be in Dingle.** You can enjoy the Dingle Races, the Dingle Regatta and, best of all, the idiosyncratic and hugely enjoyable Dingle Show, where locals gather to enjoy home-grown fun regardless of the tourists.

Hidden gem On a side road just above N86, 3km (2 miles) east of Camp, lie the ivy-smothered ruins of the village of **Killelton**, abandoned because of famine and emigration. Just off the path is a solid stone box with walls a metre thick, the remains of an ancient church built in the 7th century by St Elton himself.

At Your Leisure

❶ Old Midleton Distillery

Jameson's old whiskey distillery, in the market town of Midleton 16km (10 miles) east of Cork, has been converted into a visitor centre. In the original distillery buildings you can see the biggest copper still in the world, a great groaning waterwheel, enormous iron-bound vats to hold the mash, and a display of barrel-making in the cooperage, before enjoying a tot of hot or cold whiskey. On the far side of the yard wall the New Distillery steams away, producing 23 million bottles of the golden stuff each year and filling the air with the sweet, pervasive smell of malt and spirit.

➕ 199 E2 ✉ Midleton, Co Cork
☎ 021 4613594/6;
www.whiskeytours.ie 🕐 Frequent
tours daily 10–6, Mar–Oct; 11:30, 2:30
and 4, rest of year 💷 Moderate

❹ Kinsale

A snug little fishing town with narrow, twisting streets and old stone houses, Kinsale, due south

Kinsale fishermen sort the day's catch. The fish will be served the same evening in the town's renowned restaurants

of Cork, is incredibly popular with visitors both for its charming appearance and for its position at the head of a narrow rocky harbour, the estuary of the Bandon River. The town bears the rather commercial title of "Gourmet Capital of Ireland", but it does have some excellent fish restaurants and an annual Gourmet Festival in October that draws the crowds.

Climb Compass Hill to the south of Kinsale to enjoy a panoramic view over the town and the estuary.

🕂 199 E1 ⊠ Tourist Information Office, Pier Road, Kinsale, Co Cork ☎ 021 4772234; www.corkkerry.ie 🕓 Seasonal

5 The West Cork Coast

The Cork coast is spectacularly beautiful all the way west from Kinsale. The cliffs of the Old Head of Kinsale are followed by a succession of sandy coves, rocky bays and headlands, with villages such as Courtmacsherry and Rosscarbery tucked in picturesquely at their heads. **Castletownshend,** with a waterfront castle at the foot of the steep village street, is particularly attractive. Under a big chunk of sand-stone in the graveyard of St Barrahane's Church at Castletownshend lies Edith Somerville; alongside is the grave of her cousin Violet Martin. Under the joint *nom-de-plume* of Somerville & Ross, the cousins wrote several best-sellers around the turn of the 20th century, including the hilarious and (later) successfully televised *Some Experiences of an Irish RM.*

At the fishing village of **Baltimore** is a pub named "The Algerian". Its name is a reminder of a disastrous day in June 1631, when Barbary pirates raided the town and took scores of locals off into slavery. From Baltimore you can ride ferries out to Sherkin Island and Clear Island, Ireland's southernmost point, in the aptly named Roaringwater Bay. On the north side of the bay start the **"Five Fingers"**, rugged peninsulas cut by the Atlantic out of the coastline. From Schull you drive down to the great cliffs of

Mizen Head (➤ below), as far south as you can get on mainland Ireland; from Durrus you can reach the tip of the Sheep's Head peninsula, returning by a challengingly steep and twisty mountain road called the Goat's Path, with great views over Bantry Bay and its islands.

The **Ring of Beara** is a road circuit around the mountainous Beara Peninsula. Three island detours are worth making here: to see the sub-tropical gardens nurtured in the mild climate of **Garinish Island** off Glengarriff; to hilly **Bere Island** a little further west (both accessible by boat); and by an exhilarating cable-car crossing over a wild tide race to rocky and dramatic **Dursey Island**, off the very tip of the peninsula.

(For more information on Iveragh and Dingle peninsulas ➤ 101 and 104.)

🕂 199 D1

6 Mizen Head Signal Station

Mizen Head is Ireland's most south-westerly point, on a spectacular stretch of rocky coastline with wonderful views. A short walk leads from the car park (but there are 99 steps to climb on the way back), and you'll see seabirds, wild flowers and seals – even whales occasionally surface offshore. On the headland, you can

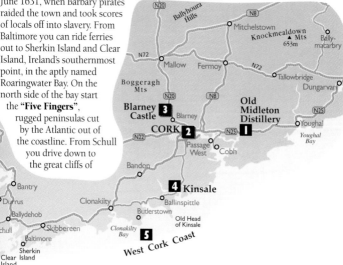

visit the signal station, established in 1931, see the various interesting displays about safety at sea, including a navigational aids' simulator and an automatic weather station, and tour the former light-keepers' quarters.

🞧 198 B1 ✉ West of Goleen ☎ 028 35115; www.mizenhead.net 🕔 Daily 10–6, Jun–Sep; 10:30–5, mid-Mar to May and Oct; Sat–Sun 11–4, rest of year 🖲 Moderate

Muckross Gardens, at the heart of Killarney National Park, are magnificent all year round

🢷 Muckross House, Abbey and Gardens

Muckross House is a handsome Victorian mansion built in Elizabethan style with high-pointed gables and tall chimneys; it contains an appealing folk museum of bygones. Close by are three farms worked by traditional methods (great fun for children). The formal gardens are full of exotic trees and shrubs; rhododendrons and azaleas are a speciality, and there's a fine rock garden. The wider grounds of the park give plenty of scope for

lakeside rambles or jaunting-car (two-wheeled carriage) rides.

North of the house, in a beautiful position, stand the impressive ruins of Muckross Abbey, established in 1340 but mostly dating to the mid-15th century. The best features are the cloisters and the big skeletal east window under the huge square tower.

Lough Leane, sometimes called the Lower Lake, in Killarney National Park

Lough Leane, the centrepiece lake of the 10,125-hectare (25,018-acre) **Killarney National Park**. You can rent a boat to get to Innisfallen Island, or venture into the hills to view the Torc Cascade waterfall and ascend from the Middle to the Upper Lake.

The area around the lakes can become uncomfortably crowded in holiday season. That's the time to put on your walking boots and follow the trails into the mountains – the

At the heart of Killarney National Park, this is a very popular and often crowded destination.

🕀 198 C2 ✉ Muckross, near Killarney, Co Kerry ☎ 064 31440; www.muckross-house.ie 🕔 House and gardens: daily 9–5:30, Jul–Aug. Farms: daily 10–7, Jun–Sep; 1–6, May; Sat–Sun 1–6, Mar, Apr and Oct 💶 House and farms: expensive. Gardens: free

🎱 Killarney National Park

While Killarney's lakes and mountains are famous for their beauty, Killarney town is infamous for its commercialisation. On the whole, it's best to get straight out into the hills. Sightseers, walkers and adventurers have been coming to the area for nearly 200 years, and things are well organised. You might consider paying the fairly high fee for a trip in a horse-drawn jaunting-car; the drivers, a smooth-talking breed known as "jarveys", know every nook and cranny. Otherwise, aim south of Killarney along the roads around

well-marked Kerry Way, perhaps, or the high and lonely Old Road to Kenmare, an adventurous 16-km (10-mile) route among scenes of wild beauty.

🕀 198 C2 ✉ Tourist Information Office, Beech Road, Killarney, Co Kerry ☎ 064 31633

For Kids
At West Cork Model Railway Village on Clonakilty Bay (open: daily 10–6, Jul–Aug; 11–5, Feb–Jun and Sep–Oct; moderate) you can play among miniature houses and a railway.

Off the Beaten Track
An hour's ride from Baltimore by ferry, Clear Island is Ireland's southernmost point. In spring and autumn the island becomes a birdwatcher's paradise as it plays host to spectacular landfalls of migrating birds.

Pretty as a picture – thatched cottage at the neat estate village of Adare

11 Adare

Adare, 19km (12 miles) south of Limerick City, is one of Ireland's prettiest villages, with thatched stone cottages and a charming riverside position. It was laid out as an estate village during the 19th century by the lords of the manor, the Earls of Dunraven, and everything here is kept neat, tidy and easy on the eye.

Monastic communities settled around Adare, and their work can still be seen in several spots: the many-arched bridge, built in about 1400; the parish church, a former 13th-century friary church; an Austin friary of about 1315, with a Dunraven mausoleum in the cloisters; and in the grounds of Adare Manor, now a luxury hotel, the very evocative ruins of a 15th-century Franciscan friary.

The manor parklands stretch for miles; there is a medieval castle, rare trees and woodland walks. **Adare Castle** is accessible only on guided tours, which must be booked at Adare Heritage Centre.

✚ 199 D3 ✉ Tourist Information Office, Adare Heritage Centre, Main Street, Limerick; www.shannonireland.travel.ie ☎ 061 396255 ☎ Adare Castle: 061 396566 ⏰ Adare Castle: Wed–Sun 11–3, Jul–Sep 💶 Adare Castle: moderate

12 Lough Gur

In quiet countryside 27km (17 miles) south of Limerick, this is one of Ireland's most extensive and best-displayed archaeological sites. An Interpretative Centre, built and thatched to look like neolithic huts, takes you through the 5,000 years that humans have been established here. There are guided tours, or you can stroll at will around the site. There are stone circles (including the mighty 45-m (148-foot) diameter Grange circle), tombs, ring forts, a *crannog* or lake island fort, and the foundations of several huts.

✚ 199 E3 ✉ Bruff Co Limerick ☎ 061 360788; www.shannonheritage.com/LoughGur.htm ⏰ Daily 10–6, May–Sep 💶 Moderate

---

Five Glorious West Cork Villages
- Courtmacsherry
- Rosscarbery
- Glandore
- Castletownshend
- Ballydehob

Where to...
Eat and Drink

Prices

Expect to pay per person for a meal, excluding drinks and service

€ up to €20 €€ up to €32 €€€ over €32

CORK CITY

Fenns Quay Restaurant €€–€€€

Right in the heart of the city, next to the Courthouse, this popular restaurant has recently been extended and refurbished to provide bright modern surroundings. Minted lamb burger with red pepper hummus is a popular choice at lunch or dinner, and there's a wide choice of equally interesting meat, fish and vegetarian dishes, plus daytime snacks, sandwiches and breakfast items.

🚹 199 E2 ✉ Shears Street, Cork
☎ 021 4279527 ◷ Mon–Sat
10 am–late

Flemings €€

Just off the main Cork–Dublin road, this large Georgian family house has linen-clad tables and windows overlooking Cork harbour. International trends are discernible in the classical cooking, but France is clearly the main influence. The seasonal menus reflect a respect for locally grown produce, some of it from the kitchen garden. There is also accommodation in four spacious bedrooms, each with its own bathroom.

🚹 199 E2 ✉ Silvergrange House, Tivoli, Cork ☎ 021 4821621
◷ Daily 12:30–2:30, 6:30–10:30; closed 25 Dec

Isaacs €€

Great flavour and attention to detail are the hallmarks at this modern restaurant in a large 18th-century warehouse. Menus have Mediterranean influences alongside Irish traditions, and plenty to please vegetarians. Stylish and relaxed, with coloured tables and fresh flowers to complement the zesty cooking, the restaurant's ambience appeals to all ages.

🚹 199 E2 ✉ 48 MacCurtain Street, Cork ☎ 021 4503805; email: isaacs@iol.ie ◷ Mon–Sat 10 am–10.30 pm, Sun 6.30–9; closed Christmas week

Jacques Restaurant €–€€

This popular restaurant is a dashing Mediterranean-toned bistro serving good, zesty international cooking. You might find risotto cakes with field mushrooms, Ardsallagh goat's cheese crostinis, or herb crusted rack of lamb. Set menus change daily and the a la carte menu is seasonal. Early dinner (6–7 pm) is good value.

🚹 199 E2 ✉ 9 Phoenix Street, Cork
☎ 021 4277387 ◷ Mon–Fri
noon–3:30, 6–10, Sat 6–10:30 pm; Sun 4:30–9; closed public hols and 25–9 Dec

CORK CITY ENVIRONS

Ballymaloe House €€€

Since 1964 Myrtle Allen of Ballymaloe has led the movement for good regional and artisan foods that brought about the current culinary revival in Ireland. The atmosphere of this comfortable house remains unspoiled and, although the food reflects current trends towards global influences, it is not over-sophisticated. A food philosophy based on allowing finest quality ingredients to take centre stage is still crucial. Reservations are essential.

🚹 199 E2 ✉ Shanagarry, Midleton, Co Cork ☎ 021 4652531; email: res@ballymaloe.ie; www.ballymaloe.ie
◷ Daily 12:30–1:15, 7:30–9:30; closed 24–6 Dec

Blairs Inn €–€€

In a quiet, wooded setting just five minutes' drive from Blarney, this delightful pub has a riverside garden for fine weather, and roaring open fires in winter. Good traditional food, based mainly on local produce such as Kerry oak-smoked salmon or Dingle crab, is served in the bar and in the separate restaurant (different menu). There's live music, too, on Sunday nights all year and Mondays from May to October.

✚ 199 E2 ⬛ Cloghroe, Blarney, Co Cork ☎ 021 4381470: email: blair@eircom.net: www.blairsinn.ie ⬤ Daily noon–midnight. Bar menu: 12:30–9:30: closed Good Fri and 25 Dec

Farmgate €–€€

The shop at the front of this establishment is a showcase for local organic produce and home baking. Behind, in an imaginative restaurant, is an irresistible display of freshly baked savouries, cakes and pastries, including creative vegetarian dishes. Later, this bustling daytime café becomes a sophisticated evening restaurant. A daytime sister restaurant, Farmgate Café (tel: 021 278134), is at the English Market in Cork.

✚ 199 E2 ⬛ The Coolbawn, Midleton, Co Cork ☎ 021 4632771 ⬤ Mon–Wed 9–6, Thu–Sat 6:45 pm–9.30 pm; closed 1 Jan and 25 Dec

Longueville House and Presidents' Restaurant €€€

This elegant, supremely comfortable Georgian mansion is renowned for warm hospitality and superb food. The river, farm and garden supply fresh salmon, Longueville lamb, fresh fruit and vegetables, and a house wine, "Coiséal Longueville", made from home-grown grapes. The cooking is among the finest in Ireland, inspired by the quality of seasonal local produce.

✚ 199 D2 ⬛ Mallow, Co Cork ☎ 022 47156: email: info@longuevillehouse.ie: www.longuevillehouse.ie ⬤ Bar lunch: 12:30–5. Restaurant: 6:30–9 pm; closed 25–8 Dec

WEST CORK COAST

Mary Ann's Bar and Restaurant €–€€

This delightful pub dates back to 1846, and renovations carried out by its current owners have respected its character. The highly regarded food includes specialities such as the platter of

Castlehaven Bay shellfish and seafood and delicious home-baked brown bread, as well as steaks and roasts. Portions are generous, and local west Cork cheeses should not be missed.

✚ 198 C1 ⬛ Castletownshend, near Skibbereen, Co Cork ☎ 028 36146 ⬤ Bar meals: daily noon–2.30, 6–9. Restaurant meals: Tue–Sun 6–9: bar and restaurant closed Good Fri and 25 Dec

Annie's Restaurant €€

You get simple, home-prepared food in this informal restaurant – perhaps seafood chowder with soda bread or scones (biscuits), or steak and salad. The surroundings are simple too, with old pine furnishings. The intimate setting makes for a pleasant atmosphere.

✚ 198 C1 ⬛ Main Street, Ballydehob, Co Cork ⬤ Tue–Sat 6:30–10:30: closed Christmas week

Crackpots Restaurant & Pottery €–€€

It's not hard to find a place to eat in Kinsale, the "Gourmet Capital of Ireland", but the gourmet tag often

means high prices and evening-only opening. Crackpots offers (at very reasonable prices) unusual and beautifully cooked meals, with ethnic and European influences brought to bear on modern Irish and International cuisine. And if you like the tableware, you can buy that too, because it is made on the premises.

✚ 199 E1 ⬛ 3 Cork Street, Kinsale, Co Cork ☎ 021 4772847: fax: 021 4773517: email: crackpts@iol.ie ⬤ Mon–Sat 6:30–10, Sun 12:30–3

La Jolie Brise €

Overlooking the harbour, this cheerful continental-style café serves good, inexpensive meals and moderately priced wines. Menus offer continental and full Irish breakfast, well-made salmon, fresh seafood, well-made pizzas (also to take out) and pastas, traditional mussels and chips, and chargrilled sirloin steaks. There's also spacious accommodation.

✚ 198 C1 ⬛ The Square, Baltimore, Co Cork ☎ 028 20600 ⬤ Daily 8 am–11 pm

Sea View House Hotel and Restaurant €€–€€€

Set in lovely gardens, this country house hotel has elegant public rooms, with family furniture lending character. Enjoy the views over Bantry Bay while tucking into dishes based on local produce, especially seafood, and have coffee and petits fours outside on fine summer evenings.

➕ 198 C1 ⊠ Ballylickey, Bantry, Co Cork ☎ 027 50073/50462; fax: 027 51555; email: info@ seaviewhousehotel.com ❂ Restaurant: daily 7–9 pm. Lunch: Sun only 12:45; closed mid-Nov to mid-Mar

KENMARE

Packie's €–€€

This stylish but unpretentious restaurant has flowers on the bar, small tables and generosity of spirit. Well known for intuitive creative cooking, Packie's produces intensely flavoured Irish-Mediterranean food, often involving local seafood. Many familiar dishes are given an original twist and there's always local cheese to finish.

The proprietors, the Foleys, also own Shelburne Lodge (▶ 116).

➕ 198 C2 ⊠ Henry Street, Kenmare, Co Kerry ☎ 064 41508 ❂ Mon–Sat 6–10; closed late Dec to mid-March

The Purple Heather €

Daytime sister restaurant to Packie's, this bar and informal restaurant serves good, simple, home-prepared food. Soups are home-made; bread is freshly baked; orange juice is freshly squeezed; and organic salads, omelettes and sandwiches are followed by comforting puddings. Choice is good, but nothing fancy.

➕ 198 C2 ⊠ Henry Street, Kenmare, Co Kerry ☎ 064 41016 ❂ Mon–Sat 10:45–6; closed Good Fri and Christmas week

KILLARNEY AND THE RING OF KERRY

The Cooperage €–€€

A relaxing haven away from all the tourist bustle of Killarney; tucked away in the Old Market Lane off the High Street, this is a charming restaurant where chef Martin McCormack produces delights such as a starter of baked Irish smokies topped with cheese and main courses like wild pheasant cooked in Irish cream liqueur. A separate lunch menu includes vegetarian choices.

➕ 198 C2 ⊠ Old Market Lane, Killarney, Co Kerry ☎ 064 37716; email: chezmar@iol.ie; ❂ Lunch: Tue–Sun noon–3 pm. Dinner: Mon–Thu 6–9:30, Fri–Sat 6–10

Gaby's €€€

Offering tempting seasonal menus in classic French style. Specialities include cassolette of prawns and monkfish in a lightly gingered sauce; Gaby's "Famous Smoked Salmon Pâté", lobster "Gaby" (made from a secret recipe), and classics like sole meunière. Availability of seafood depends on daily catches, but there's always a choice, including steaks and local lamb. Good accompaniments and service contribute to a sense of occasion.

➕ 198 C2 ⊠ 27 High Street, Killarney, Co Kerry ☎ 064 32519 ❂ Mon–Sat 6–10; closed 1 Jan, 25 Dec and mid-Feb to mid-Mar

DINGLE PENINSULA

Lord Baker's €–€€€

"Lord Baker" was the original owner of what is probably the oldest bar in Dingle. Bar food (maybe crab claws in garlic butter or chowder and home-baked bread) is served in front of the turf fire. Beyond it a restaurant opens onto a garden, serving well-cooked food.

➕ 198 A3 ⊠ Dingle, Co Kerry ☎ 066 9151277; www.lordbakers.ie ❂ Daily 12:30–2, 6–10; closed Good Fri and 24–5 Dec

The Tankard €–€€€

This pub and restaurant is noted for its seafood. Dishes on the imaginative bar menu are available from lunch onward. The seafood cooking in the restaurant is particularly good, but there is plenty more to choose from, including steaks, Kerry lamb, duckling and vegetarian dishes.

➕ 198 C3 ⊠ Kilfenora Fenit, Tralee, Co Kerry ☎ 066 7136164; email: tankard@eircom.net ❂ Bar: daily 12:30–10 pm. Restaurant: daily 6–10 pm, Sun lunch noon–4

Where to... Stay

Prices

Expect to pay per person staying

€ up to €40 €€ up to €77 €€€ over €77

CORK CITY

Assolas Country House €€–€€€

Beautifully set in peaceful riverside gardens, this gracious 17th-century manor house is renowned for thoughtful hospitality, impeccable housekeeping and wonderful food. Use of local produce is a point of honour: the productive walled garden supplies a kitchen whose cooking has achieved international acclaim. Bedrooms vary in size and outlook but have good bathrooms and all are elegantly furnished in country-house style, with many special touches.

🚹 199 E2 ⊠ Kanturk, Co Cork
☎ 029 50015; fax: 029 50795;
email: assolas@eircom.net;
www.assolas.com ⏰ Apr–Oct

Garnish House €€

Decked with colourful windowboxes, this nice little guest house is only five minutes' walk from the city centre. It's also handy for the port and airport, and offers 24-hour reception facilities. Some rooms have a Jacuzzi, and there's an extensive breakfast menu to set you up for the day.

🚹 199 E2 ⊠ 1 Aldergrove, Western Road, Cork ☎ 021 4275111; email: garnish@iol.ie ⏰ Open all year

Hayfield Manor Hotel €€€

Although built in the mid-1990s, this attractive hotel in the university area, less than 2km (1 mile) from the city centre, has the feel of a large period house. It's set in extensive gardens,

and amenities include a large bar (popular for weekday lunches), an elegant restaurant and drawing room, both overlooking a walled garden, and a leisure centre for residents only. Spacious bedrooms are furnished to a very high standard with antiques and have generous marbled bathrooms.

🚹 199 E2 ⊠ Perrott Avenue, College Road, Cork ☎ 021 4315600; fax: 021 4316839; email: enquiries@hayfieldmanor.ie; www.hayfieldmanor.ie ⏰ Open all year

Jurys Inn Cork €–€€

Like other Jurys Inns (▶ 39), this central, riverside hotel is conveniently located and provides comfort for a moderate price. There's no room service, but prices include accommodation for up to four. Rooms are well designed with good-quality furnishings and have phone, TV, tea and coffee facilities and full bathrooms. There's some private parking and the hotel also has an arrangement with a nearby parking lot.

🚹 199 E2 ⊠ Anderson's Quay, Cork ☎ 021 4276444; email: info@jurys.com ⏰ Closed 24–6 Dec

KINSALE

Trident Hotel €€–€€€

This 1960s waterfront building enjoys one of Kinsale's best locations. It's well run, hospitable and comfortable; bedrooms all have full bathrooms, and there are two suites with private balconies, directly overlooking the harbour. The food, in both the first-floor restaurant and the Wharf Tavern underneath it, is well above average hotel fare.

🚹 199 E1 ⊠ World's End, Kinsale, Co Cork ☎ 021 4772301; fax: 021 4774173; email: info@tridenthotel.com; www.tridenthotel.com ⏰ Closed 25–6 Dec

KENMARE

Shelburne Lodge €€–€€€

This fine old stone house on the edge of Kenmare has been stylishly restored and furnished. There's an elegant drawing room and well-appointed dining room where delicious breakfasts with home-baked bread and hot dishes are served. Comfortable bedrooms with bathrooms are decorated to a high standard. Guests can eat at Packie's (▶ 115).

🚹 198 C2 ☒ Killowen, Cork Road, Kenmare, Co Kerry ☎ 064 41013
Ⓒ Closed Nov–Mar

KILLARNEY

Killarney Park Hotel €€€

This luxurious modern hotel has a country-house look and an elegant atmosphere. Hands-on management and a programme of constant refurbishment and upgrading ensure that standards never slip. Spacious bedrooms, decorated in countryside colours, have large beds and lovely bathrooms. The modern, international food served is above average.

🚹 198 C2 ☒ Town Centre, Killarney, Co Kerry ☎ 064 35555; fax: 064 35266; email: info@killarneyparkhotel.ie; www.killarneyparkhotel.ie
Ⓒ Closed 24–7 Dec

DINGLE PENINSULA

The Brandon Hotel €€

This is Tralee's largest hotel and an important centre for town activities. It has spacious public areas, and the bedrooms are well equipped with direct-dial phone, radio and TV. Some bedrooms are small, but all have well-designed bathrooms. The hotel has a swimming-pool and leisure centre.

🚹 198 C3 ☒ Princes Street, Tralee, Co Kerry ☎ 066 7123333 Ⓒ Closed 23–8 Dec

Doon House €–€€

Ballybunion is famous for golf, and players staying here can get a reduction on their green fees and an early breakfast. This member of the Town and Country Homes Association is ideal for non-golfers too – it has fine views of the sea and mountains, and there are facilities near by for hill walking, horseback-riding and cycling. Doon House provides home comforts and excellent breakfasts.

🚹 198 C3 ☒ Doon Road, Ballybunion, Co Kerry ☎ 068 27411; fax: 068 27411

Heaton's €–€€

This guest house has a lovely location, right by the water with spectacular views across Dingle Bay. Cameron and Nuala Heaton are welcoming hosts, and the accommodation is exceptionally good – all rooms have bathrooms with power showers, and the mini-suites have Jacuzzis. Daughter Jackie has attracted some renown for her excellent à la carte breakfast menu, a long list which includes local smoked salmon, Irish cheeses, Dingle kippers, porridge with a topping of Drambuie, brown sugar and cream, as well as the usual breakfast fare. Bread, scones and preserves are all homemade.

🚹 198 A3 ☒ The Wood, Dingle, Co Kerry ☎ 066 9152288; fax: 066 9152324; email: heatons@iol.ie; www.heatonsdingle.com
Ⓒ Closed 6 Jan–1 Feb and 9–27 Dec

ADARE

Dunraven Arms Hotel €€€

Although it is now a large hotel, this 18th-century inn still has a relaxed country ambience. Bedrooms are beautifully furnished with antiques, and have dressing rooms and luxurious bathrooms. Amenities include a new leisure centre, and the hotel is a popular base for sporting holidays. The food is good in both the bar and the two restaurants.

🚹 199 D3 ☒ Adare, Co Limerick ☎ 061 396633; email: reservations@dunravenhotel.com; www.dunravenhotel.com

GLIN

Glin Castle €€€

The Fitzgeralds, the hereditary Knights of Glin, have lived here for 700 years (though the current house is a mere 200 years old) and now welcome guests to share their home. There are 15 bedrooms; dinner is served in the beautiful dining room, which can seat up to 30 people. The castle's garden is open to the public (as is the house at certain times of the year).

🚹 199 C3 ☒ Glin, Co Limerick ☎ 068 34173; email: knight@iol.ie; www.glincastle.com Ⓒ Closed mid-Nov to mid-Mar

Where to...
Shop

CORK

Shop for local produce at the **English Market**, off Patrick Street. Antiques are best in the **Paul Street** area. Shanagarry is home to **Ballymaloe** enterprises, and **Stephen Pearce Pottery and Emporium** (tel: 021 4646807).

BLARNEY

Blarney Woollen Mills (tel: 021 4385280) sells a huge range of goods.

KINSALE

Visit **Victoria Murphy** (Market Quay, tel: 021 4774317) for jewellery, **Kinsale Crystal** (Market Street, tel: 021 477 4463) for crystal, and **Bolands** (Barry's Place, tel: 021 4772161) for crafts.

BANTRY

Mannings Emporium (Ballylickey, tel: 027 50456) sells artisan foods.

KENMARE

Kenmare lace is famous (Heritage Centre, tel: 064 41491); buy antique lace at **Nostalgia** (Henry Street, tel: 064 41389), rugs at **Avoca Handweavers** (Moll's Gap, tel: 064 34720) and clothing at **Cleo** (Shelbourne Street, tel: 064 41410).

KILLARNEY

Look out for **Christy's Irish Stores** (Main Street, tel: 064 33222), **Bricín Craft Shop** (High Street, tel: 064 34902), and **Frank Lewis Gallery** (Bridewell Lane, tel: 064 34843) for original art.

DINGLE

The **Weaver's Shop** (Green Street, tel: 066 9151688) sells handwoven fabrics, and **Louis Mulcahy's** pottery. His factory shop is near Dingle (tel: 066 9156229).

Where to...
Be Entertained

OUTDOOR ACTIVITIES

Activities include sailing (Marine Tourism Ltd, Castlepark Marina, Kinsale, tel: 021 4774959), sea angling (notably out of Kinsale), cycling, horseback-riding and golf, especially on the Kerry links; information from tourist information offices. Kenmare's **Seafari** (The Pier, tel: 064 83171) makes an entertaining wildlife cruise on Kenmare Bay. Dingle is a base for dolphin-watching (boats depart regularly from the harbour).

SPECTATOR SPORTS

Greyhound racing (Curraheen Park, Bishopstown, tel: 021 4543095) and horse racing (Mallow, tel: 022 21592) are popular. A local sport to be aware of is road bowling, played with metal balls.

MUSIC

Pubs in every town have live music most nights in summer. Good venues include: in Kinsale, **The Spaniard** (Scilly, tel: 021 4772436) and **The Shanakee** (Market Street, tel: 021 4777077); in Kenmare, the **Lansdowne Arms** (tel: 064 41368); in Killarney, **Buckley's** (Arbutus Hotel, College Street, tel: 064 31037) and the **Grand Hotel** (Main Street, tel: 064 31159). Dingle is *the* place for traditional music, especially **O'Flaherty's** (Bridge Street, tel: 066 9151983) – but almost any bar will be humming. Contrasting musical treats are **Castletownshend's Festival of Classical Music** Thursdays in July and August (St Barrahane's Church, tel: 028 36193) and the **West Cork Chamber Music Festival** (Bantry House, tel: 027 52789) late June to July.

West and Northwest Ireland

Getting Your Bearings

The west of Ireland may not have as dense a profusion of dramatic mountains and wild peninsulas as the southwest, but it has something else – sheer magic.

A succession of remarkable landscapes blends one into another, each entirely distinctive but only a part of the whole captivating jigsaw. They include the naked grey limestone hills of the Burren in County Clare, beautiful with carpets of wild flowers in spring and summer; the Connemara district of County Galway, with its remote mountainous heart and harshly lonely coasts; and the three windswept

★ Don't Miss

At Your Leisure

Further Afield

High cross at
Clonmacnoise,
County Offaly,
displays fine
Celtic carving

Aran Islands in Galway Bay, where life
and work go on at an unhurried pace
among the tiny, rocky fields and
innumerable stone walls. The glorious
countryside round Clew Bay in County
Mayo combines gentle green hills and
forbidding mountains with ancient field monuments. And
dominating the whole area is Croagh Patrick, the Holy
Mountain. Then there's County Sligo – "Yeats Country" – and
Donegal, a ragged-edged sea county with truly wild hills and
cliffs, where people are few and far between.

This is the land that inspired playwright J M Synge and
novelist Liam O'Flaherty, painter Jack Yeats and his brother, the
poet W B Yeats. The landscape still inspires musicians; some of
the best traditional music is played in the West of Ireland, from
Clare's gently flowing tunes to the spiky reels of Donegal. Here
in the West you can play the tourist – for instance at County
Clare's Bunratty Folk Park; or you can take the other road and
savour the

Right: fishing
boats moored
at Leenane,
County Galway,
on the deep
water of Killary
Harbour

Previous page:
O'Brien's Tower
atop the
plunging Cliffs
of Moher

savour the
lonely silences
of the Nephin
Beg Mountains.
Whatever you
do, be sure to
climb Croagh
Patrick. Going
up is a hard
sweat, but
you will never
forget the
view from the
summit.

The West in Four Days

Take your time, now, take your time...the slower the better, through the wild green landscapes and the haunting traditional music of Ireland's West.

Day One

Morning Spend the day exploring the **5 Burren** (➤ 124–7). Travel the slow coast road from Ballyvaughan down to **Doolin**, stopping at one of its famous pubs for lunch (➤ 127).

Afternoon Carry on a few miles down the coast to the spectacular **5 Cliffs of Moher**. Then take your time circling back inland by way of the great ancient monuments of **Poulnabrone portal dolmen** (above) and **Gleninsheen wedge tomb**, making time for a stroll on the Burren's naked limestone hills. An hour's drive in the early evening will land you in Galway for the night.

Day Two

Morning Take the ferry from the city quays and cruise down Galway Bay to **6 Inishmore** (right, ➤ 129), the biggest of the Aran Islands. Stop for lunch at Joe Watty's friendly pub in the small port of Kilronan.

Afternoon Make your way up to the ancient fort of **6 Dún Aengus** (➤ 129) on the cliffs, preferably on foot or by rented bicycle. Be sure to be back in Kilronan in good time for the last ferry back to Galway!

Day Three

Morning You'll have plenty of time for coffee, a stroll and a look around **7 Galway City** (➤ 135) before moving on in the early afternoon.

Afternoon Take the **8 Connemara** coast road west, at first along the smooth upper shore of Galway Bay, then winding in and out around a succession of small, craggy bays. After a cup of tea in **Clifden** (➤ 130), push on 65km (40 miles) by way of dramatic Killary Harbour to **9 Westport** (➤ 133). Stay overnight here, and look for a great music session in Molloy's, Hoban's or McHale's.

Day Four

Morning Set off bright and early for the hour's run (via the bridge) out to **9 Achill Island** (coast at Dooagh above, ➤ 133). Back on the mainland, continue north on the wild coastal road to Bangor Erris, then turn east across the bleakly impressive Bellacorick bog to reach civilisation and a late lunch at Ballina, perhaps at The Broken Jug pub in the centre of the town (tel: 096 72379).

Afternoon Push on to **13 Sligo** (➤ 137; a pint in Hargadon's bar is obligatory here), and drive north towards W B Yeats's favourite mountains to pay your respects at his grave in **Drumcliff churchyard** (➤ 179). Then return through Sligo and drive on south for Galway.

Further Afield

If you have a day to spare for a bleakly beautiful and little-visited corner of Ireland (right), stay overnight in Ballybofey and spend the next day driving the really spectacular circuit of southwest Donegal's coast, out by Glencolumbkille and the Slieve League cliffs.

5 The Burren and the Cliffs of Moher

The Burren is 1,300sq km (502sq miles) of hilly ground in the north-west corner of Clare, almost water-less, all but deserted, and largely made up of naked grey limestone. Yet in this bleak setting you'll find superb wildflowers, marvellou music, hundreds of ancient monuments and a beautiful coast-line, culminating in the mighty Cliffs of Moher. And with it all comes that special laid-back County Clare atmosphere. The place is a paradox, but one you'll have unbeatable pleasure in exploring.

A Snapshot Tour

Start in **Ballyvaughan**, following the coast road down to **Doolin**, noted for its traditional music pubs, and on to the **Cliffs of Moher** for some spectacular views. Then take the road for **Lisdoonvarna** and **Kilfenora**, and on by **Corofin** to enjoy some typical laid-back Burren villages. There are carved high crosses at

Kilfenora, and the excellent **Burren Display Centre** there fills you in on the geology and flora of the region. See more early Christian remains at **Dysert O'Dea** south of Corofin, then meander north through the heart of the Burren to find the magical landscape of **Mullaghmore**, the great portal dolmen of **Poulnabrone**, and, in spring and summer, the carpets of wild flowers.

You could see the "Best of the Burren" in a long day like this. But you won't begin to see the place itself until you leave the car and wal out into the wilderness.

Ledges in the Cliffs of Moher make ideal roosting niches for fulmars

Floral Present and Stony Past

Boulders dumped by Ice Age glaciers litter the naked limestone pavements of the Burren

You don't have to be a botanist to see the beauty of the flowers of the Burren. The limestone pavements carry deep cracks, known as "grykes" to geologists. These trap water, sun and soil fragments, making them ideal hothouses for plants. The warm Gulf Stream moves offshore; sunlight bounces off the naked stone into the grykes. Whatever combination of factors makes it happen, the Burren bursts open each spring with an astonishing array of wildflowers: orchids, spring gentians, mountain avens, eyebright, bloody cranesbill. Plants that wouldn't normally be found anywhere near each other grow side by side – acid-loving and lime-loving, arctic, mountain, coastal, Mediterranean. The ferns, mosses and lichens are spectacular. Springtime and summer in the Burren are a botanist's dream, and beautiful for anyone who loves colour and variety in the landscape.

Scattered across the landscape are monuments bearing witness to five millennia of human habitation. Around 5,000 years ago, a forgotten people built the **Poulnabrone portal dolmen** – the stone uprights and cap stone of which would once have been covered with earth to form a tomb chamber.

Gleninsheen, near Caherconnell, and other wedge-shaped tombs near by date from about 1500 BC. With the introduction of Christianity came the wonderfully carved high crosses at **Kilfenora**, and in the 12th and 13th centuries respectively the monastic site of **Dysert O'Dea** in the south and the rich stonework at **Corcomroe Abbey** in the north. Round stone forts and enclosures with jaw-breaking names dot the hills: Cahermacnaghten, Caherballykinvarga, Cahercommaun. Under the hills stand fortified towers like the gaunt 16th-century **Newtown Castle** near Ballyvaughan, and imposing houses such as the picturesquely ruined 17th-century **Leamaneh Castle** outside Corofin. There are also the shells of ancient churches abandoned after Oliver Cromwell's troops invaded and subdued the Burren in the 1650s.

Archaeology

Five of the Burren's great archaeological delights:
- Poulnabrone portal dolmen
- High crosses at Kilfenora Cathedral
- Newtown Castle tower house
- Dysert O'Dea's church doorway with its carved saints and beasts
- Corcomroe Abbey

The Cliffs of Moher plunge a dizzying 200m (656 feet) to the sea

Flowers

Don't forget your flower book! Maryangela Keane's *The Burren* (an Irish Heritage Series paperback that is widely available locally) gives an excellent introduction to the Burren flora. Real enthusiasts should bring a hand lens with them; this will give wonderful close-ups of the flowers. But remember – don't pick them!

✉ Tourist information centres: Clare Road, Ennis, and Cliffs of Moher; www.shannonireland.travel.ie
☎ Ennis: 065 6828366. Cliffs of Moher: 065 7081171

Burren Display Centre
✚ 199 D5
☎ 065 7088030; www.theburrencentre.ie
🕐 Daily 9:30–6, Jun–Sep; 10–5, mid-Mar to May, Oct
💲 Moderate

Aillwee Caves
✚ 199 D5
☎ 065 7077036
🕐 Daily 10–6:30, Jul–Aug; 10–5:30, Mar–Jun, Sep–Oct; tours only Nov–Dec 💲 Expensive

Fine Scenery and a Good Time

A great way to see the Burren is to spend a couple of days walking the **Burren Way**, a 42-km (26-mile) footpath from Ballyvaughan to Liscannor. The most spectacular part is undoubtedly along the edges of the **Cliffs of Moher** at the southwestern extremity of the Burren. At their highest point these giant flagstone cliffs fall sheer into the sea: a great tourist attraction, and often a crowded one.

There are more tremendous views from **Corkscrew Hill**, a section of N67 south of Ballyvaughan that snakes back and forth as it climbs, and the whole of the steep, craggy coastline around Black Head. You can tour the underground **showcaves at Aillwee** near Ballyvaughan, with their stalagmites and stalactites; and escape other tourists at **Mullaghmore**, a magical hill reached by a country road north of Corofin, to enjoy strange land formations and delicious solitude.

TAKING A BREAK

In Kilfenora, try **Vaughan's** or **Linnane's**, and in Lisdoonvarna, the **Roadside Tavern**: you're guaranteed conversation and laughter. If you fancy a singalong in Doolin, **O'Connor's** is a good bet. If your taste is for traditional tunes and you're staying in Doolin overnight, try **McGann's** at around 10 pm.

THE BURREN: INSIDE INFO

Top tips Five of the **Burren's chief tourist attractions** lie on or very near N67: Ballyvaughan, Newtown Castle, Aillwee Caves, Corkscrew Hill, and the spa town of Lisdoonvarna. The Cliffs of Moher are 10km (6 miles) along R478.
• Anyone with enough skill not to spoil the tune is welcome to join a pub **music session**. Don't be shy, ask if you can join in!

Hidden gems Holy wells, rock chairs that cure the backache, Mass rocks and forgotten church ruins: the Burren is packed with them, and you can find them all (or almost all) with the help of **Tim Robinson's wonderful** *Folding Landscape*, a hand-drawn, large-scale, meticulous map of the Burren, widely available locally.

One to miss Don't bother with the **Cliffs of Moher on a high-season weekend** – the clifftops will be crowded, and all sense of awe will be on hold.

⑥ The Aran Islands

Seeming to float in the mouth of Galway Bay like three low grey boats in line astern, the Aran Islands resemble no other part of Ireland. Here Irish is still spoken as an everyday language, the traditional black hide-covered boats called *currachs* are used for fishing (though now they're canvas covered and often motorised), transport is mostly on foot or bicycle, homespun clothing is still worn by some of the older folk, and the pace of life is driven not so much by the clock as by the tides and winds, and by tasks done and not done.

Aran Island houses are built low and small-windowed to give maximum protection from bad weather

The islands are made not of Galway granite but of Clare limestone, which means that their spring and summer flower displays are glorious. Countless thousands of stone walls march in parallel lines across the bare grey and black rock, squaring off the islands into hundreds of tiny fields. Partly these walls show ownership; partly they are built of necessity, as handy repositories for stones picked laboriously from the fields by hand. The soil of the islands has been created by hand, too, a precious mixture of sand, seaweed and dung that grows the best potatoes in Ireland. Life out here on these windswept, barren rocks has always been hard, and still is.

Inisheer, nearest to County Clare (reached from Doolin), is the smallest of the Aran Islands at just over 3km (2 miles)

Great Aran Reading

- *Skerrett* by Liam O'Flaherty – titanic, tragic struggle between Inishmore's priest and schoolmaster, written by a native and based on a true story.
- *The Aran Islanders* by J M Synge – classic account of the islands and their people at the turn of the 20th century, garnered during the playwright's sojourns on Inishmaan, 1898–1902.

across, and has a splendid 15th-century fort built by a chieftain of the O'Brien clan. **Inishmaan**, in the middle, is 5km (3 miles) across and is the most traditional and the most remote. For island specialists with a couple of days in hand, these two offer unforgettable delights. But most visitors will opt for **Inishmore**, the biggest Aran island at 13km (8 miles) long and the most easily accessible.

Inishmore has a small port at Kilronan, and a tiny airstrip. You could drive from Galway to Rossaveal for a 40-minute ferry crossing, or fly over by Aer Arann from Connemara Airport, just outside Galway City, and be in Inishmore in six minutes. But the most leisurely and enjoyable way to get there is by ferry from Galway City, with a 90-minute cruise down Galway Bay.

The island's chief attraction is the dramatically perched clifftop fort of **Dún Aengus** with its three giant rings of battlements; but the island is covered in pre-Christian and early Christian remains. Take plenty of time to walk, talk, listen, sit and stare. Even in Ireland, you won't find a more peaceful spot.

Seaweed is gathered from the shores of Inishmore to be used as fertiliser on the rocky fields

🚗 198 C5　✉ Tourist information offices:
Kilronan, Inishmore ☎ 099 61263; www.visitaranislands.com
Aras Fáilte, Forster Street, Galway ☎ 091 537700;
www.westireland.travel.ie
🕐 All year round (both)

Dún Aengus
☎ 01 647 2455/2453
🎟 Free

TAKING A BREAK

Stop for lunch in **Joe Watty's** friendly pub in Inishmore's tiny port of Kilronan.

Folding Landscape
The Tim Robinson map and guide – *Folding Landscape* (Oileáin Arann), at 2.2 inches to the mile – will serve you best and show you most in the Aran Islands.

THE ARAN ISLANDS: INSIDE INFO

Top tips A minibus will take you from Kilronan, Inishmore's port village, to Dún Aengus clifftop fort in 5 minutes.
• If you are planning to visit Inishmaan, **check the weather forecast first**. Fog, mist or very high winds can suspend all travel between island and mainland.
• Note that there are no ATMs on Inishmore, so take some money with you.

Hidden gem On Inishmore, about 6km (4 miles) east of Dún Aengus, is the far less visited stronghold of **Dún Dúchathair** in a spectacular setting on the cliff edge.

⑧ Connemara

Connemara in northwest County Galway is the romantic heart of the west, a harsh land of boggy fields, knobbly mountains and savage sea coasts. Dublin schoolkids come here to learn Irish; the rest of us visit for the wild and beautiful scenery. But make no mistake, this is a tough place to live, with poor soil stretched thinly over beds of unyielding granite. As the locals say: "You can't eat scenery."

North of Galway stretches the immense inland sea of **Lough Corrib**. Here angling-oriented Oughterard is a pretty spot to base yourself for good trout fishing, while **Cong Abbey** on the north shore is worth the detour – a glorious little 12th-century building.

West of here is Joyce Country, so named because much of the population belonged to the Joyce clan, where the sister ranges of the **Maumturk Mountains** and, to their west, the magnificent **Twelve Bens** (or Twelve Pins) pierce the sky with hard quartzite peaks. This is a cruelly beautiful landscape, and wonderful walking country, bounded on the north by mountains sweeping down to the narrow inlet of Killary Harbour.

Going west again, you are confronted by classic Connemara landscapes, a hard land of wide bog vistas, rugged brown hills and innumerable little lakes. **Clifden**, a Victorian holiday

Enjoying a good gallop through the Connemara surf

Clifden, the charming 19th-century seaside resort that developed when the railway reached West Galway

resort, sits out west in the centre of a wheel of craggy coastline, where a coast road crawls and climbs around the indentations. Follow it east at a nice slow speed, stopping at **Roundstone** to visit the workshop at Roundstone Musical Instruments, where Malachy Kearns makes the world's best *bodhráns* (goatskin drums). Then carry on in increasingly desolate and magnificent scenery towards Galway City. Before getting there, spare a couple of hours to turn right at Casla/Costelloe, where a causeway road takes you through the Irish-speaking islands of **Lettermore**, **Gorumna** and **Lettermullan**. This wild, lonely back country gives a true flavour of Connemara.

TAKING A BREAK

Destry's Café-Restaurant in Clifden is a fun and inexpensive place to eat. In Roundstone, **O'Dowd's Seafood Bar and Restaurant** (► 140) serves a good pint and inexpensive bar food.

🞦 194 B1 ✉ Tourist Information Office, Aras Fáilte, Forster Street, Galway City
☎ 091 537700; email: user@western-tourism.ie; www.irelandwest.ie

---

CONNEMARA: INSIDE INFO

Top tips To get straight from Galway City to Clifden, the "capital" of West Connemara, take N59. This road whisks you straight there on a 80-km (50-mile) run through the heart of the region.

• Bring your fly and coarse rods if you are an angler; the **coastal rivers of Connemara are some of the best in Ireland** for salmon, and the loughs provide excellent trout fishing.

• If you are visiting in August, try to get to the **Clifden Show**, where appealing, long-haired Connemara ponies are brought for sale.

Hidden gem The little **6th-century oratory on St Macdara's Island**, 9.5km (6 miles) south of Roundstone (where you may charter a boat to visit the island).

One to miss Avoid **Salt Hill in holiday season**, when it becomes a crowded, very average seaside resort. There are better, quieter beaches a little further west.

9 **West Mayo**

Above: the stunning view from the summit of Croagh Patrick

West Mayo is one of Ireland's most atmospheric corners. While not exactly undiscovered, it is far enough distant from Dublin and walled in by serious enough mountains and bog-lands to retain (and flaunt) its own character.

Centrepiece of the region is broad **Clew Bay**, reputed to have 365 islands. Certainly there are several dozen of them, little drumlins (heaps of Ice Age rubble) with grassy backs turned to the land and yellow clay teeth bared to the west. At the mouth of Clew Bay is **Clare Island**, hump-backed and greenly beautiful, a great place to spend a few days away from it all; the ferry leaves from Roonagh Quay on the southwest-ern extremity of the bay and, depending on the weather, takes between 30 minutes to an hour to reach the island.

On Clew Bay's south shore stands the 765-m (2,510-foot) cone-shaped mountain of **Croagh Patrick** (known locally as "The Reek"), Ireland's Holy Mountain, focus of a massed

🔲 194 C2
✉ Tourist Information Office, The Mall, Westport, Co Mayo
☎ 098 25711; www.westireland.travel.ie

Westport House
🔲 194 C2
☎ 098 25430/27766; www.westireland.travel.ie
🕐 Daily 11:30–5:30, Jul–Aug; Mon–Fri 11:30–5:30, Sat–Sun 1:30–5:30, rest of year
💶 Expensive

National Museum of Ireland – Country Life
🔲 195 D2
✉ Turlough Park, Castlebar, Co Mayo
☎ 094 903 1773 or 01 648 6392; www.museum.ie
🕐 Tue–Sat 10–5, Sun 2–5; closed Good Fri and 25 Dec
💶 Free

annual pilgrimage and one of Ireland's classic hill hikes (➤ 176–7). The top of The Reek is the best vantage point to view Clew Bay.

At the southeastern corner of Clew Bay lies **Westport**, a small town of great charm and character, planned in the latter part of the 18th century by celebrated Georgian architect James Wyatt at the request of the Marquess of Sligo, on whose estate it was built. **Westport House** (1730–34), beautifully furnished and with a fine collection of paintings, is worth a look around, and its grounds are lovely. A zoo and atmospheric dungeons are a bonus for visitors with children. But the great attraction of Westport is its town life – gossip, storytelling, music-making. It is one of the best towns in Ireland for traditional music and each year, in late September, hosts an excellent arts festival, showcasing home-grown and invited talent.

Over near Castlebar is the only national museum outside Dublin, the **National Museum of Ireland – Country Life**, appropriately located in one of Ireland's most rural counties. It contains the national Folklore Collection, comprising around 50,000 objects, and the displays reflect traditional rural life in Ireland between 1850 and 1950. The specially built museum is in the grounds of Turlough Park House, which is itself open to the public to show how the landowners lived.

Out at the northwest corner of Clew Bay is **Achill Island**, a big ragged outline attached to the mainland by a road bridge across Achill Sound. This Irish-speaking island, superbly mountainous, is Ireland's largest. You can climb 672-m (2,205-foot) Slieve More, Achill's highest peak, from Doogort on the north coast, or join a boat-rental party for a jaw-dropping inspection of some of Ireland's highest cliffs at the island's northwestern tip. Boats can be rented from Doogort Pier; for information contact Alice's Harbour Inn tourist office (tel: 098 45384).

TAKING A BREAK

Stop for a drink at **McGing's** pub in Westport, in the high street. John McGing is a fountain of knowledge on local history, and serves the best stout in town. Alternatively, try **Quay Cottage** (➤ 140), an informal waterside restaurant on Westport's harbour.

At Your Leisure

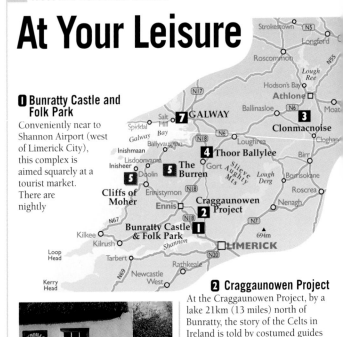

❶ Bunratty Castle and Folk Park

Conveniently near to Shannon Airport (west of Limerick City), this complex is aimed squarely at a tourist market. There are nightly

❷ Craggaunowen Project

At the Craggaunowen Project, by a lake 21km (13 miles) north of Bunratty, the story of the Celts in Ireland is told by costumed guides amid clever reconstructions of Celtic buildings that include a *crannóg* or lake dwelling, a stone ring fort, round

At Craggaunowen, reconstructed Celtic buildings surround a 16th-century building

Buildings of a bygone Ireland, in Bunratty Folk Park, County Clare

mead'n'minstrels medieval banquets in the castle (reservations are essential), and a crowded "19th-century Irish village" in the grounds with costumed guides and demonstrations of traditional skills, which many visitors seem to take for the real thing. Come here well out of season, however, and you can appreciate the atmosphere and the authentic touches without having your toes trodden on. The castle itself, built in about 1425, is a very fine restoration, with plenty of good tapestries and beautiful furniture, some dating back as far as the building.

🕂 199 D4 ✉ Bunratty, Co Clare ☎ 061 360788; www.shannonheritage.com
🕒 Daily 9:30–5:30 (Folk Park also 5:30–6:30, Jun–Aug) 💶 Expensive

thatched huts and burial places. The leather-hulled boat *Brendan*, built by adventurer Tim Severin and sailed by him from the Dingle Peninsula to Newfoundland in 1976–77, is on display: it was this voyage that showed how St Brendan might have discovered America back in the 6th century AD.

➕ 199 D4 ✉ Quin, Co Clare ☎ 061 360788; www.shannonheritage.com ⏱ Daily 10–6, Apr–Oct; 9–6, mid-May to Aug 💷 Moderate

❸ Clonmacnoise

Clonmacnoise is one of Ireland's finest and most interesting ecclesiastical sites. It was the most influential centre in pre-Norman Europe in its day. Several Irish kings are buried here. Within the site are two Round Towers (the lightning-blasted 10th-century O'Rourke's Tower and the almost perfect MacCarthy Tower of 1124), eight ancient churches and a largely 14th-century cathedral. Of three notable high crosses, the best is the richly carved Cross of the Scriptures, also known as the Great Cross, which dates from the early 10th century and stands over 4m (13 feet) tall.

➕ 199 F5 ✉ On R444, north of Shannonbridge, Co Offaly ☎ 090 967 4195; www.shannonheritage.com ⏱ Daily 9–7, mid-May to Sep; 10–6, mid-Mar to mid-May, Sep–Nov; 10–5:30, rest of year 💷 Moderate

❹ Thoor Ballylee

I the poet William Yeats,
With old millboards and sea-green slates
And smithy work from the Gort forge
Restored this tower for my wife George.
And may these characters remain
When all is ruin once again.

This inscription at Thoor Ballylee tells the story of the medieval stone tower house bought by W B Yeats in 1916 for £35, and intermittently inhabited (and written about) by him. It is now a beautifully restored museum housing Yeats memorabilia and first editions.

➕ 199 D5 ✉ Gort, Co Galway ☎ 091 631436 ⏱ Mon–Sat 10–6, Jun–Sep 💷 Moderate

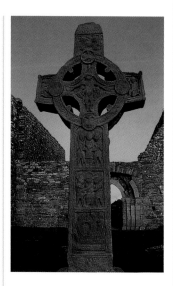

The Cross of the Scriptures at Clonmacnoise monastic site is a thousand years old

❼ Galway City

Galway is a thriving place with a lively atmosphere thanks to its university and the large number of job-providing industries that have sprung up around the town. During Galway Arts Festival late in July, and the Races that follow it, is a good time to visit. Everything centres on Eyre Square; in the streets to the south and west you'll find most of the bars, restaurants and shops. Worth exploring are medieval Lynch's Castle (now a bank) in Shop Street and the waterways of Claddagh to the south.

➕ 199 D5 ✉ Tourist Information, Eyre Square ☎ 091 537700; email: user@western-tourism.ie; www.irelandwest.ie

For Kids

Leisureland, a modern pool complex in Salt Hill, has a waterslide, Treasure Cove complete with pirate ship, a tropical beach pool and playground.

✉ Salt Hill, Galway ☎ 091 521455 ⏱ Daily 8 am–10 pm, in summer; 12:30–2, 5:45–7:15, 8–10, in winter 💷 Moderate

Four Lonely Headlands with Wonderful Views
• Malin Head, Donegal
• Achill Head, Achill Island, Mayo
• Mace Head, Connemara, Galway
• Hags Head, Clare

⑩ Strokestown Park House, Garden & Famine Museum

Allow a good half-day to explore this fascinating place. The big, white-fronted Palladian mansion, approached through a grand arch, dates back to the 1660s, though it was remodelled in the 1730s. The original 18th-century furnishings are still in place. Tunnels concealed the movement of servants from the patrician gaze of the Mahon family, owners of Strokestown. There was even a gallery constructed around the kitchen so that the lady of the house could observe what went on without being seen herself.

Money and privilege did not save Major Denis Mahon. He was murdered on his estate during the Great Famine of 1845–50 after he had tried to evict most of his starving tenants and ship them off to America. An excellent, if harrowing, Famine Museum, housed in the old stable yard, explores the tragic sequence of events of which this was a small part.

Outside in the grounds is a fine walled garden with an immensely long herbaceous border.

➕ 195 F2 ✉ Strokestown, Co Roscommon ☎ 071 9633013; www.strokestownpark.ie 🕐 Daily 10–5:30, mid-Mar to Oct; rest of year by appointment 💶 Expensive

⑪ Nephin Beg Mountains

These roadless mountains in northwest Mayo fill a triangle of 200sq km (77sq miles) north of Westport, flanked by the wild Atlantic coast on the west and the great bog of Bellacorick on the east. It is the remotest range in Ireland, crossed by one dramatic and demanding footpath, the 48-km (30-mile) Bangor Trail from Newport to Bangor Erris. A yearly challenge walk in June tackles the trail in celebratory style. The path can be followed at any time of year, but only by experienced walkers with plenty of stamina. Don't attempt it on your own or in very bad weather. For more information, contact the tourist office in Westport, tel: 098 25711.

➕ 194 C2

⑫ Céide Fields

A pyramidal eyesore of a visitor centre, housing a good exhibition, is the focal point of the world's largest Stone Age site – 1,500 hectares

(3,706 acres) of stone-walled fields, enclosures, dwelling areas and tombs dating back 5,000 years, all painstakingly unearthed since the 1970s from the blanket bog that swallowed them.

➕ 194 C3 ✉ Ballycastle, Co Mayo
☎ 096 43325; www.heritageireland.ie
🕐 Daily 10–6, Jun–Sep; 10–5, mid-Mar to May and Oct–Nov 💶 Moderate

🔢 Sligo

Sligo is a delightful town, full of history and well supplied with restaurants and pubs. The small library, museum and art gallery contain paintings by Jack Yeats and manuscripts of poems by his brother, William; the brothers spent their holidays with cousins in Sligo, a place they loved (▶ 178–80 for a tour of Yeats Country). An annual Yeats Summer School fills the town with fans of the poet each August. There's superb medieval stonework in the ruined **Dominican Friary** church of **Sligo Abbey**. Among the town's other attractions are Hargadon's (a classic pub where chat is firmly on the agenda – ▶ 141) and Furey's (excellent sessions of traditional music); and opposite the Court House in

Alcock and Brown

Just off R341 coast road south of Clifden in western Connemara, a limestone cairn stands in Derrigimlagh bog as a monument to Sir John Alcock and Sir Arthur Whitten Brown. It was here that their Vickers-Vimy bomber biplane came to rest on its nose on 15 June, 1919, having completed the first non-stop flight across the Atlantic.

Teeling Street the much-photographed window of solicitors Argue and Phibbs.

➕ 195 E3 ✉ Tourist Information Centre, Aras Reddan, Temple Street ☎ 07191 61201; www.ireland-northwest.travel.ie

Read the runes on Sligo's monument to W B Yeats

Off the Beaten Track

Out beyond Clifden in westernmost Connemara lies the village of Claddaghduff. You can cross the sands here at low tide, with the aid of markers, to Omey Island, a secluded place where you'll find a hidden church, a holy well, ancient burial grounds and a beautiful circular walk. Keep an eye on the time – and tide – for getting back. For tide information contact the Connemara Walking Centre in Clifden, tel: 095 21379.

Further Afield

Glencolumbkille Folk Village, outside the town, shows life as it was in rural Ireland

Donegal

Donegal forms the northwestern corner of Ireland, almost cut off from the Republic to which it belongs by the thrusting heel of Fermanagh in Northern Ireland. Of all the counties of western Ireland, it is probably the least explored, but if you enjoy rugged and lonely country and have time to spare, it shouldn't be missed.

Two parts of the county are particularly striking: the southwest coast, famous for its majestic cliffs, and the little-visited Inishowen Peninsula, whose flattened spear-blade shape forms the northernmost tip of Ireland.

The Southwest Coast

A 120-km (75-mile) drive will show you the best of southwest Donegal, starting west from Donegal town to reach the village of **Killybegs**. This is a big fishing port where fish-processing factories line the roads and sturdy little red-and-blue trawlers ride side by side in the harbour. A tumbled landscape follows – heathery hillsides, cragged headlands and pine forests – through which side roads take you around spectacular coastal inlets. In Carrick a left turn (signed "Teelin Pier") takes you via "Bunglass: The Cliffs" signs to a steep gated lane. This climbs eventually to a thrilling viewpoint high above the cliffs of Slieve League, rearing some 600m (1,970 feet) out of the sea in a blotched wall of yellow, black, orange and brown.

Now the main road swoops across wild bogland to **Glencolumbkille**, huddled in a long green valley under rugged headlands. St Columba of Iona established a monastery here, and the secluded valley is full of monuments that attest to its Christian heritage: stone slabs and pillars incised with crosses, cairns, early Christian chapels. Annually on 9 June pilgrims walk a 15-part Stations of the Cross route that links up several of these monuments. Glencolumbkille is an exceptionally peaceful and haunting place.

Return via the beautifully sited little town of Ardara, and the mountain road back to Donegal town.

Inishowen Peninsula

Inishowen is even more isolated than Donegal's southwestern coast. Northeast of Letterkenny you pass **Grianan of Aileach** in the neck of the peninsula, a circular stone fort 6m (20 feet) high, perched in a dominant position high on a hill overlooking Lough Swilly. Grianan of Aileach was sacked in 1101 by Murtagh O'Brien, King of Munster, who ensured its demolition by ordering his soldiers to remove a stone for every sack of provisions they carried. From here the road runs north past the sandy beach at Buncrana into the bog and hills of northern Inishowen. Up at the peak of the peninsula you climb to the old signal-tower on **Malin Head** and look out on wind-whipped headlands and sea, with nothing between you and the Scottish islands of the Outer Hebrides 160km (100 miles) to the north.

Where to...
Eat and Drink

Prices

Expect to pay per person for a meal, excluding drinks and service

€ up to €20 €€ up to €32 €€€ over €32

THE BURREN

Hyland's Hotel €-€€

This delightful old family-run establishment close to Ballyvaughan harbour has open fires, well-crafted furniture and a welcoming atmosphere. Their reputation for good food is growing – specialities include freshly caught seafood, Burren lamb, organic vegetables and herbs, and local farmhouse cheeses. Caring service and a genuine sense of hospitality add to the enjoyment. The accommodation is also very comfortable, with good amenities.

🚩 199 D5 🖾 Ballyvaughan, Co Clare
☎ 065 7077037; fax: 065 7077131;
email: hylands@eircom.net 🍴 Bar
food: daily noon–9.30 pm; closed
Christmas–early Feb

Sheedy's Country House Hotel €€

The hotel has been run by the Sheedy family for generations, and their hands-on approach shows in attractive furnishings, open fires and well-equipped bedrooms with bathrooms. However, good food is perhaps the major draw, with dishes such as traditional chowders and crab salads in the Seafood Bar, and more formal dining in the Sheedy's Restaurant. Exacting standards of produce and cooking apply to both.

🚩 198 C5 🖾 Lisdoonvarna, Co Clare
☎ 065 7074026; email:
info@sheedys.com; www.sheedys.com
🍴 Bar food: daily 6:30–8:30; closed
mid-Oct to Easter

Whitethorn Restaurant €

This terrific seaside craft shop and restaurant serves delicious home cooking, including tempting vegetarian dishes and desserts. There's also an unusual visitor centre here: "Burren eXposure". Dinner is more formal, when a fine wine list can be appreciated – and the sun setting over the sea can be magic.

🚩 199 D5 🖾 Ballyvaughan, Co Clare
☎ 065 7077044; email:
whitethorne@eircom.net 🍴 Daily
9:30–6; dinner on selected days – call
for information. Closed Nov–Mar

GALWAY CITY & SURROUNDING AREA

Kirbys of Cross Street €-€€

This dashingly informal two-storey restaurant shares premises with two of Galway's leading pubs, Busker Browne's and The Slate House. Lots of light wood, bare tables, and cheerful young staff give it a youthful atmosphere. The attractively presented contemporary cuisine is based on Irish themes, seasoned with influences from further afield. Cooking is sound and prices reasonable.

🚩 199 D5 🖾 Cross Street, Galway
☎ 091 569404 🍴 Daily 12:30–2:30,
5–10:30; closed 25 Dec

Kirwan's Lane Restaurant €€

This stylish modern restaurant in the trendy Spanish Arch area of Galway City offers a wide choice of international dishes and some exciting new creations based on traditional Irish themes. The confident, concise menus are good value, especially the lunch menu; in the evening there's a little more formality but the colourful, zesty style is the same. Service and surroundings match the smart food and reservations are advised.

🚩 199 D5 🖾 Kirwan's Lane, Galway
☎ 091 568266 🍴 Mon–Sat
12:30–2:30, 6–10:30, Sun 6–10;
closed 25 Dec

Moran's Oyster Cottage €-€€€

An idyllic thatched pub on Galway Bay, with its own oyster beds, Moran's attracts a loyal following from all over Ireland and beyond. The seafood is wonderful; the native oysters – in season from September to April – are a treat. You can have the farmed Gigas oysters all year, however, along with other specialities like chowder, smoked salmon and delicious crab sandwiches and salads.

🚹 199 D5 🗺 The Weir, Kilcolgan, Co Galway ☎ 091 796113; email: moransthewier@eircom.net 🕓 Bar food: noon–10 pm; closed Good Fri and 25 Dec

White Gables Restaurant €€€

Open stonework and soft lighting create a soothing atmosphere in this attractive restaurant on the main street of Moycullen, 8km (5 miles) north of Galway City. The hearty cooking is consistently good, with tempting freshly made soups, specialities such as black and white pudding with wholegrain mustard sauce, and a good choice of seafood, including lobster fresh from the tank. The set Sunday lunch is particularly popular.

🚹 199 D5 🗺 Moycullen, Co Galway ☎ 091 555744; fax: 091 556004; email: wgables@indigo.ie 🕓 Lunch: Sun 12.30–2.30. Dinner: Mon–Sat 7–10; closed Dec 23–Feb 14, Mon low season

ATHLONE

Wineport Lakeshore Restaurant €€-€€€

Attractions are the ten luxury guestrooms, the waterside location on Lough Ree, not far from Clonmacnoise (▶ 135), the hospitality, and the seasonal menus. These are based on such local delicacies as Irish Angus beef, game, eels, home-grown herbs and wild mushrooms. The style of cooking is International and Modern Irish, some creative vegetarian cooking and an Irish farmhouse cheeseboard. Bar food is available 1–5 pm in summer.

🚹 195 F1 🗺 Glasson, Nr Athlone, Co Westmeath ☎ 090 6485466; email: restaurant@wineport.ie 🕓 Closed Mon, Tue, Nov–Feb, Good Fri and 24–6 Dec

CONNEMARA

O'Dowd's Seafood Bar and Restaurant €-€€

This traditional bar serves a good pint; the bar menu is reasonably priced. The restaurant serves more substantial meals. There is also a coffee shop serving Irish breakfast and speciality teas and coffee.

🚹 194 B1 🗺 Roundstone, Co Galway ☎ 095 35809; email: odowds@indigo.ie 🕓 Bar food: noon–9.30. Restaurant: noon–10, Apr–Sep; noon–3, 6–10, rest of year. Closed 25 Dec; no food Good Fri

O'Grady's Seafood Restaurant €-€€

This is Clifden's oldest restaurant, and it has won all kinds of awards, including the Bord Fáilte Tourist Excellence Award. Chef Elliot Fox produces modern Irish cuisine, with seafood specialities and vegetarian choices.

🚹 194 B1 🗺 Lower Market Street, Clifden, Co Galway ☎ 095 21450; fax: 095 21994 🕓 Mon–Sat 12.30–2.30, 6.30–10; closed Nov–Apr

WESTPORT

Quay Cottage €€

This charming, stone waterside restaurant never fails to delight. Its maritime theme is strongly reinforced by the imaginative menu, with such items as chowder and seafood platter. There is much else of interest, including mountain lamb and innovative and creative vegetarian options. Tempting desserts or a farmhouse cheese selection, and freshly brewed coffee by the cup, make a fitting finale.

🚹 194 C2 🗺 The Harbour, Westport, Co Mayo ☎ 098 26412; fax: 098 28120; email: reservations@quaycottage.com; www.quaycottage.com 🕓 Daily 6 pm till late; closed 24–6 Dec and 4 weeks off season

CAVAN

MacNean House Bistro €€

This little family restaurant is right on the Cavan–Fermanagh border, not far from Florence Court (▶ 164–5). The sassy international menus here invariably surprise first-time visitors. Locally produced ingredients, including lamb, beef, guinea fowl, quail, seafood and organic produce, find their way into skilfully executed international dishes. If you want to try a little of everything, there's a no-choice tasting menu served to complete tables. Delicious desserts are a speciality, and Sunday lunch is especially good value. Simple but comfortable bedrooms with bathrooms are also available.

🗺 196 B3 ⊠ Blacklion, Co Cavan
☎ 071 9853022; fax: 072 53404
🕐 Wed–Sat 6:30–9:30, Sun 12:30–3:30, 6:30–9:30 (closed Wed, Oct–May); closed Good Fri and 25 Dec

SLIGO

Cromleach Lodge €€€

Fine views from this modern building on a hill overlooking Lough Arrow are a bonus: Moira and Christy Tighe's genuine hospitality ensures comfort and relaxation for guests. The best of local ingredients – organically grown vegetables and herbs, goat's cheese, or tender, succulent, local loin of lamb – underlie a light, elegant style with excellent saucing. Simple table settings complement a growing number of mouthwatering house specialities. Details, in both restaurant and the comfortable accommodation also available, are superb throughout.

🗺 196 A2 ⊠ Castlebaldwin, via Boyle, Co Sligo ☎ 071 9165155; email: info@cromleach.com
🕐 Dinner: Mon–Sat 7–8:30 pm, Sun 6:30–8 pm; closed Nov–Jan

Hargadon's €

This is one of Ireland's greatest old pubs. The best time to see it properly is early in the day, when it's quiet. They'll give you a cup of coffee and provide you with a newspaper to read while you relax and take in the detail of this remarkable old place. It still has the shelves that used to hold the groceries when it was a grocer-bar, along with the snugs and the old pot-belly stove. Wholesome food including soups, salads and casseroles is available.

🗺 196 A3 ⊠ O'Connell Street, Sligo, Co Sligo ☎ 071 9170933 🕐 Closed Good Fri and 25 Dec

Where to... Stay

Prices

Expect to pay per person staying
€ up to €40 €€ up to €77 €€€ over €77

THE BURREN

Gregans Castle €€€

This remote hotel on the direct inland road between Ballyvaughan and Lisdoonvarna may seem as grey and stark as the landscape; but appearances are deceptive. In fact, warmth, elegance and tranquillity are the keynotes, both in spacious public rooms and luxurious accommodation. Non-residents are welcome in the restaurant, and also for lunch or afternoon tea in the Corkscrew Room bar. In fine weather you can sit out beside the Celtic Cross rose garden.

🗺 199 D5 ⊠ Ballyvaughan, Co Clare
☎ 065 7077005; fax: 065 7077111;
email: stay@gregans.ie; www.gregans.ie
🕐 Restaurant: daily 7–8:30 pm, light meals from noon; closed 25 Oct–20 Mar

Temple Gate Hotel €€–€€€

This hotel right in the centre of Ennis is a clever conversion of a building that formerly served as a gentleman's residence, then a convent. It retains some of its Gothic-style features, and the 70 rooms are simple but comfortable, with specially designed furniture emphasising the medieval theme, and neat en-suite bathrooms. There is a restaurant.

🗺 199 D4 ⊠ The Square, Ennis, Co Clare ☎ 065 6823300; email: info@templegatehotel.com; www.templegatehotel.com
🕐 Closed 25 Dec

Ardilaun House Hotel €€€

Set in wooded grounds about 5 minutes' drive from the city centre, Ardilaun House Hotel has elegantly furnished, spacious public rooms, plus a leisure centre with an indoor pool. The bedrooms are well decorated – those with bay views are the most popular, though others are equally attractive. The pleasant dining room overlooks the pretty gardens.

✚ 199 D5 ☒ Taylor's Hill, Galway
☎ 091 521433; fax: 091 521546;
email: ardilaun@iol.ie ◉ Closed
Christmas week

Glenlo Abbey €€€

This restored 18th-century abbey, 4km (2 miles) from the centre of Galway City on the N59 Clifden road, is set in extensive landscaped grounds and overlooks a beautiful loch. Wooden floors and leather sofas give an exclusive air to the main reception area. The bedrooms are housed in a modern wing, which also has a library, restaurants and bars. Leisure facilities are extensive and include golf, fishing and clay-pigeon shooting. Irish and French cuisine is served in the hotel's restaurant.

✚ 199 D5 ☒ Bushypark, Galway
☎ 091 526666; fax: 091 527800; email:
info@glenloabbey.ie; www.glenlo.com

Jurys Inn Galway €€–€€€

This good-value choice, perfectly located to enjoy the river and the bustling Spanish Arch area of Galway City centre, provides a high standard of basic accommodation. Rooms are large and provide every comfort and convenience: neat bathroom, TV, phone and hospitality tray – but with no room service or other extras. However, there's a pleasant bar, a restaurant, and adjoining parking.

✚ 199 D5 ☒ Quay Street,
Galway ☎ 091 566444; email:
bookings@jurysdoyle.com
◉ Closed 24–6 Dec

Killeen House €€

This lovely house, built in 1840, is set in 10ha (25 acres) of private grounds which go down to the shores of Lough Corrib. Each of the six spacious bedrooms is carefully and individually furnished in the style of a different period. The excellent breakfasts are served in the dining room, which overlooks the garden.

✚ 199 D5 ☒ Bushypark, Galway
☎ 091 524179; fax: 091 528065;
email: killeenhouse@ireland.com;
www.killeenhousegalway.com
◉ Closed 25 Dec

Hodson Bay Hotel €€€

Overlooking Lough Ree, this modern hotel adjoins Athlone Golf Club and has lovely lake and island views. Good amenities include boating, fishing and a fine leisure centre. Comfortable bedrooms are decorated in a bright contemporary style, and there are well-finished bathrooms, plus all the necessary extras (phone, TV, hospitality tray). The hotel's food in L'Escale Restaurant is excellent.

✚ 195 F1 ☒ Hodson Bay, Athlone,
Co Westmeath ☎ 090 6480500; email:
info@hodsonbayhotel.com; www.
hodsonbayhotel.com ◉ Open all year

Hotel Westport €€€

This modern hotel, just a short walk from the centre of Westport, is set in its own grounds. Major expansion has recently made this the largest hotel in the area, and it is the only one with a swimming pool and leisure centre. Its excellent conference and leisure facilities attract a business clientele, though not exclusively so. Wheelchair access throughout the hotel is good and seven rooms have been specifically designed for wheelchair use.

✚ 194 C2 ☒ The Demesne, Newport
Road, Westport, Co Mayo ☎ 098
25122; fax: 098 26739; email:
sales@hotelwestport.ie
◉ Open all year

Olde Railway Hotel €€–€€€

This former coaching inn, on the river-side Mall in Westport, is the best town-centre choice. It has been modernised to provide bathrooms in all bedrooms, satellite TV and private parking, but the antiques and some mild eccentricities have helped to ensure that its original Victorian character is preserved intact. The food served in the front bar makes this a great spot to take a break.

➕ 194 C2 ☒ The Mall, Westport, Co Mayo ☎ 098 25166; fax: 098 25090; email: railway@anu.ie; www.theoldrailwayhotel.com ⓒ Closed 25 Dec and mid-Jan to mid-Feb

SLIGO

Markree Castle €€€

Home to the Cooper family for 350 years and set in park and farmland, this is a real traditional Irish castle. A huge welcoming log fire always burns brightly in the lofty hall – generosity with heating is one of the castle's most attractive features. There's a very beautiful dining room (non-residents welcome) for more formal dining and a large double drawing room where delicious light food, including afternoon tea, is served. Two floors of attractively furnished bedrooms provide guests with all the necessary comforts and amenities

and there is the added bonus of pleasant parkland views.

➕ 195 E3 ☒ Collooney, Co Sligo ☎ 071 9167800; fax: 071 67840; email: markree@iol.ie ⓒ Closed Dec 24–6

DONEGAL

Kee's Hotel €€–€€€

Established as a coaching inn in 1845, and in the Kee family since 1892, this comfortable hotel is well placed for touring County Donegal. Rooms at the back of the hotel are quieter and more desirable than those at the front; some have views of the Blue Stack Mountains. There's an excellent leisure centre for guests and a stylish, fine restaurant, **The Looking Glass**, where imaginative Franco-Irish cuisine is served.

➕ 196 B4 ☒ Stranorlar, Ballybofey, Co Donegal ☎ 074 9131018; email: info@keeshotel.ie; www.keeshotel.ie ⓒ Restaurant: daily 6:30–9:30 pm (till 10 pm Fri, Sat). Lunch: Sun 12:30–2:15. Also breakfast for non-residents 7:30–10 am

Where to...
Shop

A high proportion of the quality goods on sale in western Ireland are locally made. Ennis rewards a leisurely browse in relatively uncrowded streets. The **Clare Craft & Design Centre** (Parnell Street, tel: 065 684723) is an outlet for all kinds of high-quality work produced within the county, including paintings, pottery, patchwork, wood turning, baskets, jewellery and stained glass. At Doolin, the **Doolin Crafts Gallery** (Ballyvoe, tel: 065 7074309) sells a similar range of goods, including leatherware, ceramics, glassware and clothing, some of which are made on the site. Go 5km (3 miles) east to the spa town of Lisdoonvarna and you can visit the

Burren Smokehouse Ltd (tel: 065 7074432) to see how oak-smoking of Atlantic salmon is done (and buy a vacuum-packed side to take back home).

GALWAY CITY

In Galway, a one-stop shop for the best in Irish design is **Design Concourse Ireland** (Kirwan's Lane, tel: 091 566016). If you're in the city on a Saturday, the **Galway Market** at St Nicholas Collegiate Church is a must; it has a great atmosphere, and sells everything from organic vegetables, cheeses and fresh eggs to flowers, home baking and preserves. The excellent **Kenny's Bookshop and Art Galleries** (High Street, tel: 091 562739) is also worth a visit. It has five floors of Irish-interest books, mainly second-hand and antiquarian, plus prints and maps, as well as a little art gallery. Also a bit different is **Claddagh Jewellery** (Eyre Square, tel: 091 562310), where you'll find a wide selection of attractive traditional Celtic jewellery.

COUNTY CLARE

Where to...
Be Entertained

CONNEMARA

Connemara Marble Industries Ltd (Moycullen, tel: 091 555102) sells locally quarried marble items crafted on site, and **Joyce's** of Recess has a wide range of quality goods. Musicians could head for **Roundstone Musical Instruments** (Roundstone, tel: 095 35808), where traditional *bodhrán* drums are made.

Clifden has good gift shops, including **Linda's Spinning Studio** (Derrylea, tel: 095 21888), where you can see serious examples of the craft. At Letterfrack, **Connemara Handcrafts** (tel: 095 41058), a branch of the Wicklow-based Avoca Handweavers, sells fabrics, clothing, crafts and specialist foods and has a pleasant coffee shop. Even better, perhaps, is **Kylemore Abbey** (Kylemore, tel: 095 41146), where there's a particularly good craft shop (stocking some quite serious clothing, including menswear) and an excellent informal restaurant.

Foxford Woollen Mills (Foxford, tel: 094 56104) is a good place to buy tweeds and blankets; there's a shop, a restaurant and The Foxford Experience, detailing the mills history from the mid-19th century, when it was founded to combat the poverty and hardship caused by the Famine.

Over at Achill Island, you could take a break at **The Beehive** (Keel, tel: 098 43134 or 43018), an attractive craft shop and restaurant that serves home-made food all day.

SLIGO AND DONEGAL

The counties of Sligo and Donegal are famous for sweaters, tweeds and parian china (so called after the marble from the Greek island of Paros, which it resembles), all widely available. Useful addresses include the **Donegal Craft Village**, five minutes' walk from the town centre and **Magee's** (Donegal town, tel: 073 21100), renowned for tweeds; they also sell quality gifts and have a good self-service restaurant. Tiny, characterful Ardara is chock-full of shops selling keenly priced local knits and weaves.

MUSIC

You'll find great pubs in the west of Ireland doing organised and impromptu music sessions. In Ennis, try **Cruise's** (Abbey Street, tel: 065 6841800) and **The Temple Gate** (The Square, tel: 065 6823300); **O'Connors** (tel: 065 7074168) of Doolin is highly regarded, while **Vaughan's** of Kilfenora (tel: 065 7088004) is famous for set dancing and music. Galway is packed with music pubs: **Tigh Neachtain** (Cross Street, tel: 091 568820) is one of the best. In early May, Kinvarra runs a **Cuckoo Fleadh**, with traditional music at **Winkles Hotel** (The Square, tel: 091 637137). Siamsa Company performs traditional music and dance in the summer at **Claddagh Hall** (tel: 091 755479) and at **Town Hall Theatre** (tel: 091 569777). Westport is noted for its music pubs (▶133). Sligo is another musical hot spot; **The Thatch** pub (Ballisadare, tel: 071 9167288) is popular with locals. There's also **Killoran's Traditional Lounge**, near Collooney (Tubbercurry, tel: 071 85111). Look out for the **Ballyshannon International Folk Festival** in Co Donegal (tel: 071 9851088).

OUTDOOR ACTIVITIES

The West and Northwest of Ireland offers fine scenic drives, golf, cycling, riding and horse racing. There's surfing on Atlantic beaches such as Strandhill on Sligo Bay (rent boards and suits from **Strandhill Surf Club**, tel: 071 9168332). Fishing is superb, particularly in County Mayo.

Northern Ireland

Getting Your Bearings

As you explore the cliffs, hills, country lanes and city streets of Northern Ireland, you will find that all the attributes of landscape and people that make the Republic so appealing are here in abundance, along with a remarkably traffic-free road system and a good number of uncrowded visitor attractions.

Northern Ireland remains part of the United Kingdom, and no one coming here can be unaware of the deep divisions between loyalists, those who want to maintain links with Britain, and nationalists, who wish to sever them. As a guest north of the border, it's good to inform yourself about recent history. Violence and hatred flared during the past 30 years or so between small extremist sections of the nationalist and loyalist communities in Northern Ireland, and between hardline nationalists insisting on a united Ireland and the security forces of army and police whom they saw as reinforcing the North's links with Great Britain. This poisonous period in Ulster's history has come to be known as "The Troubles". Paramilitary groups on both sides declared ceasefires in 1994 – loyalists have largely maintained theirs since then, and the Republican IRA, despite a brief return to violence, has observed a renewed ceasefire since 1997. The 1998 Good Friday Agreement, signed by all the interested political parties, brought hope of peace, along with the establishment of a partly autonomous Northern Ireland Assembly made up of Ulster politicians from both sides of the divide.

As a visitor to Northern Ireland you are bound to notice wall graffiti, and flags of allegiance proudly flown. But there is no need to feel uneasy. Outside the nationalist and loyalist inner-city and housing estate strongholds, no one would dream of burdening you with their opinions – unless you specifically ask them to do so! After more than three decades of negative publicity, the people of Northern Ireland are delighted to welcome visitors to their country and all it has to offer.

Belfast has its cheerful black humour, vibrant nightlife and superb Botanical Gardens. The east coast is carved by the Glens of Antrim into beautiful deep valleys, and the Antrim Coast in the north is celebrated for the Giant's Causeway, one volcanic extravaganza among many along this spectacular line of cliffs. Swing across the hair-raising Carrick-a-Rede rope bridge. Take a hike over the wild Sperrin or Mourne mountains, watch the geese and wading birds on Strangford Lough, or lazily cruise the great inland waterway of Lough Erne among islands crammed with ancient churches, round towers and enigmatic stone carvings. And spare a day to enjoy welcoming and optimistic Derry.

LONDONDERRY 5

INISHO

Lifford

B536

Plumbridg

Newtownstewart A5

Ulster-American Folk Park 7

Drumquin Omagh

A47 8

Dromore

Irvinestown

Belleek Pottery 8

Lough Erne 8

Castle Coole 11

B52

Enniskillen

Lisbellaw

Blacklion Belcoo

A32 A509 Lisnaskea

Marble Arch Caves 9

Florence Court 10

Upper Lough Erne

Swanlinbar Newtownbutler

★ Don't Miss

At Your Leisure

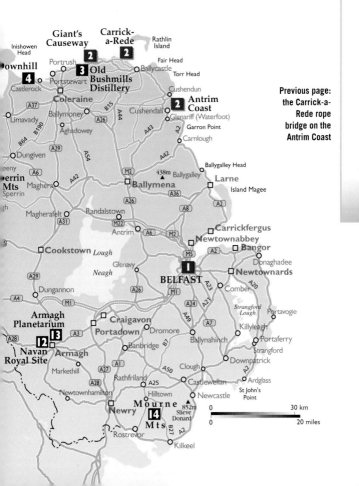

Previous page: the Carrick-a-Rede rope bridge on the Antrim Coast

Northern Ireland in Three Days

This varied round trip takes you from Belfast's atmospheric streets by way of spectacular coasts and lonely moorland hills to the shores and islands of Fermanagh's lakeland.

Day One

Morning Explore **1 Belfast** (► 150–3), making sure not to miss the Grand Opera House (right), Botanic Gardens, Ulster Museum and wall paintings along the Shankill and Falls roads.

Afternoon After an early lunch in the Victorian splendour of the Crown Liquor Saloon (► 167), head north around the spectacular Antrim Coast by way of the deep-cut **2 Glens of Antrim** (right, ► 154–5). Stick to the minor coast road round Torr Head. Signposted turnings lead to **Carrick-a-Rede rope bridge** (► 155–6), a nerve-tingling crossing above a 24-m (79-foot) drop, and the **Giant's Causeway** (► 156), from whose slippery basalt promontory there are memorable cliff views. Overnight on the coast at Portstewart or Portrush.

Day Two

Morning 5 **Derry City** (► 164, 181) lies to the
west – if you have a little more time, walk
around the city walls. To continue the itiner-
ary from Portstewart, head south via
Coleraine and Limavady to Dungiven, then on
to Feeny (B74). A further 5km (3 miles) south
(B44), take the mountain road that crosses the
rugged 6 **Sperrin Mountains** (► 164) to reach
Sperrin village. Head west along the Glenelly
Valley for a drink and a snack at Leo McCullagh's
pub in Plumbridge, then southeast to Newtonstewart and south to Omagh.

Afternoon About 5km (3 miles) north of Omagh lies the 7 **Ulster-American Folk
Park** (► 158–9), well worth an hour's exploration to see the carefully reconstructed houses and the striking emigration exhibition. From Omagh drive
southwest (A32) to Irvinestown, then west on A35 or A47 to 8 **Belleek** (► 160)
and its world-famous pottery (above). A drive along the south shore of beautiful
Lough Erne will land you in Enniskillen for the night.

Day Three

Morning Drive east for 65km (40 miles) to Armagh City, where there is the
excellent Armagh Planetarium and nearby historic Navan hill fort (► 166),
then on to Newry and the A2 coast road. At Kilkeel bear left (B27) on side
roads through the wilderness of the 14 **Mountains of Mourne** (below, ► 166),
then head northeast to Downpatrick with its cathedral and St Patrick's Grave.

Afternoon Take the car ferry from Strangford to Portaferry, and drive north up the
Ards Peninsula beside island-dotted and bird-haunted **Strangford Lough**
(► 184–6); then continue from Newtownards into Belfast.

① Belfast

Belfast has had more than its share of bad publicity since the early 1970s. There's no denying that Northern Ireland's chief city has been the setting for some atrocious events, but visitors today need have no qualms about whether they will be welcome here. Belfast humour is black and mordant, but its people are particularly keen to put the bleak past behind them. Every new visitor is a symbol of a return to normal life, and especially welcome because of that. What you will find in Belfast is a fairly old-fashioned looking place, a city of the Industrial Revolution, with red-brick terraces and grandiose public buildings. It doesn't have the instant appeal of Dublin, but well repays a couple of days' exploration.

The Golden Mile

Many of the attractions of city-centre Belfast are within a few minutes' walk of each other. You could start and finish your sightseeing on Great Victoria Street at the **Crown Liquor Saloon**, now in the care of the National Trust, a splendidly maintained Victorian pub, complete with stained-glass windows, carved-wood booths, an elaborately tiled front, and a fine mosaic of a crown at the front door (► 167). The story goes that Patrick Flanagan, the pub's

Belfast's ponderously magnificent 19th-century City Hall

Drinking in opulent surroundings at the Crown Liquor Saloon

Emerald Poet

Poet William Drennan (1754–1820) was born in Belfast. His output is forgotten these days but for one phrase, which has become the most fondly quoted cliché about Ireland – "The Emerald Isle".

original owner and a passionate Irish nationalist, put the crown in that position so that anyone who wished could wipe their feet on it.

Across from the Crown is the **Grand Opera House** of 1894, bombed and neglected in the past, but now restored to its overblown best with gilt plaster and woodwork, a ceiling writhing with golden apes, and viewing boxes supported by gilt elephants with immense trunks. Nearby stands the **Europa Hotel**, favourite watering-hole and office-from-home of journalists covering the Troubles, which until recently revelled in its title (thoroughly earned) of "Europe's Most Bombed Hotel".

Great Victoria Street forms the west side of a triangle of streets known as the Golden Mile, where chic eateries and nightspots are clustered. At the top of the triangle is Donegall Square, with the remarkable **Linenhall Library** – a real old-fashioned library with thousands of shelves of well-thumbed books, a splendid curved wooden staircase, an atmosphere of holy hush, and a Members' Room and decent Tea Room tucked away. Opposite stands the very grand **City Hall** of 1906, under a magnificent dome. Queen

Victoria stares imperiously across the square from a plinth in front of the building, and around the side you'll find a fine memorial to the city's crewmen who lost their lives when the Belfast-built *Titanic* sank on 15 April, 1912. The interior of the City Hall is baroque, with a handsome central dome seen above a hollow galleried ceiling, and a Council Chamber full of heavily carved wood, stained glass and padded red leather benches.

The University Area

South of the city centre – a 10-minute bus ride – stands the early Victorian, mock-Tudor pile of **Queen's University**. Just beyond are Belfast's very enjoyable **Botanic Gardens**, a quiet and leafy spot with hundreds of tree species and the splendid Palm House, whose rounded prow and long side wings in cast iron and glass hold tropical vegetation in a hot, steamy atmosphere.

The *Titanic* in construction at the Harland and Wolff shipyard, East Belfast

Nearby is the 9m (30-foot) deep Tropical Ravine, housed inside a glass-roofed building dating from the 1880s, where fish and terrapins swim in the dripping shadows of cinnamon tree, dombeya, loquat and banana. In the **Ulster Museum**, alongside, the industrial history of Belfast is illustrated with mighty

---

➕ 197 E3
✉ Belfast Welcome Centre, 47 Donegall Place
☎ 028 9024 6609; www.gotobelfast.com

Crown Liquor Saloon (NT)
✉ 46 Great Victoria Street
☎ 028 9027 9901

Botanic Gardens
✉ Stranmillis Road/Botanic Avenue
☎ 028 9032 4902
🕐 Main garden open without restrictions. Palm House and Tropical Ravine: Mon–Fri 10–5, Sat–Sun 1–5, Apr–Sep; Mon–Fri 10–4, Sat–Sun 1–4, rest of year 💷 Free

City Hall
✉ Donegall Square
☎ 028 9027 0456 🕐 Tours Mon–Fri 11, 2, 3, Sat 2:30, Jun–Sep; Mon–Fri 11, 2:30, Sat 2:30, rest of year; closed public holidays 💷 Free

Linenhall Library
✉ Donegall Square North
☎ 028 9032 1707; www.linenhall.
🕐 Mon–Fri 9:30–5:30, Sat 9:30–4
💷 Free

Ulster Museum
✉ Botanic Gardens
☎ 028 9038 3000; www.ulstermuseum.org.uk
🕐 Mon–Fri 10–5, Sat 1–5, Sun 2–5 💷 Free

calendering (pressing) and fulling machines from the textile trade, photos of great ships being launched, tobacco and snuff samples – all reminders of the heavy industry that made this place.

Away from the Centre

Don't leave Belfast without seeing some of the work of the **gable-end artists** thrown up by the Troubles. Out west along the loyalist **Shankill Road** and nationalist **Falls Road** the polemic is fierce: even more so just east of the river in the Short Strand or Lower Newtownards roads. You can buy postcards showing the best examples of this "people's art".

On the eastern outskirts of Belfast stands the imposing mansion of **Stormont**, home of the Northern Ireland Assembly. And north of the city centre on the quays of the ship-yards stand **Samson and Goliath**, two giant yellow cranes that symbolise the past industrial might and the dogged four-square strength of this most resilient city.

Troubles Taxis

Regular buses were withdrawn in the 1970s due to hijackings, and though some services have been reinstated, black taxis, part of Belfast life, still run what amount to cut-price minibus services to West Belfast. The cab drivers pack their vehicles, and the passengers split the fare, which is in any case quite modest.

Loyalist colours in the Lower Newtownards Road

TAKING A BREAK

Stop for lunch at the **Crown Liquor Saloon** (➤ 167) and try the delicious "champ" – mashed potatoes and spring onions. **Roscoff Café** on Fountain Street is also a good place for light lunches.

Fragrant Flats

Laganside, once a riverside slum area polluted by the smell from the mudflats at low tide, has been redeveloped as high-class residences since the creation of Lagan Weir in the early 1990s has kept river levels constant and the stink away.

BELFAST: INSIDE INFO

Top tips Avoid the Golden Mile, and particularly Great Victoria Street, in the early hours at weekends if you are likely to get upset by the rowdy behaviour of young clubbers.

Hidden gem Often seen, but seldom noticed with appreciation: the **Marks & Spencer department store** opposite the City Hall, a magnificent Italianate building in red Dumfries sandstone that used to house the Water Office.

One to miss If pushed for time, give **Stormont** a miss – the best thing about it is the long view of the building from way down the drive, and you can see that on any postcard stand in Belfast.

2 The Antrim Coast

The Antrim Coast is Northern Ireland's best-known scenic attraction, with the Giant's Causeway as the plum in the pudding. But don't rush straight to that celebrated piece of volcanic freakery; take your time getting there, and enjoy the beautiful journey north from Belfast through wild glens and along a wonderful coast road.

The Glens of Antrim

Take A2 north from Larne to Carnlough, a pretty little fishing harbour where the cliffs rise in a foretaste of what's in store. The road hugs the shore under steep hillsides for the next 16km (10 miles), curving into Red Bay at Waterfoot with some really striking big hills rearing inland. This is the place to turn aside up **Glenariff**, most spectacular of the series of deep glens carved into the basalt of North Antrim by rivers. Glenariff is bounded by granite cliffs over which waterfalls pour in rainy weather, a dark and rugged cleft. Drive up it and park at the Glenariff Forest Park Visitor Centre, amid mountain scenery. Various waymarked walking trails start from here: short garden and nature trails, a longer scenic trail, and a gorgeous 5km (3-mile) waterfall trail that leads you beside and over some of Glenariff's torrents.

The most spectacular of the Glens of Antrim, Glenariff has dozens of lovely waterfalls

Watching the sunset from the basalt grandstand of the Giant's Causeway

Back on the coast road you go through neat little Cushendall. If you take A2 inland here, you can turn off left shortly and make a back-road loop up **Glenaan** by way of Ossian's Grave (► 157), before returning to the coast down quiet and lovely **Glendun**. From Cushendun among its trees there's an exhilarating alternative to A2 – a very rough and bouncy side road in marvellous coastal scenery via Torr Head to Ballycastle.

Carrick-a-Rede Rope Bridge

Carrick-a-Rede rope bridge is well signposted from Ballycastle; but you won't find it if you visit in the winter between October and March, for this clever cat's cradle of rope with a board floor is in position only during the salmon fishing season. It's a good 800-m (880-yard) walk from where you park to the bridge, with 161 stone steps, before you arrive at the entrance gate and look down on the nervous visitors swinging across the rope bridge, 25m (82 feet) above the sea. The National Trust has now "improved" the bridge's safety by installing a cage structure.

It's quite safe ...but you'll need some nerve to cross the Carrick-a-Rede rope bridge

The bridge is the only means of crossing the 20-m (66-foot) gap between the cliff and the Carrick-a-Rede basalt stack offshore. The name means "rock-in-the-road" – the stack stands in the path of the salmon, who turn aside to pass it and swim into a net stretched out from the stack and anchored in the sea. It's a thrill to cross the bridge (come early or late to avoid the hordes), and a great photo opportunity.

Spanish Treasure

The Spanish Armada galleon *Girona* was wrecked in Port na Spaniagh ("Spaniard's Bay"), just east of the Giant's Causeway in 1588. Out of 1,300 men, only five were saved. A fabulous treasure went to the bottom with the ship, and stayed there until 1968 when much of it was recovered: gold, silver, jewels, implements. You can see the best of what was salvaged on display in Belfast's Ulster Museum.

The Giant's Causeway

So to the Giant's Causeway, a short distance along the coast. Here the cliffs are at their most spectacular as they rise almost 100m (330 feet) around a series of rocky bays. The Causeway itself is formed of some 37,000 basalt columns, mostly hexagonal, that slope in a narrowing and declining shelf into the sea. They were made by cooling lava after a volcanic eruption some 60 million years ago. Up in the cliffs of the bay are more formations. The most striking, reached by a footpath, is the Giant's Organ, a cluster of basalt "organ pipes" weathered into vertebra-like rings that rise 12m (40 feet) high. As for the Giant: he was the mythological hero Fionn MacCumhaill (Finn McCool), who, legend has it, laid down the causeway as stepping stones to the island of Staffa

Dare one say it? The Giant's Causeway, after all the publicity and raised expectations, can strike visitors as rather an anticlimax. Don't expect too much, and do make the footpath circuit if you can, up by the Organ and back along the clifftop footpath, to enjoy one of the best views of the Causeway from on high.

TAKING A BREAK

Stop at the **National Trust Tea Room** in the Giant's Causeway Centre (► 168).

✉ Tourist Information Centre, Sheskburn House, 7 Mary Street, Ballycastle
☎ 028 2076 2024; www.discovernorthernireland.com

Carrick-a-Rede Rope Bridge and Larrybane Visitor Centre
✚ 197 E5
✉ On B15 between Ballycastle and Ballintoy
☎ 028 2073 1582; www.ntni.org.uk
🕐 Daily 10–6, mid-Mar to Sep; 9:30–7:30, Jul–Aug 🎫 Free; moderate parking fee

Giant's Causeway
✚ 197 D5
✉ Giant's Causeway Centre, 3.2km (2 miles) north of Bushmills
☎ 028 2073 1855 or 028 2073 2972; www.ntni.org.uk
🕐 Giant's Causeway always open for exploration. Shop and tea room: daily 10–7, Jul–Aug; 10–6, Jun; 10–5, Mar–May and Sep–Oct; 10–3, rest of year; closed 1 Jan and 25 Dec 🎫 Free; moderate parking fee

Top: cooled basalt formed the hexagonal columns of the Giant's Causeway

Right: high cliffs overlook the promontory of stumpy columns that noses out into the sea

THE ANTRIM COAST: INSIDE INFO

Top tips If you want to avoid the 10-minute walk down the road from the Giant's Causeway Visitor Centre to the Causeway itself, **hop on the minibus** and be whisked down in a couple of minutes.

• Don't take a large shoulder-bag or hold anything in your hands when you cross Carrick-a-Rede rope bridge, as you'll find you need both hands free for the crossing.

Hidden gem Signposted off A2 near the bottom of Glenaan is **Ossian's Grave**. This impressive "horned" cairn (with an entrance courtyard and two inner chambers) lies in a field at the top of a steep, rough lane better walked than driven, and commands a great view. Ossian was a warrior-poet, the son of the great hero Fionn MacCumhaill (Finn McCool).

One to miss The **coast road north** between Belfast and Larne is none too exciting; a better route is M2 to Junction 4, then the pleasant hill-and-valley A8 via Ballynure to Larne.

7 **Ulster-American Folk Park**

This collection of reconstructed and replica buildings gives a graphic idea of life in 18th- and 19th-century Ireland, of the miseries of emigration, and of the long, hard struggle that emigrants had to face before they could prosper in America.

The collection is split into two halves, Old World and New World.

In the **Old World section** you stroll among buildings brought from their original locations and rebuilt here. Among these are a **weaver's cottage** with a fixed loom, and a **Mass House** where Roman Catholics in the days of the Penal Laws (a collection of laws passed in the 18th century strictly limiting the rights of Catholics in all spheres) were permitted to attend the proscribed Mass. Don't miss **Castletown National School** with its graffiti-scarred desks – though it's a good idea to delay your visit if a school party is swarming there. Also here are the modest **homesteads** of two Irish emigrants who made spectacularly good in America: that of Judge Thomas Mellon (who emigrated 1818), whose son Andrew Mellon founded the Pittsburgh steel industry, and John Joseph Hughes, Archbishop of New York and founder of St Patrick's Cathedral there. When the Folk Park's Visitor Centre was opened in 1980, the ceremony was attended by the benefactor, Dr Matthew T Mellon. He impressed everyone present by recalling his boyhood conversations with his great-grandfather Judge Thomas Mellon, who would tell tales of the miseries of the three-month Atlantic crossing he had endured way back in 1818.

The **New World section** includes the primitive cabin of a Midwest settler, a smoke house and barn, and a Pennsylvania farmhouse, all built of logs. Both Old and New World collections are brought to life by costumed guides who inform and entertain as they bake and keep sweet-scented turf fires burning.

Left: live demonstration of cottage handicrafts

Below: a retired post box

Water Weary
People who lived in old-time rural Ireland will tell you that one of the toughest aspects of a tough life was having to ration the water, which had to be carried so laboriously from spring or well to the house.

Particularly poignant is the indoor reconstruction of a 19th-century Ulster street, complete with post office, draper, pawn-broker and chemist. The dockside booking office leads to a gangplank into the gloomy hold of an emigrant ship, where the imagination soon re-creates the experience of the passengers, as they pitched westward across the Atlantic in such a dark, cramped, stinking, noisy hellhole.

TAKING A BREAK

There is a restaurant at the Folk Park.

A log house typical of those built by early Irish-American settlers in the wild Midwest

➕ 196 C4
✉ Mellon Road, Castletown, Omagh, Co Tyrone
☎ 028 8224 3292; www.folkpark.com
🕐 Mon–Sat 10:30–6, Sun, public hols 11–6:30, Apr–Sep; Mon–Fri 10:30–5, rest of year (last admission 90 mins before closing)
💷 Moderate

ULSTER-AMERICAN FOLK PARK: INSIDE INFO

Top tips The Mellon Homestead and the ship and Dockside Gallery are two of the Folk Park's most popular sites. For the former, keep ahead as you leave the Information Centre and then bear right; for the latter, bear left from the Centre.
• Forget your diet, and try any goodies that the guides may offer you: they are all freshly made on site.

Hidden gem Don't overlook the **raised viewpoint** behind the Mellon Homestead. From here you get an excellent view over the whole park, with roofs peeping charmingly out of the trees.

8 Lough Erne and Belleek Pottery

One-third of County Fermanagh is under water. The centre of the county is entirely filled by the island-dotted waters of Upper and Lower Lough Erne. You can follow winding lanes along the shores in a car, on foot or by bicycle. Alternatively, you could rent a cruiser at Belleek, and spend a couple of days drifting lazily among more than 200 islands and their tangled backwaters – a wonderfully relaxing way to see Fermanagh. Now that the Victoria Canal linking Upper Lough Erne with the River Shannon has been re-opened, you could actually cruise 480km (300 miles) from Belleek to Killaloe, in sheltered water all the way.

Fine China

Belleek and its celebrated pottery stands at the seaward end of the Lower Lough Erne. They have been making gleaming basket-weave pottery at **Belleek Pottery** since 1857, and in much the same way, with traditional tools made by the workers themselves. Wander around the factory and watch the crafts-people teasing the raw material – Cornish china clay and glass – into long snakes, then painstakingly constructing the delicate bowls and plates of latticework that will be decorated with tiny,

Right: a delicate masterpiece of Belleek pottery

Below: the calm waters of Upper Lough Erne from Knockninny Hill

handmade china flowers and painted to perfection. Of course you can buy a piece if you want, after the tour.

The Lough and Its Islands

Once, legend says, Fermanagh was a dry plain, with a fairy well that was always kept covered. Two lovers, hastening to elope, drank at the well and forgot to replace the cover. As the first rays of sun touched the water it over-flowed, and went on flowing until it had formed Lough Erne.

The county town of **Enniskillen** sits on an island in the narrow waist between Upper and Lower Lough Erne. This is a great spot to base yourself when you explore the lough and its islands. Apart from their beauty, visitors are attracted by the little islands' extraordinary wealth of relics of the past, Christian and pre-Christian.

Devenish Island is reached by ferry from Trory Point just downstream of Enniskillen. On Devenish you'll find the ruins of a 13th-century parish church, a fine high cross, the beautiful shell of St Mary's Priory (1449), and a very well preserved round tower dating from about 1160 from whose uppermost window, 25m (82 feet) up, you get a marvellous view over the lough and islands. A small museum

Tough Guy

The story is told that when Belleek Pottery was being built, a construction worker fell from the roof to the ground, miraculously landing on his feet. He swallowed a glass of whiskey and was sent straight back up again to carry on with the job.

Enigmatic Janus figure on Boa Island

"Janus" by Heaney

God-eyed, sex-mouthed,
its brain
A watery wound…

Nobel Prize-winning poet Seamus Heaney responds to the Janus figure on Boa Island.

explains the layout and history of this monastic site, founded during the 6th century by St Molaise, "Little Flame the Beautiful from multitudinous Devenish". This island is exceptionally peaceful, with its own magic.

A different aura of pre-Christian enchantment hangs round the old cemetery at Caldragh on **Boa Island**, reached by bridge from the north shore of Lower Lough Erne. Here you'll find a much-photographed pagan "Janus figure", dating perhaps from the 5th to the 6th century AD, with two faces looking in opposite directions, and a hollow in the "skull" between them that some have speculated might have been made to hold ceremonial blood.

On **White Island**, reached by a ferry from Castle Archdale marina, are more enigmatic figures: seven stone statues over a thousand years old, built into a wall side by side. One holds a priest's bell and crosier; one has his hand on his chin; another is a *sheela-na gig* – a cross-legged woman in a sexually blatant attitude. These may signify the Seven Deadly Sins, but no one knows for sure…

TAKING A BREAK

You'll find simple, tasty sustenance such as casseroles with baked potatoes, quiches and salads at the **Belleek Pottery Tea Rooms** (tel: 028 6865 9300). For Enniskillen's best music and hospitality, visit **Blake's Of The Hollow** (tel: 028 6632 2143), a wonderful pub in a dip of the main street.

LOUGH ERNE: INSIDE INFO

Top tips If you have to select just one of Lough Erne's islands, go for **Devenish Island**: the ecclesiastical remains there are stunning.

Hidden gem Take binoculars to Devenish Island, to see what most visitors miss: the **four stone heads** looking out from under the cap of the round tower.

Belleek Pottery
✛ 196 A3
✉ Belleek Pottery Visitors' Centre, Belleek, Co Fermanagh ☎ 028 6865 9300; www.belleek.ie
🕐 Mon–Fri 9–6, Sat 10–6, Sun 2–6, Apr–Oct; Mon–Fri 9–5:30, rest of year; Sat 10–5:30,
   Nov–Christmas. Pottery tours: Mon–Fri, every 30 mins all year 💷 Inexpensive

Lough Erne
✛ 196 B3
✉ Lough Erne information: Tourist Office, Shore Road, Enniskillen, Co Fermanagh
☎ 028 6634 6736; www.discovernorthernireland.com

At Your Leisure

swan-shaped pot stills, and a warehouse where wooden kegs give off the smell of the evaporating "angels' share". In the shop you can buy Original or Black Bush blends, or classic malts.

🔢 197 D5
✉ Bushmills, Co Antrim ☎ 028 2073 1521; www. whiskeytours.ie
🕐 Tours: Mon–Sat 9:30–5:30, Sun noon–5:30 (last tour 4), Apr–Oct; Mon–Fri 10:30, 11:30, 1:30, 2:30, 3:30, Sat–Sun 1:30, 2:30, 3:30, rest of year 🎟 Moderate

4 Downhill

This is as eccentric and fascinating a cluster of buildings as you'll find in Ireland. Now in the care of the National Trust, and connected by scenic footpaths, they were built on the cliff tops just west of Castlerock by a highly idiosyncratic Bishop of Londonderry. The **Mussenden Temple** on the cliff edge is a classical rotunda, built 1783–85 by Frederick Hervey, 4th Earl of Bristol and Bishop of Londonderry, perhaps to accommodate one of his mistresses. Inland stands the roofless, gaunt ruin of **Downhill House**, the Bishop's country seat, and nearby are a restored walled garden, dovecote and ice-house, and the **Lion Gate** topped with one of Hervey's armorial leopards.

🔢 197 D5 ✉ Mussenden Road, Castlerock, Co Londonderry ☎ 028 7084 8728; www.ntni.org.uk 🕐 Temple: daily 11–7:30, Jun–Aug; Sat–Sun and public hols 11–6, Mar–May and Sep. Grounds: always open 🎟 Free; parking inexpensive when Temple open

A big-bellied copper whiskey still at Old Bushmills Distillery, County Antrim

3 Old Bushmills Distillery

Some of Ireland's best malt and blended whiskey is made here in the world's oldest licensed distillery (1608), housed in an attractive huddle of whitewashed buildings in the shadow of two pagoda towers.

The tour takes you around big copper tuns full of steaming mash,

5 Londonderry/Derry

Known as Londonderry to loyalists, and Derry to nationalists, this picturesque walled city has been split by politics. Its streets saw major disturbances in the 1970s, but it has emerged as one of the most forward-thinking cities in Ireland. Chief attraction is the walk around the 17th-century city walls (▶ 181–3), but there are plenty of other things to enjoy, including the **Tower Museum**; a looming 19th-century **Guildhall** (▶ 183); **St Columb's Cathedral** with relics of the epic siege of 1688–89, when the Protestant citizens defied the army of Catholic James II (▶ 182); and a **Craft Village** where shops and eateries cluster around a square in the heart of the city.

➕ 196 C4 ✉ Tourist Information Centre, 44 Foyle Street ☎ 028 7126 7284; www.discovernorthernireland.com 🚌 Foyle Street 🚉 Waterside Station, Duke Street

Tower Museum

✉ Union Hall Place ☎ 028 7137 2411; www.derry.net/tower 🕐 Mon–Sat 10–5, Sun 2–5, Jul–Aug; Tue–Sat 10–5, rest of year; closed for refurbishment until spring 2005 💷 Moderate

Guildhall

☎ 028 7137 7335 to arrange a visit; www.discovernorthernireland.com 🕐 Guided tours: Mon–Sat 9–5, Apr–Oct; Mon–Sat 9–4, rest of year 💷 Free

6 Sperrin Mountains

In the Sperrin Heritage Centre at Cranagh you can learn about geology, local history, wildlife and folklore; you can even pan for gold in the nearby stream. All good stuff – but it's better

Political Pot

In the Countess's Bedroom at Florence Court the chamber pot is of finest Belleek china. Strategically placed at the bottom is a portrait of 19th-century prime minister William Gladstone, unpopular with the ruling Anglo-Irish classes because of his support for Home Rule and land reform.

Stalactites and limestone extravagances at Marble Arch Caves, County Fermanagh

still to get out and explore this wild range of hills that straddles the Tyrone/Derry border. Even the highest peak (Sawel, at 683m/2,241 feet) is easily climbed with good walking shoes; golden plover, raven, peregrine and red grouse breed on the moors; and twisting roads soon put you deep into unfrequented back country.

➕ 196 C4 ✉ Sperrin Heritage Centre, 274 Glenelly Road, Cranagh, Co Tyrone ☎ 028 8164 8142; www.strabanedc.org.uk 🕐 Mon–Fri 11:30–5:30, Sat 11:30–6, Sun 2–6, Apr–Oct 💷 Inexpensive

9 Marble Arch Caves

The entrance to this system of semi-flooded caves lies about 8km (5 miles) due west of Florence Court. You can walk much of the system, and boats carry you the rest of the way, through caverns and chambers with glistening mineral walls and plenty of stalactites. Phone before visiting, as the caves can be closed for safety after heavy rain.

➕ 196 B3 ✉ Marlbank Scenic Loop, Florence Court, Enniskillen, Co Fermanagh ☎ 028 6634 8855; www.discovernorthernireland.com 🕐 Daily 10–5, Jul–Aug; 10–4:30, mid-Mar to Jun and Sep 💷 Expensive

10 Florence Court

A few kilometres southwest of Enniskillen, the big square central block and arcaded wings of Florence Court look out over immaculate gardens and parkland. This mid-18th-century house belonging to the Earls of Enniskillen was gutted by fire in 1955, but has been superbly restored by the National Trust. Rich plasterwork in the hall, on the dining room ceiling and above the staircase is notable; as are the portraits of the Earls of Enniskillen with their red hair and imperious eagle noses. There's a fine cutaway scale model of the basement in Florence Court.

The grand arcaded façade at Florence Court

+ 196 B3 ✉ Florence Court, Enniskillen, Co Fermanagh ☎ 028 6634 8249; www.ntni.org.uk ① House: daily noon–6, Jun–Aug; Sat–Sun and public hols noon–6, rest of year. Grounds: daily 10–8, May–Sep; 10–4, rest of year ⓦ Moderate

Ⅺ Castle Coole

Designed between 1790 and 1798 by James Wyatt, this is Ireland's finest neoclassical mansion. Behind the giant portico of this National Trust property lie superb furnishings, Irish oak floors and silk-hung state rooms. In the library, note the camels' heads on the gilt curtain pole, installed to celebrate Admiral Nelson's victory over Napoleon at the Battle of the Nile in 1798. As you go around, the guide will tell you the sad story of the 1st Earl of Belmore, whose wife ran off and left him desolate and alone in this huge house.

+ 196 B3 ✉ Enniskillen, Co Fermanagh ☎ 028 6632 2690; www.nationaltrust.org.uk ① House: daily noon–6, Jul–Aug; Sat–Sun, hol Mon noon–6, Mar to mid-May, Sep; Wed–Mon noon–6, Jun. Grounds: daily 10–8, May–Sep; 10–4, rest of year ⓦ Moderate

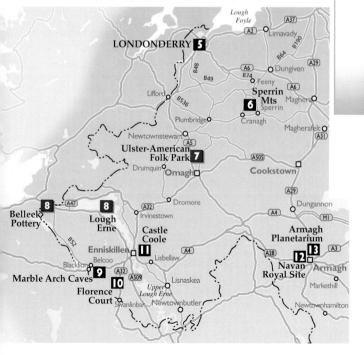

🔞 Navan Royal Site

The Lords of ancient Ulster ruled from the Hill of Navan, just outside Armagh City, from *c*700 BC to the 4th century AD. Misty figures of legend – bold King Conor's Knights of the Red Branch, the Ulster hero Cuchulainn and his arch-foe Queen Mebh of Connacht, beautiful Deirdre of the Sorrows – walk the domed green hill.

Beneath the turf lies an extraordinary structure built by Iron Age tribes-people: a vast mound of pebbles packed inside a gigantic timber hall, which the builders then deliberately burned down. In the Navan Centre below the hill, a well laid-out exhibition explores the myth and mystery.

🗺 197 D3 ✉ Killylea Road, Armagh
☎ 028 9181 1491;
www.nics.gov.uk/ehs/ 🕐 Open access
🎟 Free

🔞 Armagh Planetarium

Several features form the Armagh Planetarium. In the Star Theatre you can "voyage" among the stars, choosing your own route, and on selected nights there are special "sky at night" viewings using powerful

telescopes. The Hall of Astronomy takes you through the technology and history of the science; in the Eartharium you can study star formation, forecast the weather, or gape at stunning close-up images of cities and landmarks relayed by satellite. Out in the grounds you can walk the universe, laid out to scale in miniature form to bewilder your mind with the distances involved.

🗺 197 D3
✉ College Hill,

Armagh
☎ 028 3752 3689;
www.armaghplanet.com 🕐 Call for opening hours 🎟 Moderate

🔞 Mountains of Mourne

The beautiful Mountains of Mourne fill Northern Ireland's southeast corner. Their conical profiles give the impression of mountains, but at an average height of just over 600m (1,968 feet), these are really tall fells. They offer wonderful walking and backroad exploring.

The A2 coast road skirts the mountains from Newcastle, the area's main tourist centre, to Rostrevor, and there are numerous side lanes that can lead you up to the reservoir lakes of Silent Valley and over by Spelga Dam in wild scenery.

At the Mourne Heritage Centre in Newcastle, you can buy a pack of ten laminated cards that detail walks ranging from easy to strenuous.

🗺 197 E2 ✉ Mourne Heritage Centre, 87 Central Promenade, Newcastle, Co Down ☎ 028 4372 4059

Off the Beaten Track

If you have a little more time to spare, take half a day to drive south of Armagh City through the lanes of South Armagh. This pretty area of tumbled small hills and quiet farming villages was branded "Bandit Country" by the world's media during 25 years of the Troubles. This strongly Republican area of the province has been almost entirely neglected by the tourist industry, but its people are as friendly as anywhere else in Ireland (if you don't broach politics in conversation, neither will they), and steeped in traditions of story-telling and music-making.

Where to...
Eat and Drink

Prices

Expect to pay per person for a meal, excluding drinks and service
£ up to £15 ££ up to £25 £££ over £25

BELFAST

Crown Liquor Saloon £–££

Belfast's best-known pub (► 150–1), this former Victorian gin palace is now owned by the National Trust and run by Bass Taverns. A visit to one of its booths to sample a thirst-quenching pint and half a dozen oysters served on crushed ice, or a bowl of steaming, tasty Irish stew, should be on your schedule. The Britannic Lounge upstairs, built with the timbers from the SS *Britannic* (sister ship to the *Titanic*), is worth a look.

🔒 197 E3 ⊠ 46 Great Victoria Street, Belfast BT2 7BA ☎ 028 9027 9901

Genoa ££

Right by the marina in Bangor, this friendly restaurant is named after a type of sail, not the Italian city, though you will find a few Italian influences on the menu. Chef Gary Beattie, formerly at Deanes in Belfast, cooks in contemporary style with some interesting combinations, and uses only the finest and freshest ingredients, mostly from individual local sources, including vegetables and herbs from the owner's own garden. Seafood is a speciality.

🔒 197 F4 ⊠ 1a Seacliff Road, Bangor, Co Down ☎ 028 9146 9253; www.genoarestaurant.com ☺ Lunch: Tue–Fri 12–2:30. Dinner: Tue–Sat 6–9:30 (5:30–10 Fri and Sat)

Nick's Warehouse ££

This lively, air-conditioned restaurant makes the most of a clever warehouse conversion. Attentive, friendly service and excellent food are the hallmarks, in both the wine bar and restaurant. Cooking is seasonal and modern, but with a less formal feel than that of many contemporary restaurants (dishes include duck with apple): international influences are certainly discernible, but Irish ingredients and traditional themes are not overlooked. An interesting and fairly priced wine list adds to the appeal.

🔒 197 E3 ⊠ 35–39 Hill Street, Belfast BT1 2LB ☎ 028 9043 9690; fax: 028 9023 0514; email: nicks@warehouse.dnet.co.uk; www.nickswarehouse.co.uk ☺ Lunch: Mon–Fri noon–3. Dinner: Tue–Sat 6–9:30

Restaurant Michael Deane ££–£££

Deanes' exclusive first-floor restaurant with its open kitchen serves exciting "fusion" food. In the more accessible brasserie downstairs, you get stylish but reasonably priced Thai-influenced food. It is open for both lunch (reservations are recommended) and dinner.

🔒 197 E3 ⊠ 36–40 Howard Street, Belfast BT1 6PF ☎ 028 9033 1134 ☺ 1st-floor restaurant: Wed–Sat 7–9:30 pm. Deanes Brasserie: Mon–Sat noon–2:30 pm, 5:30–11 pm

Shanks ££–£££

The setting – an architecturally controversial modern golf club – may be unlikely, but this is indisputably one of Ireland's finest restaurants. The main restaurant is downstairs, where the decor is smartly minimalist and bright. The cooking is done in a windowed kitchen, providing entertainment while you wait. Mediterranean and Asian influences integrate local ingredients with produce from afar in the stylish, assured cooking. Lunch is especially

☺ Flannigan's Bar and eatery: Mon–Sat 11:30–11:30, Sun 12:30–10 good value. This is a no-smoking environment.

⊞ 197 F4 ⊠ Blackwood Golf Centre, Crawfordsburn Road, Bangor, Co Down BT19 1GB ☎ 028 9185 3313 ⊘ Lunch: Tue–Fri 12:30–2:30. Dinner: Tue–Sat 7–10; closed 1 Jan, 25 Dec and 2 weeks around 12 Jul

THE ANTRIM COAST

National Trust Tea Room £

Enjoy simple, tasty food – soup and snacks, good home baking – at the "eighth wonder of the world". There's another National Trust Tea Room at the lovely harbourside village of Cushendun (tel: 028 2076 1506), open off-season weekends and daily after Easter.

⊞ 197 D5 ⊠ Giant's Causeway Centre, Co Antrim ☎ 028 2073 2282 ⊘ Daily 10:30–4:30 (till 5:30 Jul–Aug)

Wysners £–££

After a bracing walk around the nearby Giant's Causeway, you'll enjoy this restaurant on Ballycastle's main street as a good place to refuel. The downstairs café has a lengthy choice of meals and snacks, and the upstairs restaurant offers more sophistication. Here you can feast on local salmon from Carrick-a-Rede a mile or two along the coast and indulge in a slice of Jackie Wysner's Bushmills malt cheesecake.

⊞ 197 E5 ⊠ 16 Ann Street, Ballycastle, Co Antrim ☎ 028 2076 2372 ⊘ Mon–Sat 9–5, 7–9:30

MOUNTAINS OF MOURNE

The Buck's Head ££

This attractive restaurant/bar has a conservatory at the back and a garden for use in fine weather, with views of Dundrum Bay from the top. Good food and service plus long opening hours make this a great place to stop on a tour. Local produce, especially seafood from Dundrum Bay, is prominent and there's always imaginative vegetarian food.

⊞ 197 E3 ⊠ Main Street, Dundrum, Co Down ☎ 028 4375 1868 ⊘ Lunch: noon–2:30. High tea: 5:30–6:45. Dinner: 7–9 (Sun till 8:30 pm); closed 25 Dec

Where to... Stay

Prices

Expect to pay per person staying
£ up to £30
££ up to £60
£££ over £60

BELFAST

Jurys Belfast Inn £££

Close to the major shopping areas of Donegall Place and Castle Court Centre, this centrally located budget hotel provides comfort without service, at a modest price. Rooms big enough to accommodate a family of four (or three adults), at a fixed price, are well designed and furnished to a high standard, with good amenities including bath and shower. There's no private parking, but there is an arrangement with a nearby car-park (parking lot).

⊞ 197 E3 ⊠ Fisherwick Place, Great Victoria Street, Belfast BT2 7AP ☎ 028 9053 3500; fax: 028 9053 3511; www.jurysdoyle.com ⊘ Closed 24–6 Dec

The McCausland Hotel £££

At night, the façade of this fashionable hotel is gloriously floodlit. Formerly a warehouse, the Victorian landmark building was designed in Italianate style – in contrast to the classic contemporary design of the interior. Rooms are finished to a high standard and the restaurant is among Belfast's best.

⊞ 197 E3 ⊠ 34–8 Victoria Street, Belfast BT1 3GH ☎ 028 9022 0200; email: mccausland@slh.com; www.slh.com ⊘ Closed 24–7 Dec

Tara Lodge £££

This stylish modern hotel has 18 rooms and friendly, intimate atmosphere. An advantage is the secure parking – rare so close to the city centre. Each of the comfortable bedrooms has a bathroom, and facilities include satellite TV, Internet access and beverages.

✚ 197 E3 ✉ 36 Cromwell Road, Botanic Avenue, Belfast BT7 1JW
☎ 028 9059 0900; www.taralodge.com

ENNISKILLEN

Abocurragh Farm Guesthouse £-££

All Ireland Agri-Tourism winner, this lovely bed-and-breakfast is on a working dairy farm in a very beautiful part of Fermanagh. Spacious bedrooms have wonderful views, and there are facilities for children, such as special meals and a babysitting service.

✚ 196 B3 ✉ Letterbreen, Enniskillen, Co Fermanagh BT74 9AG
☎ 028 6634 8484; fax: 028 6634 8288; email: abocurragh@yahoo.com; www.abocurragh.com

THE ANTRIM COAST

Bushmills Inn £££

Thoughtful development has added to the appeal of this well-run 19th-century coaching inn near the Giant's Causeway. A turf fire and traditional country-style furniture in the hall set the tone, and public rooms are all in keeping with the country theme. Bedrooms are furnished in a comfortable country style, and even the new bathrooms seem to belong to an earlier era. There is a Taste of Ulster restaurant and a gas-lit bar.

✚ 197 D5 ✉ 9 Dunluce Road, Bushmills, Co Antrim BT57 8QG
☎ 028 2073 2339; fax: 028 2073 2048; email: mail@bushmillsinn.com; www.bushmillsinn.com

GLENS OF ANTRIM

Greenhill House £

This Georgian farmhouse is at the centre of a working farm. Bedrooms include two family rooms; the bedrooms are not luxurious, but they have bathrooms and their furnishings make them far more comfortable than one might expect in farmhouse accommodation. Dinner is available for residents by arrangement.

✚ 197 D5 ✉ 24 Greenhill Road, Aghadowey, Co Antrim BT51 4EU
☎ 028 7086 8241; fax: 028 7086 8365; email: greenhill.house@btinternet.com; www.greenhill.house.btinternet.co.uk
⊘ Early Mar–Oct

LONDONDERRY/DERRY

Beech Hill Country House Hotel £££

Just outside the city walls, this 18th-century house has retained many of its original details, but now has a new fitness suite too. Bedrooms vary in size and outlook but all have bath or shower rooms and are furnished with antiques. The bar is popular, and good food is served.

✚ 196 C4 ✉ 32 Ardmore Road, Londonderry BT47 3QP ☎ 028 7134 9279; email: info@beech-hill.com; www.beech-hill.com ⊘ Closed 25 Dec

DUNGANNON

Grange Lodge £££

The comfort and hospitality provided at this lovely Georgian house make this a good base for touring. Bedrooms (and bathrooms) are exceptionally comfortable and the food (residents' dinner and breakfast) is superb.

✚ 197 D3 ✉ 7 Grange Road, Dungannon, Co Tyrone BT71 1EJ
☎ 028 8778 4212; fax: 028 8778 4313; email: grangelodge@nireland.com
⊘ Closed 20 Dec–1 Feb

MOUNTAINS OF MOURNE

Hastings Slieve Donard Hotel £££

This prestigious Victorian hotel in Newcastle stands in grounds beneath the Mountains of Mourne and beside the Royal County Down Golf Links. Renovated in the late 1990s, the accommodation is furnished to a high standard, and every bathroom sports a yellow Hastings duck! There's a health club, and Tollymore Forest Park provides excellent walking.

✚ 197 E3 ✉ Downs Road, Newcastle, Co Down BT33 0AH ☎ 028 4372 1066; fax: 028 4372 4830; email: res@sdh.hastingshotel.com; www.hastingshotel.com

Where to... Shop

The North, with its long tradition of craftsmanship, is the best part of Ireland for buying linen, hand-made lace and parian china. Look out, too, for beautifully made woollen goods and hand-cut Tyrone crystal.

BELFAST

Belfast's main shopping area is around Donegall Place, High Street and Royal Avenue; **Castle Court** (Royal Avenue) is the most interesting shopping mall. Old-established **Hoggs** (Donegall Square West) has fine linen, and a good selection of Tyrone crystal and Belleek pottery; **Smyth's Irish Linens** (59 Boundary Street, tel: 028 9032 1065) has beautiful linen goods, and **Smyth & Gibson** (Bedford House, Bedford Street, tel: 028 9023 0388) sells its own brand of luxurious linen shirts and accessories. For superb modern jewellery, **The Steensons** (Bedford House, Bedford Street, tel: 028 9024 8269) is a must. The in-place for up-to-the-minute clothes is **Apache** (Wellington Place, tel: 028 9032 9056), with funky gear and an instore DJ to entertain customers. If you like flea markets, browse around the bric-a-brac at **St George's Market** on May Street (Tue and Fri mornings; farmers' market Sat).

LONDONDERRY/DERRY

In Derry, **The Donegal Shop** (Shipquay Street, tel: 028 7126 6928) does great Irish linen, tweeds and knitwear, and the **Derry Craft Village** (off Shipquay Street) has interesting workshops and demonstrations of craftspeople plying their trade in an 18th-century setting. **Austins** (The Diamond, tel: 028 7126 1817) is a large shop stocking a wide range of high-quality Northern Irish goods, including Tyrone crystal and Belleek china.

Where to... Be Entertained

The Arts Council of Northern Ireland (tel: 028 9038 5200) produces a monthly publication, *Artslink*. Additional information is available at Northern Ireland Tourist Board information offices and in newspaper listings.

SPORT

In addition to the usual sporting pursuits of greyhound racing, horse racing, soccer, rugby and cricket, the Northern Irish love watching and participating in their native sports, hurling and Gaelic football; in Armagh you might see "bullets" (or "road bowling") being played, which involves hurling metal balls along country lanes. Other activities on offer include golf, cycling, fishing, walking and riding. Details on all these and many other options – including cruising on Lough Erne and birdwatching on Strangford Lough – are available from tourist offices.

MUSIC

There's plenty of informal music in Northern Ireland. In Belfast, one of the best places to experience traditional music sessions is **Pat's Bar** (Prince's Dock, tel: 028 9074 4524). **The Rotterdam** (54 Pilot Street, tel: 028 9074 6021) has regular folk, jazz and blues, and the **Kitchen Bar** (16–18 Victoria Square, tel: 028 9032 4901) has traditional music sessions on Friday nights. Club fashions move fast, but **Manhattan** (Bradbury Place, tel: 028 9023 3131) is always a good bet, with celebrities flown in to perform every week to liven up the regular mix.

Walks & Tours

1 HILL OF HOWTH
Walk

DISTANCE 11km (7 miles) **TIME** 3 hours (4 if you stop…and you should)
START/END POINT Howth DART railway station (24 minutes from Connolly Station in central Dublin). For information tel: 01 836 6222 ⊞ 201 E5

This delightful walk is a favourite weekend stroll of Dubliners. It is easily reached by train, varies between hill slopes and coastal paths, and has tremendous views over the city, Dublin Bay and the coast and hills for 50km (30 miles) around. It makes an ideal change of pace when you are feeling jaded with central Dublin and long to get some fresh sea air into your lungs.

1–2
Turn left out of the DART station in Howth to pass the **harbour**. This was where Erskine Childers, author of the classic spy thriller *The Riddle of the Sands*, landed guns and ammunition from his little yacht *Asgard* in July 1914 to help foment a nationalist uprising.

2–3
In a few hundred metres turn right up Abbey Street. Beside Ye Olde Abbey Tavern climb steps on the right to reach the ruins of the

abbey – a seat of learning famed throughout medieval Europe. There's a great view here over the packed white houses of Howth to the crooked crab-claws of the harbour breakwaters.

Howth has long been a favoured dwelling place for writers, Trinity College dons, poets and artists, and more recently for well-heeled commuters who want to live conveniently close to, but not actually in, Ireland's capital city.

3–4
Turn down Church Street into Abbey Street, and take the next right up St Lawrence's Road. In 100m (110 yards) keep ahead along Grace O'Malley Road, then turn left up Grace O'Malley Drive. At a telephone booth on a left bend keep ahead up a path to a road; go ahead for 20m (22 yards), then turn right up steps.

4–5
Turn right at the top, and ascend a ramp beside house No 53 ("Ballylinn"). Keep ahead up a grassy slope, go through trees, then up a steep bank and on southward up the edge of a rough field, with a golf course and a banked reservoir to your right.

5–6

Bear right around the top edge of the golf course; follow the path into the trees, across the aptly named Bog of Frogs, and on under the crags of Dun Hill. Cross the golf course and

From the ruins of 11th-century Howth Abbey there is a splendid view out across the harbour to the rocky island of Ireland's Eye

climb the steep heathery slope ahead (red-and-white striped poles) on a rough path that leads to the top of Shielmartin.

Take time up here to admire the superb views across Dublin Bay and the city to the Wicklow Hills. Knobby, white quartzite boulders form a ring round the crown of **Shielmartin**. They were placed here 2,000 years ago to mark the burial place of an Irish warrior king, Crimhthan

Niadhnair. Helped by his wife, Nar of the Brugh (some say she was a goddess), he became rich beyond dreams of avarice by making frequent raids across the Irish Sea to plunder the Romans who had newly arrived in Britain. Whether his golden treasure is buried on Shielmartin is open to romantic speculation.

6–7

A clear path leads off the summit, steeply down to Carrickbrack Road. Turn left; in 300m (330 yards) cross the road, go through a swing gate ("Dangerous Cliffs" sign – but don't be alarmed!) and take the path down to the shore.

7–8

Here you turn left and follow the narrow but well-defined coastal path for 8km (5 miles), past the Baily Lighthouse on its promontory and on all the way round Howth Head and back to the DART station.

Taking a Break

There are many pubs and restaurants in Howth. Try **Ye Olde Abbey Tavern** in Abbey Street (tel: 01 839 0307) for delicious fish and an excellent pint of stout.

2 BLACKWATER BOG

Tour

DISTANCE 8km (5 miles) **TIME** Around 1 hour
START/END POINT Bord na Mona's Blackwater peat works, 1·6km (1 mile) beyond Shannonbridge on R357, 13km (8 miles) east of Ballinasloe; Bog tour daily, on the hour every hour 10–5, Apr to early Oct ⊞ 200 A5 **INFORMATION** tel: 090 9674114/9674172/9674121; www.bnm.ie **COST** Moderate

At first glance, the great boglands of central Ireland do not look like interesting places. In fact, most visitors hurry past these blankets of brown emptiness, their imaginations fixed on the glorious mountains and coasts of the west. But allow yourself an hour aboard the cranky little green-and-yellow bog workers' train grandiosely named the Clonmacnoise & West Offaly Railway, and you'll have your eyes opened to the rich wildlife and sullen beauty of an environment that very few are privileged to penetrate.

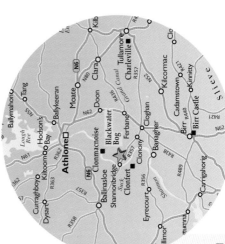

Plants such as bogbean thrive in the Blackwater Bog

Sphagnum Sponge

Sphagnum moss, the main building material of a raised bog such as Blackwater, is amazingly absorbent: it can hold up to 20 times its own weight in water, trapped in its myriad pores and cells.

Beautiful Bogland

"On a day of bright sky the bogland is a lovely, far-reaching expanse of purple and rich brown; and the lakelets take on the quite indescribable colour that comes from clear sky reflected in bog-water."

– Robert Lloyd Praeger, *The Way That I Went*

One-seventh of all Ireland is bog – sodden peat moss, laid down thousands of years ago and hardly touched until the Irish Peat Board, Bord na Mona, was formed in 1946 to harvest the stuff for burning in the electricity-generating stations of Ireland, a country largely without timber and wholly without coal. Bord na Mona, having wreaked havoc across Ireland's bogs, has only 28 years to run before peat extraction has

to stop, and has now begun to make some conservation moves.

The snail's pace of the little train allows you plenty of time to get down and explore – and even to have a go at cutting turf (the Irish term for peat), by hand with a slane (sharp-edged turf spade). You can see for yourself how vegetable matter has remained unrotted for thousands of years in the acid environment of the bog. Down in a huge drainage gash, 10m (33 feet) below the surface, lie great trunks and boughs of "bog oak" – twisted, silvery limbs of yew,

oak, birch and pine trees that were growing here long before the pharaohs began to build their pyramids in Egypt.

Duckboard trails lead off across the heathery bosom of the bog. Looking closely, you can spot patches of brightly coloured flowers: bog asphodel, heath spotted orchids, bog cotton, lousewort and insect-eating sundew. Birds love the wide spaces of the bog and its scrub trees. It's one of the most peaceful places on earth, something you will appreciate if you come here out of season and have the whole bog, horizon to horizon, to yourself.

Back at the Blackwater works there's a display centre explaining the formation and wildlife of the bog, and a museum of the outlandish machines that have worked it over the years. When harvesting finishes around the year 2030, Ireland's worked bogs are due to become the centrepiece of a wetland landscape with lakes, fens and forests, part recreational, part conservational – not a bad outcome for such a destructive industry.

Taking a Break

There is a pleasant **café** back at the Blackwater works.

Mini songbirds find shelter in the reed pools of the bogland

3 CROAGH PATRICK
Walk

The ascent of Croagh Patrick (or The Reek) is one of Ireland's classic hill climbs. The climb itself is not technically challenging, although the second half forms a stamina-sapping scramble up loose scree. The view from the summit – a huge slice of coastline, hundreds of small islands, Clew Bay, and the Nephin Beg and Connemara mountains – will take your breath away.

Most visitors opt for the short climb from Murrisk, but the 37-km (23-mile) pilgrimage route, beginning at Ballintober Abbey, repays the effort.

Maps
If you are following 37-km (23-mile) Tochar Phadraig from Ballintober Abbey, you will find these Irish OS 1:50,000 maps useful: 30, 31, 37, 38.

DISTANCE 7km (4 miles) up and down; ascent of 765m (2,510 feet) **TIME** 4–5 hours. The Pilgrimage Route takes 2 days **START POINT** Murrisk, on R355 9km (5 miles) west of Westport, for the ascent of The Reek; Ballintober Abbey, 11km (7 miles) south of Castlebar, off the N84 Ballinrobe road, for the full pilgrimage route ⊞ 194 C2 **END POINT** Murrisk

Short Climb
1–2
Leave your car by Owen Campbell's pub in Murrisk and turn up the signposted lane towards Croagh Patrick.

2–3
Walk past the statue of St Patrick and continue along the well-worn path that leads to the saddle at 500m (1,640 feet).

Ireland's Holy Mountain
Croagh Patrick is a place of pilgrimage and penance. Each year on Garland Sunday, the last Sunday in July, whatever the weather, as many as 50,000 people (many of them barefoot), ranging in age from 8 to 80, climb the mountain and offer prayers to St Patrick in the little church at the summit.

St Patrick (▶ 14) is said to have climbed up Croagh Patrick's steep slopes in AD 441, preaching from the summit and breaking the power of a cloud of demons by hurling his bell through them. He also begged successfully for deliverance of the souls of the Irish people on Doomsday, and banished all snakes from the island by driving them over a precipice.

2-3

The Tochar, an ancient pilgrim route, runs west for 37km (23 miles), aiming for the cone of Croagh Patrick. *En route* it passes holy wells, standing stones, monastic sites, prehistoric burial mounds and inscribed rocks.

3-4

You can break your journey halfway at the village of Aghagower, or accomplish the whole thing in one go, but take into account the stiff ascent up loose scree that awaits you.

4-5

Once under The Reek itself, follow the track up the south flank to the saddle, then sweat up the rock slide to the summit. You'll be rewarded with spectacular views of Clew Bay and the Nephin Beg and Connemara mountains.

Taking a Break

As you return to Murrisk, refreshed in spirit but leg-weary and footsore, stop at **Owen Campbell's pub** at the foot of the path. The interior of the pub is hung with photographs of Reek pilgrims.

The distinctive profile of Croagh Patrick dominates the view of pilgrims approaching from Owen Campbell's pub in Murrisk

3-4

Take a deep breath and tackle the loose, rubbly and very steep slope to the summit. Return on the same path.

Pilgrimage Route

1-2

For this longer route, start at Ballintober Abbey, and follow the marker stones incised with crosses. These will lead you along the field paths and lanes of St Patrick's Causeway, known in Irish as Tochar Phadraig.

4 YEATS COUNTRY
Tour

William Butler Yeats (1865–1939), winner of the 1923 Nobel Prize for Literature and arguably Ireland's greatest poet, had the flat-topped mountains and sea-beaten shores of County Sligo always in his mind. This beautiful and weathered countryside, where Yeats spent happy childhood months with his grandparents and cousins, inspired many of his best-known poems, and symbolised the mystery, strangeness and strength of his native land.

Most of the ragged circuit of this Yeats Country route is signposted by brown roadsigns showing a writer's quill and inkstand.

DISTANCE 160km (100 miles)
TIME Half-day
START/END POINT Sligo town 🗺 195 E3

1–2

Having first got into the mood by visiting the many W B Yeats sites in Sligo town (➤ 137), leave the town along Castle Street and make your way west towards the distinctive 328-m (1,076-foot) mound of Knocknarea

Just outside Sligo, a brown notice points left for **Carrowmore Tombs**. Sprawling across fields a couple of kilometres down this side road is the largest concentration of megalithic monuments in Ireland – stone circles, dolmens and cairns, most of them now reduced to a few stones but one or two still nearly intact. It is a haunting place, which would be even more impressive were it not for the huge orange-hued riding centre that dominates this ancient site.

Back on the Sligo road, turn left to pass close under Knocknarea; a side road is sign-posted "Meascán Meadhba", and leads via a 45-minute walk to "**Queen Mebh's tomb**" and a wonderful 80-km (50-mile) view. Mebh or Maeve was the 1st-century warrior queen of Connacht who initiated the "Cattle Raid of Cooley". The big green cairn that stands out against the sky on the summit of Knocknarea, said to be her tomb, is in fact a passage grave, filled with 40,000 boulders, that predates Queen Mebh by at least 2,000 years.

3–4
Continue 8km (5 miles) up N15, then bear left for **Lissadell House**, ancestral home of the Gore-Booth family. Two members of the family befriended Yeats. One was the poet Eva Gore-Booth; the other, her sister Constance, Countess Markievicz, who would win a place in the pantheon of nationalist heroes for her active part in the 1916 Easter Rising. She was subsequently elected to Westminster as the first female Member of Parliament (though she never took her seat).

Horseback-riding on a quiet Sligo lane, with the great bulk of Benbulbin as a backdrop

The main road drops to an intersection; turn right here, and beside the Sancta Maria Hotel go left to reach the stony shore, enormous grassy dunes and splendid hill views of Strandhill beach. The cliffs and domed brow of Knocknarea hang behind Strandhill, on whose shore W B Yeats saw and heard the Atlantic waves crash during storms:

"The wind has bundled up the clouds high over Knocknarea,
And thrown the thunder on the stones for all that Maeve can say."

2–3
Return into Sligo and take the N15 Bundoran–Lifford road north out of town. On the outskirts bear left on R291 to **Rosses Point**, a neat little seaside village with a really beautiful view and some fine sandy beach walks.

Return to N15 and go north to **Drumcliff**. The stump of a round tower stands by the road, and a heavily carved high cross dating from about AD 1000 forms part of the churchyard wall. But the focal point is W B Yeats's grave, next to the northwest corner of the tower. A gravel walk leads to a plain limestone slab which is inscribed with the words:

> Cast a cold Eye
> On Life, on Death.
> Horseman, pass by.
>
> W B YEATS
>
> June 13th 1865
> January 28th 1939

"Cast a cold Eye
On Life, on Death
Horseman, pass by!"

These are the last lines of the epitaph poem composed by Yeats for himself. It begins:

"Under bare Ben Bulben's head
In Drumcliff Churchyard Yeats is laid..."

And the view is just that: the simple gravestone, a line of trees, and Benbulbin in the distance.

Return to N15 and turn left to run through **Cliffony**, with Benbulbin's profile changing from that of a lion couchant to a perfect flat-topped table. On the right at the far end of the village is a parking place; from here it's just a step to the well-signposted **Creevykeel court tomb**. This complicated cairn was built between 3000 and 2000 BC with a central court and several burial chambers, all approached through massive stone portals. One even has its rugged lintel still in place.

4–5

Turn back along N15, and immediately left (brown "Ballintrillick" sign) on a long, straight country road. Under Ben Wisken, cross a lane and follow "Gleniff Horseshoe" signs. **Gleniff** is a remote upland valley hemmed in by great basalt crags, where sheep graze under huge fellsides rushing with waterfalls.

The great dark rock arch that hangs high over the top end of Gleniff is said to be the bed of runaway lovers Diarmuid and Gráinne. Diarmuid had the bad luck to cross swords with the right Fionn MacCumhaill, a former fiancé of Gráinne, and suffered the posthumous indignity of having his severed head sent to his true love by the implacable Fionn.

Back on the lane, turn left and continue for 8km (5 miles). Turn left on N15 for Sligo. In 3.2km (2 miles) sidetrack left to **Glencar** to view the fine waterfall in its wooded cleft. It is superb after rain, but a beautiful spot in any weather.

5–6

Return to Sligo and take N16 out of town, following R286 for "Dromahair" signs, and also brown "Lough Gill" and "Parke's Castle" signs. You pass beautiful little Colgagh Lough below, and are soon down on the thickly wooded shore of **Lough Gill**, one of the most attractive stretches of water in County Sligo. Follow the road along the north shore of the lough. You pass the turreted, fortified 17th-century stately home of Parke's Castle, a picture of grim impregnability. Boat trips run from the inlet by the castle to the **Lake Isle of Innisfree**, subject of Yeats's most widely known poem, but you can reach the shore much nearer this tiny island by way of Dromahair. On the far edge of the village bear right (following the "Ballintogher/Sligo" sign); then after 1km (half a mile) take the first narrow lane on the right to wriggle down to the lake shore. Some 200m (220 yards) out lies the tree-smothered round blob of an islet whose peaceful beauty, pictured in the midst of city bustle, brought great solace to Yeats:

Taking a Break

Hargadon's Bar in O'Connell Street, Sligo, is a traditional pub with old-fashioned wood-panelled bars.

Places to Visit

Carrowmore Tombs

⊞ 195 E3 ☎ 071 61534 🕙 Daily 9:30–6:30, May–Sep 💲 Inexpensive

Lissadell House

⊞ 195 E3 ☎ 071 63150; www.castlesireland.com/lissadell-house 🕙 Mon–Sat 10:30–12:15, 2–4:15, Jun–Sep 💲 Moderate

"I will arise and go now, and go to Innisfree,
And a small cabin build there, of clay and wattles made:
Nine bean-rows will I have there, a hive for the honey-bee,
And live alone in the bee-loud glade…"

Yeats never did build his wattle cabin on Innisfree, of course. But he truly loved this peaceful lake, and you can well appreciate why, as you complete the circuit of Lough Gill before returning to Sligo town on R287.

WALLS OF DERRY

Walk

This circuit of the city walls of Derry gives insight into much of the passion and tribalism that divides society in Northern Ireland. The walk is best known, not so much for the historical interest or beauty of the 17th-century walls themselves as for the bitter emotions stirred up annually throughout the 1950s and 1960s when the Orange Order carried out its ritual Apprentice Boys' Marches around the circuit (for the historical background see panel, ▶ 182).

DISTANCE 1.6km (1 mile) **TIME** 2 hours
START/END POINT The Tower Museum, Union Hall Place, near Magazine Gate ✚ 196 C4

taken over the running of the city and were determined to see it prosperous and properly protected against all potential enemies – chiefly local clans resistant to the rule of the British Crown. The walls created an enclave based on a cross of streets that ran from a diamond-shaped central marketplace – The Diamond – to four great gates: Shipquay Gate (northwest), Butcher's Gate (northeast), Bishop's Gate (southwest) and Ferryquay Gate (southeast). Three more gates were added later.

1–2

Walk into the old city through **Shipquay Gate**, and turn to your right to climb to the top of the walls by the Tower Museum in Union Hall Place. The walls of Derry, 6–8m (19–26 feet) tall and the same thickness, form a belt of solid stone that buckles the city into its high defensive position. They were built during the five years 1613–18 by guilds from London that had

2–3

Set off southwest above **Magazine Street**, looking down on the tangled roofs of the walled city. Cross over **Castle Gate**, then **Butcher's Gate**. A little further along, pause on the **Royal Bastion**, a stout outward bulge, and look west across the roofs of the Bogside to the far-off hills of Donegal, a beautiful backdrop. "No Sectarian Marches" says the house-wall graffiti in the Bogside, and "No Consent, No Parade". Other gable-end paintings put the inhabitants' views on the police, army and politicians in graphic if unflattering style. Down on them frown the bastion cannon presented to the city in 1642. Up here stood Walker's Pillar, a great local landmark that offered wonderful wide views from the top until the IRA blew it up in 1973. The Apprentice Boys on their December marches would string up from the pillar an effigy of Robert Lundy, Governor of Derry during the Great Siege of 1688–89 and a folk devil to all Orangemen.

Bearded river god, crowned with water weeds, on Bishop's Gate

3–4

Walk on to **Bishop's Gate**, and climb down to admire the gate itself, rebuilt in classical style in 1789. Two local river gods, bearded and crowned with water-weeds, adorn its arch, Foyle looking out and Boyne looking into the city.

It was to Bishop's Gate that Britain's deposed Catholic King James II rode on 18 April, 1689, to demand the surrender of 30,000 Protestants walled up inside Derry. The Great Siege began then; but the citizens of Derry had been locked in since the previous December, when the celebrated 13 Apprentice Boys seized the keys of the four gates and locked them against the Jacobite army.

4–5

Walk down Bishop Street Within, then right up St Columb Court, to reach **St Columb's Cathedral**, a veritable museum to the Great Siege. It was from the tower that the cry of "No Surrender!" was launched in response to King James's demands. Once Governor Robert Lundy had been ejected, the defenders found a champion in the formidable Reverend George Walker.

In the Chapter House are displayed the keys seized by the Apprentice Boys, brick cannon balls, and a portrait of George Walker in armour. In the church is a plaque to Captain Michael Browning, killed on 28 July, 1689, as his ship *Mountjoy* smashed through the boom built by the besiegers across the river, bringing relief supplies into the city. For 7,000 of the 30,000 defenders (who had eaten every dog, cat and rat in the place), it was too late. The cathedral's entrance hall contains a stand holding the "First Air Mail Letter", an iron mortar bomb which was

Apprentice Boys' Marches

In the 1950s and 1960s, up to 15,000 Orangemen from all over Northern Ireland would turn up with flutes and mighty lambeg drums to parade on the walls of Derry in full sight of the depressed and decaying Roman Catholic Bogside district below. Provocative triumphalism, said the Bogsiders; a celebration of history, responded the Orangemen. Tensions culminated in a riot in August 1969 that became known as the Battle of the Bogside – the catalyst for the recent Troubles, many think. To get an idea of just how bad living conditions in the Bogside were for its Catholic residents, take a look at the collection of black-and-white contemporary photographs on display in the Tower Museum at the end of your walk. They show barefoot children with rickets, ragged-trousered men and overtired women on slum streets in the shadow of crumbling, derelict houses – a fertile breeding ground for resentment and anger. These days, things are different. After a lengthy ban on the Apprentice Boys' parades, a small band of locals now performs the ritual march in August and December, to general indifference among the city's Catholics. Now the dust has settled, you can enjoy this stroll around the 17th-century walls of Derry, among the best preserved in Europe.

fired into the city with the Jacobites' surrender demands sticking out of its fuse hole.

Don't leave St Columb's without enjoying some of its other treasures: ancient regimental flags, carved pew-ends, the great oak tabernacle over the Bishop's chair, and the beautiful late Victorian "Garden of Gethsemane" window.

5–6

Return to Bishop Street Within and continue down to The Diamond. Turn right along Ferryquay Street to rejoin the walls at Ferryquay Gate. Complete your circuit, to finish at the **Tower Museum.** The museum was dreamed up, and built, as an act of faith and optimism at the height of the Troubles when over a quarter of the walled city's buildings had been destroyed.

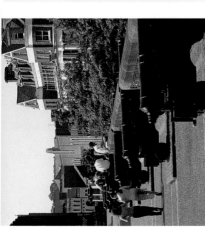

Martyrs' Mound

Outside the east end of the cathedral is the Martyrs' Mound, a green burial hump where 4,500 victims of the Great Siege lie. They were interred there a century after the siege, having been exhumed from the city cellars in which they had been hastily buried during the emergency.

Symbol of ancient defiance: 17th-century cannon line Derry's city walls

It has amply repaid the vision. This is an excellent museum, taking you by way of curving "time tunnels" into various phases of Derry's history. The Troubles are not shirked, but given even-handed treatment.

Taking a Break

The **Dungloe Bar** in Waterloo Street is a good place to stop for a light lunch, and there is sometimes live music.

Places of Interest

Guildhall

Make sure you pop into the splendidly florid Victorian Guildhall. A bombing in 1972 destroyed the stained-glass windows, but by some miracle the original 19th-century watercolour designs had been preserved in London, and the windows were painstakingly reconstructed.

028 7137 7335 to arrange a visit

St Columb's Cathedral

028 7126 7313
Mon–Sat 9–5, Apr–Sep; Mon–Sat 9–1, 2–4, rest of year
Inexpensive

Tower Museum

028 7137 2411
Closed for refurbishment until spring 2005 Moderate

6 STRANGFORD LOUGH

Tour

The 37-km (23-mile) Ards Peninsula hangs down like an elephant's trunk east of Belfast. This narrow seaward outpost of County Down shelters the great tidal inlet of Strangford Lough and all but encloses it. At its southern end, the ferry villages of Portaferry and Strangford face each other across a gap only 500m (550 yards) wide.

Strangford Lough is home to millions of geese, ducks and wading birds, while the peninsula's east coast faces out into the Irish Sea as a run of huge sandy beaches interspersed with rocky coves. It's a beautiful place, unknown to most visitors to Ireland.

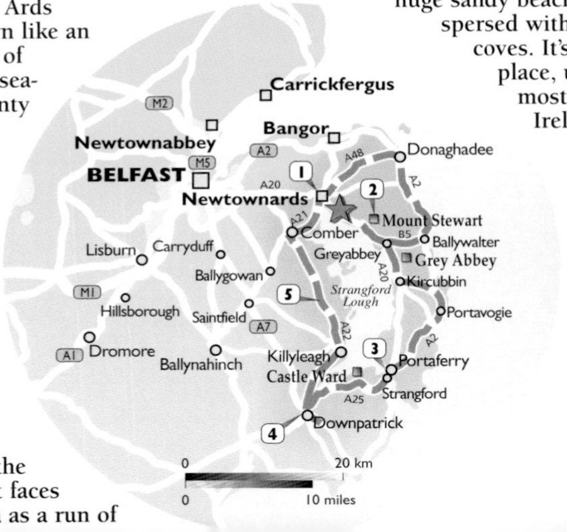

DISTANCE 160km (100 miles). This includes the 10-minute car ferry ride between Portaferry and Strangford (operates half-hourly)

TIME 1 day

START/END POINT Newtownards (on A20, 10km/6 miles east of Belfast) ✚ 197 F3

1–2

Starting at **Newtownards** at the northern end of Strangford Lough, take A48 across the shoulder of the peninsula to the fishing village of

Wildfowl flock to the tidal margins of Strangford Lough

binoculars and admire the **bird life** of Strangford Lough – godwit, redshank, curlew and plover, and in winter huge flocks of pale-bellied brent geese all the way from Greenland. At Kircubbin, weave your way back across the peninsula and continue your coast drive south through small fishing villages such as Ballyhalbert and Portavogie.

When you reach Cloghy, you can either carry on south to the rugged tip of the peninsula at Ballyquintin Point, or cut back again inland to Dorn on Strangford Lough, a national nature reserve and another excellent birdwatching spot. Either way, aim to end up at the pretty little port of **Portaferry**, where you catch the car ferry over the narrows to Strangford.

Crossing the mouth of Strangford Lough, you enter what is known as "St Patrick's Country". Here Ireland's patron saint is said to have landed in AD 432 on his great mission to convert the heathen Irish; and here in the abbey at the monastery of Saul he died in AD 461. It's worth spending a couple of hours cruising around the back roads of this quiet green landscape.

3–4

Follow A25 from Strangford to pass **Castle Ward**. The house, now a National Trust property,

Water features are prominent in the beautifully kept gardens at Mount Stewart

Donaghadee, whose harbour was extended in the 1820s to cope with a flourishing ferry trade to Portpatrick in southwest Scotland. Many famous people have stepped ashore or embarked at Donaghadee: among them are the poet John Keats, biographer James Boswell, composer Franz Liszt, writer Daniel Defoe, and Peter the Great, Tsar of Russia, who (locals will tell you) stayed at Grace Neill's pub in the High Street while touring Europe in 1697–98.

Follow A2 down the coast, admiring the fine beaches, to Ballywalter, where you strike inland along B5 to Greyabbey on the shore of Strangford Lough. There's the ruin of 12th-century **Grey Abbey** to explore here; then bear right up the A20 shore road to **Mount Stewart**. This splendid National Trust house, still lived in by a member of the Stewart family, feels warm and domestic notwithstanding the chandeliers and fine inlaid wood floors. Its gardens are among the National Trust's best, developed by Lady Londonderry from 1921 onwards in dashingly idiosyncratic style, and ornamented with weird stone sculptures of freakish beasts.

2–3

Return along A20 through Greyabbey and on south, stopping now and then to get out the was built in 1762–68 by Bernard Ward and his wife, Anne. He liked the Palladian style, she romanticism; and both wanted their own way. So Castle Ward has a graceful Palladian front and some tastefully furnished classical rooms, while around the back are Moorish windows, pinnacles, and rooms with extravagant pointed door arches and elaborate plasterwork fan vaulting. As for the ill-matched couple, they eventually separated.

Continue along A25 into **Downpatrick**. On a mound outside the cathedral lies a giant slab inscribed "PATRIC". Does St Patrick lie under this stone together with Ireland's other two major-league saints, Brigid and Columb? Historians say no: folklorists and others say yes, and strew the slab with daffodils on St Patrick's Day. It's a lovely spot, whatever the truth.

4–5

Two or three kilometres (2 miles) southeast of Downpatrick, signposted off the Ardglass road, you'll find **Struell Wells**, a curious and peaceful spot where ancient stone bathhouses conceal ice-cold springs in which Patrick is said to have immersed himself.

Return to Downpatrick, from where A22 takes

you back north to Newtownards up the west shore of Strangford Lough. Spare time for a stroll along the waterside track at **Quoile Pondage National Nature Reserve** just outside Downpatrick, and be sure to detour out across the causeways to lonely little **Mahee Island**. Here you'll find a broken round tower, grave slabs of monks, ancient walls and hut foundations – relics of the 5th-century monastery of Nendrum, one of Ireland's earliest Christian foundations,

A massive grave slab, which many people believe marks St Patrick's burial place, lies just outside **Downpatrick Cathedral (below)**

Places to visit

Grey Abbey

✛ 197 F3 ☎ 028 9054 3037
🕐 Tue–Sat 10–7, Sun 2–7, Apr–Oct; Sat 10–4, Sun 2–4, rest of year 💷 Free

Mount Stewart

✛ 197 F3 ☎ 028 4278 8387;
www.ntni.org.uk 🕐 House: Wed–Mon noon–6, Jul–Aug; Mon, Wed–Fri 1–6, Sat–Sun noon–6, May–Jun; Sat–Sun and public hols noon–6, mid-Mar to Apr and Oct. Formal gardens: daily 10–8, May–Sep; 10–6, Apr; Sat–Sun and public hols 10–4, Mar and Oct–Dec. Lakeside gardens and walks: daily 10–8, May–Sep; 10–6, Apr and Oct; 10–4, rest of year. Temple of the Winds: Sat–Sun 2–5, Apr–Oct 💷 Moderate

Castle Ward

✛ 197 F3 ☎ 028 4488 1204; www.ntni.org.uk 🕐 House: daily noon–6, Jul–Aug; Mon–Fri 1–6, Sat–Sun noon–6, May; Sat–Sun and public hols noon–6, mid-Mar to Apr and Sep–Oct. Grounds: daily 10–4 (till 8, May–Sep) 💷 Moderate

Quoile Countryside Centre

✛ 197 F3 ☎ 028 4461 5520; www.fjordlands.org/strngfrd/quoile 🕐 Daily 11–5, Apr–Sep; Sat–Sun 1–5, rest of year 💷 Free

Telefón

Websites
- Bord Fáilte (Irish Tourist Board): www.ireland.travel.ie
- Northern Ireland Tourist Board: www.discovernorthernireland.com

In the Irish Republic
Bord Fáilte (Dublin)
☎ 01 602 4000
Northern Ireland Tourist Board (Dublin)
☎ 01 679 1977

In Northern Ireland
Bord Fáilte (Belfast)
☎ 028 9032 7888
Northern Ireland Tourist Board (Belfast)
☎ 028 9023 1221

BEFORE YOU GO

WHAT YOU NEED

● Required
○ Suggested
▲ Not required

	UK	Germany	USA	Canada	Australia	Ireland	Netherlands	Spain
Passport/National Identity Card	▲	●	●	●	●	▲	●	●
Visa	▲	▲	▲	▲	▲	▲	▲	▲
Onward or Return Ticket	○	○	○	○	○	▲	○	○
Health Inoculations (tetanus and polio)	▲	▲	▲	▲	▲	▲	▲	▲
Health Documentation (▶ 192, Health)	●	●	●	●	●	▲	●	●
Travel Insurance	○	○	○	○	○	○	○	○
Driving Licence (national)	●	●	●	●	●	●	●	●
Car Insurance Certificate	●	●	n/a	n/a	n/a	●	●	●
Car Registration Document	●	●	n/a	n/a	n/a	●	●	●

WHEN TO GO

Dublin

High season Low season

JAN	FEB	MAR	APR	MAY	JUN	JUL	AUG	SEP	OCT	NOV	DEC
8°C	8°C	10°C	13°C	15°C	18°C	20°C	19°C	17°C	14°C	10°C	8°C
46°F	46°F	50°F	55°F	59°F	64°F	68°F	66°F	63°F	57°F	50°F	46°F

☀ Sun   ☁ Cloud   🌧 Wet

Temperatures are the **average daily maximum** for each month.
The best weather is in spring and early summer (April and June) when the countryside looks its best. Winter (November to March) can be dark, wet and dreary, especially in the mountainous west, but good-weather days can be magical. In high summer (July and August) the weather is changeable and often cloudy. Autumn (September and October) generally sees good weather. The cities are great places to visit at any time, regardless of the weather, and Christmas and New Year are particularly popular.
It will almost certainly rain at some time during your stay, no matter when you visit. Be prepared, but try to accept the rain as the Irish do, as a "wet blessing".

In mainland UK
Bord Fáilte (London)
☎ 0800 039 7000
Northern Ireland Tourist Board
(London)
☎ 0800 039 7000

In the USA and Canada
Bord Fáilte and NITB
(New York)
☎ 1-800 223 6470
(Toronto)
☎ 1-800 223 6470

In Australia and New Zealand
Bord Fáilte and NITB
(Sydney)
☎ (02) 9299 6177
(Auckland)
☎ (0) 379 8720

GETTING THERE

By Air Scheduled flights operate from Britain, mainland Europe and North America to Dublin, Cork, Knock, Shannon and Belfast. **Aer Lingus** (tel: 0845 0844 444; www. aerlingus.ie) operates services from London and regional UK airports, many European countries and the US. **Ryanair** (tel: 0871 246 0000; www.ryanair.com) flies to Dublin from airports all over Britain and **British Midland BD** (tel: 0870 60 70 555; www.britishmidland.com) from Heathrow to Dublin and Belfast. Check with your travel agent, the airlines or the Internet for details of other carriers. **Flying time to Dublin:** from mainland UK (1–2 hours), from Europe (2–4 hours), from USA/Canada (8–11 hours), from Australia/New Zealand (24-plus hours). **Flying time to Belfast:** from mainland UK (1–2 hours), from Europe (2–3 hours), from USA/Canada (8–11 hours), from Australia/New Zealand via London (24-plus hours). Some long-haul carriers may offer the London–Belfast section free of charge.

By Sea Most ferry services **from Britain** arrive at Dun Laoghaire and Belfast. **Crossing times:** Holyhead–Dun Laoghaire (99 minutes by HSS); Holyhead–Dublin (3 hours 45 minutes, or under 2 hours by fast ferry); Fishguard–Rosslare (3 hours 30 minutes); Swansea–Cork (10 hours); Stranraer–Belfast (3 hours 30 minutes, or 1 hour by SeaCat, 1 hour 45 minutes by HSS); Cairnryan–Larne (2 hours 15 minutes, or 1 hour by Jetliner); Campbelltown–Ballycastle (3 hours). There are also services **from France** to the Republic: Roscoff–Cork (15 hours); Cherbourg–Rosslare (18 hours). **Ferry companies** operating services to Ireland are **Irish Ferries** (tel: 0870 5171717), **Stena Lines** (tel: 0870 5707070), **Swansea/Cork Ferries** (tel: 01 792 456116) and **Brittany Ferries** (tel: 0870 5360360).

TIME

Ireland is on Greenwich Mean Time (GMT) in winter, but one hour ahead of GMT from late March until late October.

CURRENCY AND FOREIGN EXCHANGE

Currency The monetary units are (in the Republic) the Euro (€), and (in Northern Ireland) the pound sterling (£).
Euro: notes are issued in denominations of 5, 10, 20, 50, 100, 200 and 500 Euros, and **coins** in denominations of 1 and 2 Euros, and 1, 2, 5, 10, 20 and 50 Euro cents.
Pounds sterling: notes are issued in £5, £10, £20 and £50 denominations and **coins** in 1p, 2p, 5p, 10p, 20p, 50p, £1 and £2 denominations by the Bank of England, and in notes of £5, £10, £20 and £50 by the provincial banks. Provincial bank notes are not accepted in other parts of the UK. There are 100 pence in each pound.
Sterling or US dollar **travellers' cheques** are the most convenient way to carry money. All major **credit cards** are recognised.
Exchange Currency exchange bureaux are common in Dublin, Belfast, at airports, sea ports and some rail stations. They often operate longer hours but offer poorer rates of exchange than banks. Many banks have ATMs for cash withdrawals; check with your bank for details.

TIME DIFFERENCES

GMT	Ireland	London	USA (NY)	USA (West Coast)	Sydney
12 noon	12 noon	12 noon	← 7 am	← 4 am	→ 10 pm

WHEN YOU ARE THERE

CLOTHING SIZES

Australia/UK	Rest of Europe	USA	
36	46	36	Suits
38	48	38	
40	50	40	
42	52	42	
44	54	44	
46	56	46	
7	41	8	Shoes
7.5	42	8.5	
8.5	43	9.5	
9.5	44	10.5	
10.5	45	11.5	
11	46	12	
14.5	37	14.5	Shirts
15	38	15	
15.5	39/40	15.5	
16	41	16	
16.5	42	16.5	
17	43	17	
8	34	6	Dresses
10	36	8	
12	38	10	
14	40	12	
16	42	14	
18	44	16	
4.5	38	6	Shoes
5	38	6.5	
5.5	39	7	
6	39	7.5	
6.5	40	8	
7	41	8.5	

NATIONAL HOLIDAYS

1 Jan	New Year's Day
17 Mar	St Patrick's Day
Mar/Apr	Good Friday (RI)
Mar/Apr	Easter Monday/Easter Tuesday (NI)
First Mon May	May Holiday
Last Mon May	Spring Holiday (NI)
First Mon Jun	June Holiday (RI)
12 Jul	Orangeman's Day (NI)
First Mon Aug	August Holiday (RI)
Last Mon Aug	Late Summer Holiday (NI)
Last Mon Oct	October Holiday (RI)
25 Dec	Christmas Day
26 Dec	Boxing Day/St Stephen's Day

OPENING HOURS

○ Shops	● Post Offices
● Offices	● Museums/Monuments
● Banks	● Pharmacies

8 am 9 am 10 am noon 1 pm 2 pm 4 pm 5 pm 7 pm

☐ Day   ☐ Midday   ☐ Evening

Shops Some open until 8 or 9 pm for late-night shopping on Thursday and Friday. Smaller towns and rural areas have an early closing day (1 pm) on one day a week.
Banks Nearly all banks are closed on Saturday. In smaller towns they may close for lunch (12:30–1:30 pm).
Post Offices Many close at 1 pm.
Museums/Tourist Sites Hours vary. Many smaller places close Oct–Mar or have limited opening.

POLICE 999

FIRE 999

AMBULANCE 999

COASTAL RESCUE 999

PERSONAL SAFETY

The national police forces are:
RI – Garda Siochána
(pronounced *sheekawnah*) in
black-and-blue uniforms.
**NI – Police Service of Northern
Ireland** (PSNI) in dark green
uniforms.

- Be wary in suburban areas
  of Belfast, which may be
  prone to sectarian violence.
- Take care of personal
  property in Dublin.
- Avoid leaving property
  visible in cars.

Police assistance:
 999 from any phone

TELEPHONES

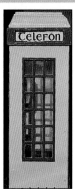

Telephone boxes
are: (RI) grey, or
green-and-white;
(NI) red, or Perspex-
and-metal booths. Payphones
accept: (RI) 10, 20 and 50
cents and €1 coins; (NI) 10p,
20p, 50p and £1 coins.
Callcards (RI) or phonecards
(NI) are also widely accepted,
sold at post offices and newsstands. For the domestic operator, dial: (RI) 10; (NI) 100. For
the international operator, dial:
(RI) 114; (NI) 155.

International Dialling Codes
Dial 00 followed by

UK:	**44** (from RI only; no code from NI)
USA/Canada:	**1**
Australia:	**61**
Germany:	**49**
Spain:	**34**

POST

In the Republic, mail boxes
and vans are painted green.
You can buy stamps from post
offices, machines or some
newsstands. In the North, mail
boxes and vans are red; British
stamps are used and British
postal rates apply.

ELECTRICITY

The power supply is: 230
volts (RI); 240 volts (NI).

Type of socket:
3-square-pin (UK
type). Parts of the
Republic also
have 2-round-pin
(continental type).
Overseas visitors
should bring an adaptor.

TIPS/GRATUITIES

Yes ✓   No ✗

Restaurants (service not included)	✓	10%
Bar service	✗	
Tour guides	✓	(RI) €1; (NI) 50p/£1
Hairdressers	✓	(RI) €1; (NI) 50p/£1
Taxis	✓	10%
Chambermaids	✓	discretion
Porters	✓	discretion
Lavatories	✗	

EMBASSIES AND CONSULATES

UK	**USA**	**Australia**	**Canada**	**Germany**
01 269 5211 (RI)	01 668 8777 (RI)	01 676 1517 (RI)	01 478 1988 (RI)	01 269 3011 (RI)
	028 9032 8239 (NI)	020 7379 4334 (NI)	020 7258 6600 (NI)	028 2954 4188 (NI)

HEALTH

Insurance
Nationals of EU and certain other countries can get medical treatment in Ireland with Form E111 (not required by UK nationals), although medical insurance is still advised, and is essential for all other visitors.

Dental Services
EU nationals, or nationals of other countries with which Ireland has a reciprocal agreement, can get dental treatment within the Irish health service with Form E111 (not needed for UK nationals). Others should take out private medical insurance.

Weather
The sunniest months are May and June (average 5–7 hours of sun a day in the southeast), although July and August are the hottest. During these months you should "cover up", use a good sunscreen and drink plenty of fluids.

Drugs
Prescription and non-prescription drugs are available from pharmacies. Pharmacists can advise on medication for common ailments. When closed, most pharmacies display notices giving details of the nearest one that is open.

Safe Water
Tap water is safe to drink. Mineral water is widely available but is often expensive, particularly in restaurants.

CONCESSIONS

Students Holders of an International Student Identity Card can buy a Travelsave Stamp which entitles them to travel discounts including a 50 per cent reduction on Bus Éireann, Iarnród Éireann and Irish Ferries (between Britain and Ireland). Contact a student travel agency for further details. The Travelsave Stamp can be purchased from USIT, 19 Aston Quay, O'Connell Bridge, Dublin 2 (tel: 01 602 1600).

Senior Citizens Discounts on transport and admission fees are usually available on proof of age.

TRAVELLING WITH A DISABILITY

Increasing numbers of hotels and other public buildings are being adapted or specially built to cater for travellers with disabilities. Helpful booklets for further information are *Guide for Disabled Persons* and *Accommodation Guide for Disabled Persons*, both available from National Rehabilitation Board, 25 Clyde Road, Dublin 4 (☎ 01 668 4181).

CHILDREN

Well-behaved children are generally made welcome everywhere. Public houses operate individual admittance policies. In the North there are designated areas for children in most pubs. Concessions on transport and entrance fees are available.

LAVATORIES

Public lavatories are usually clean and safe. Some are coin-entry, others are free.

WILDLIFE SOUVENIRS

Importing wildlife souvenirs sourced from rare or endangered species may be illegal or require a special permit. Before purchase, you should check your home country's customs regulations.

Atlas

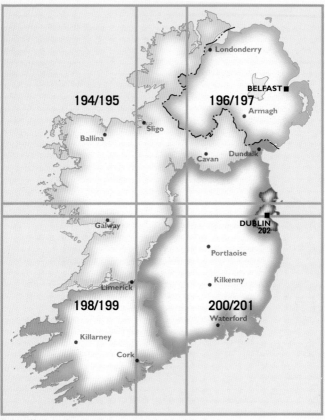

194/195

196/197

Londonderry

BELFAST ■

Armagh

Sligo

Ballina

Cavan

Dundalk

Galway

DUBLIN ■
202

Portlaoise

Kilkenny

198/199

200/201

Limerick

Waterford

Killarney

Cork

To identify the regions see the map on the inside of the front cover

Key to Regional Maps

—··—··— International boundary

▭▭▭▭▭ Motorway

━━━━━ Major route

░░░░░ Main road

————— Other road

  Built-up area

□ City

▫ Major town

○ Other town

○ Village

▨ Featured place of interest

■ Place of interest

✈ Airport

| 0 | 10 | 20 | 30 | 40 km |
| 0 | | 10 | 20 | 30 miles |

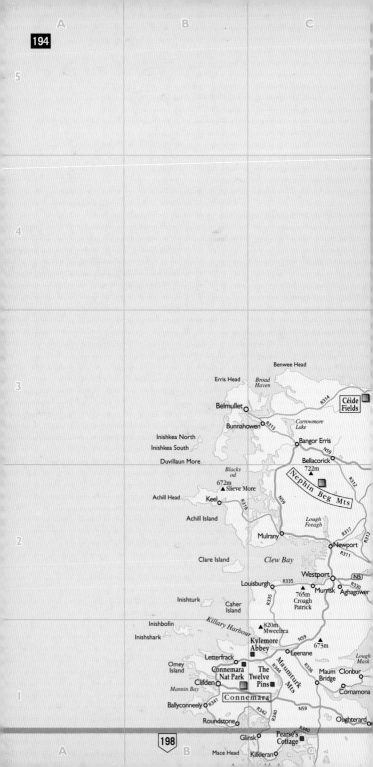

Benwee Head

Erris Head · *Broad Haven*

Belmullet

Bunnahowen · R313 · *Carrowmore Lake*

Inishkea North

Inishkea South

Duvillaun More

Bangor Erris

N59 · Bellacorick

R314 · **Céide Fields**

722m · **Nephin Beg Mts** · R312

Blacks od

672m ▲ Slieve More

Achill Head · Keel · R319 · N59

Achill Island

Lough Feeagh · R317 · R312

Mulrany · Newport · R311

Clare Island · *Clew Bay*

Westport · N5

Louisburgh · R335 · R335 · Murrisk · R330 · Aghagower

765m · Croagh Patrick

Inishturk · Caher Island

Inishbofin

Inishshark

Killary Harbour · ▲820m Mweelrea

Kylemore Abbey · N59 · 673m ▲ · *Lough Mask*

Leenane

Letterfrack · **Maumturk Mts** · R336 · Maum Bridge · Clonbur

Omey Island · **Connemara Nat Park** · The Twelve Pins · R344 · Cornamona

Clifden · *Mannin Bay* · **Connemara** · N59 · Oughterard

Ballyconneely · R341 · R342 · R340

Roundstone · R340

198

Glinsk · **Pearse's Cottage**

Mace Head · Kilkieran

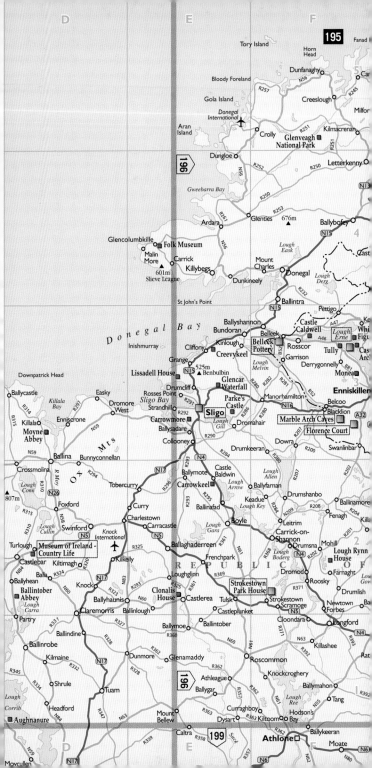

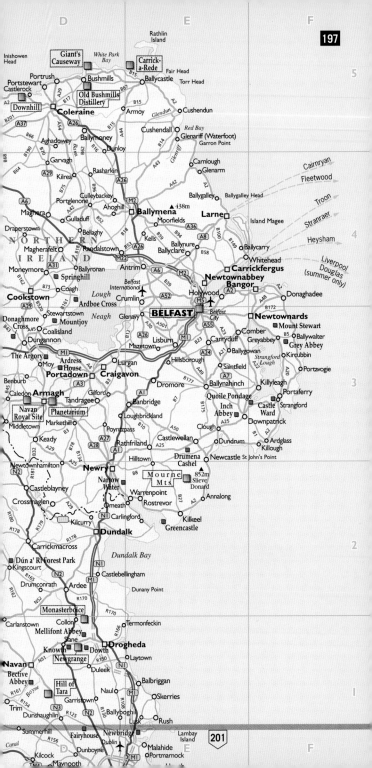

Glinsk
Cottage
Mace Head   Kilkieran
Lettermore Island
Costelloe
Gorumna
Island   Lettermullen
R336
Spiddal

North Sound
Inishmore
Dunaengus   Kilronan
Aran Islands   Inishmaan   Newtown
Inisheer
Lisdoonvarna
Doolin   R478
R477
The

Cliffs of Moher
Liscanor
Hags Head   Ennistymon
Mal Bay   N67
Milltown Malbay   R460
Mutton
Island
Doo Lough
Doonbeg
Donegal Point   N68
Kilkee   Cooraclare
R483
R487   N67   R466
Kilrush   N67
Loghill
Loop Head   Tarbert
Mouth of the
Shannon   Ballylongford   R551   Glin
Ballybunion   R553   Glin
Castle
Ballyduff   Listowel
Kerry Head   Causeway   R551   Feal   R555
Ballyheige   N69   Abbeyfeale   N21
Ballyheige   Kilinlea   Mullagh
Bay   R551   357m   M
Rough   Ardfert
Point   Stacks Mts   R576
Brandon   Tralee Bay   Tralee
Head
Ballydavid Head   953m   Cloghane   R560   N21   Castleisland
Brandon Mtn   828m   Camp   852m   N22   R577   R578
Sybil Point   Gallarus   Beenoskee   Slieve Mish Mts   N70   Scartaglen
Oratory   Kilmalkedar   Anascaul   R561   Farranfore   N23   Ballydesmond
Dunquin   R559   Church   Castlemaine   R561   Kerry County
Great Blasket   Ventry   Dingle   Killorglin   Milltown   N22   Rathmore
Island   Slea Head   N72   Lough   Killarney   Muckross   R582
Dingle Bay   Glenbeigh   N70   Caragh   Leane   Killarney   N72
Ring of Kerry   1041m   Killarney   Muckross   Poulgorm
Doulus Head   Carrauntoohil   National Park   Muckross   Bridge
774m   N71   House   Derrynasaggart
Valentia   Cahersiveen   Mullaghanattin   R568   Kilgarvan   R569   Mts
Island   Macgillycuddy's Reeks   Kilgarvan   Lee   R584
Portmagee   R565   N70   Ring of Kerry   Kenmare   Ballingeary
Skellig   Waterville   Staigue   Sneem   N70   R571   Ballingeary
Michael   Bolus Head   Fort   Tahilla   707m   R585
Caherdaniel   Castlecove   R573   Laragh   Knockboy   Bandon   R585
Derrynane   Kenmare   Glengarriff   Garinish   Dunmanway
Scariff   Ardgroom   River   Caha Mts   Glengarriff   Island   R586
Island   R571   R574   Bantry   R593
Cod's   686m   Adrigole   R572   Leap   Drimoleague
Head   Allihies   R575   Castletown   Durrus   N71   Glandore
Dursey   R572   Bearhaven   Bantry Bay   Ballydehob   Castle
Island   Bear Island   Dunmanus Bay   Schull   Skibbereen   R595
Muntervary or   R592   Toormore   Glandore
Sheep's Head   Goleen   R595   Toe Head
Mizen Head   Crookhaven   Baltimore
Signal Station   Mizen Head   Sherkin
Roaringwater Bay   Island
Cape   Clear
Fastnet   Clear   Island   Castle
Lighthouse

A   B   C

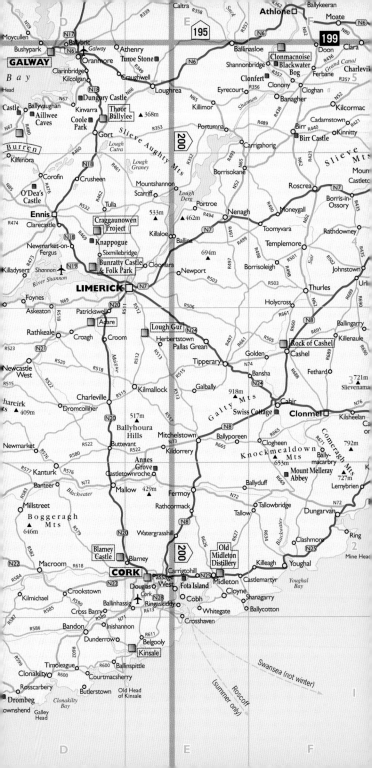

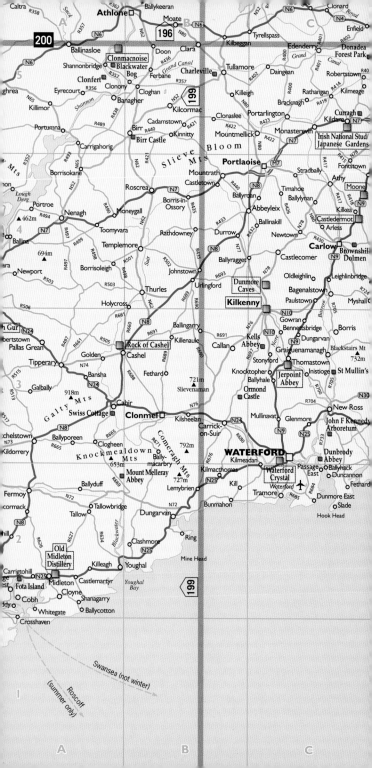

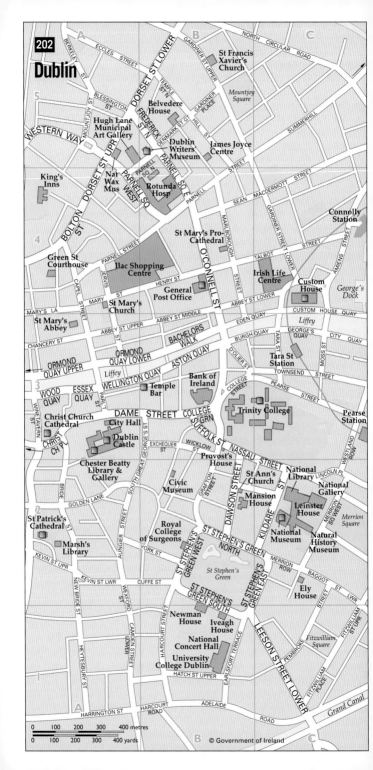

Index

Picture credits

Abbreviations for terms appearing below: (t) top; (b) bottom; (l) left; (r) right; (c) centre.

Front and back cover (t), AA Photo Library/Steve Whitehorn; (ct), AA Photo Library/ Stephen Hill; (cb), AA Photo Library/Christopher Hill; (b), AA Photo Library/Michael Diggin.

The Automobile Association wishes to thank the following photographers, libraries and associations for their assistance in the preparation of this book.

AKG, London 16t, 26, 27t; BORD FAILTE-IRISH TOURIST BOARD 81, 96b, 106; BRIDGEMAN ART LIBRARY, LONDON 48t MS 58 fol.291v Portrait of St. John, page preceding the Gospel of St. John, Irish (vellum) Book of Kells, (c.800) The Board of Trinity College Dublin, 50/1 MS 58 fol.34r Chi-Rho (Greek initials for Christ) Gospel of St. Matthew, chapter 1 verse 18, Irish (vellum) Book of Kells, (c. 800) The Board of Trinity College Dublin; BRUCE COLEMAN COLLECTION 174, 175; CORBIS UK 2 (i) (Michael St Maur Sheil), 2 (ii) (Michael St Maur Sheil), 2 (iii) (Macduff Everton), 5 (Michael St Maur Sheil), 6b (Werner Forman), 33 (Michael St Maur Sheil), 45 (Macduff Everton), 49t (Michael St Maur Sheil); MICHAEL DIGGIN 132/3, 191cl; MARY EVANS PICTURE LIBRARY 14, 15t, 16/7, 16c, 18/9, 19, 20/1t, 20, 20/1c, 21, 27b; GUINNESS ARCHIVES, St James' Gate, Dublin 8. 15r; ROBERT HARDING PICTURE LIBRARY 124/5; CHRISTOPHER HILL PHOTOGRAPHIC LIBRARY 9b, 13b, 148c; HULTON GETTY 8, 152; ILLUSTRATED LONDON NEWS 52b; IMAGES COLOUR LIBRARY 13t, 30, 104/5, 149b, 154/5, 183; IMAGOS/CHRIS COE 3 (i), 86, 107, 110, 119, 124, 126/7; NATIONAL MUSEUM OF IRELAND 54, 54/5, 56; REX FEATURES LTD 17, 29l, 29r, 31c; SLIDEFILE 3 (iii), 12, 24/5, 49b, 55, 75 t, 83r, 97t, 101, 102/3, 134 b, 138, 148b, 160/1, 163, 164, 171; SPECTRUM COLOUR LIBRARY 99; TONY STONE IMAGES 130/1; WATERFORD CRYSTAL 75c, 78; WORLD PICTURES LTD 2 (v), 22, 48c, 93, 98, 98/9.

The remaining photographs are held in the Association's own photo library (AA PHOTO LIBRARY) and were taken by Chris Coe with the exception of the following: Liam Blake 130, 177; Jamie Blandford 100; Steve Day 10/11, 64, 121b; Michael Diggin 102, 105, 122t, 191cr; Derek Forss 63b, 108; Chris Hill 23t, 31t, 123b, 137, 179r; Stephen Hill 6/7, 96t, 109, 122b, 128, 129, 134c, 187, 191t; Caroline Jones 23b; Tom King 48b; Jill Jennings 149t; Simon McBride 47b; George Munday 3 (ii), 145, 155, 184, 185, 186; Michael Short 2 (iv), 23c, 28/9, 63t, 71, 74c, 76/7, 80, 88, 135; SlideFile 53, 62, 87; Bernard Stonehouse 97b; Stephen Whitehorne 15r, 32, 47t, 52t, 57t, 57b, 58, 58/9, 60t, 60b, 173; Peter Zöeller 7cr, 81/2/3, 112.

Acknowledgements

The author would like to thank John Lahiffe and Katrina Doherty of the Irish Tourist Board for their help during the research of this book and Olcan Masterson for contributing his personal view of Ireland on page 6.

Extract from *Decline and Fall* by Evelyn Waugh (Copyright ©Evelyn Waugh 1928) on page 9 reproduced with kind permission of Peters, Fraser & Dunlop on behalf of the Evelyn Waugh Trust.

Extract from *Experiences of an Irish RM* on page 8 reproduced with permission of Curtis Brown Group Ltd, London, on behalf of the Estate of Somerville & Ross. Copyright ©Somerville & Ross, 1908.

Extract on page 9 from *An Evil Cradling* by Brian Keenan, published by Hutchinson. Reprinted by permission of The Random House Group Ltd.

Questionnaire

Dear Traveler

Your comments, opinions and recommendations are very important to us. So please help us to improve our travel guides by taking a few minutes to complete this simple questionnaire.

Send to: Spiral Guides, MailStop 66, 1000 AAA Drive, Heathrow, FL 32746–5063

Your recommendations...

We always encourage readers' recommendations for restaurants, nightlife or shopping – if your recommendation is added to the next edition of the guide, we will send you a FREE AAA Spiral Guide of your choice. Please state below the establishment name, location and your reasons for recommending it.

_____

_____

_____

_____

_____

Please send me AAA Spiral_____

(see list of titles inside the back cover)

About this guide...

Which title did you buy?

_____ **AAA Spiral**

Where did you buy it? _____

When? m m/ y y

Why did you choose a AAA Spiral Guide? _____

_____

_____

_____

Did this guide meet your expectations?

Exceeded ☐   Met all ☐   Met most ☐   Fell below ☐

Please give your reasons _____

_____

_____

_____

continued on next page...

Were there any aspects of this guide that you particularly liked?

Is there anything we could have done better?

About you...

Name (Mr/Mrs/Ms) ______

Address ______

______ Zip ______

Daytime tel nos. ______

Which age group are you in?

Under 25 ☐ 25–34 ☐ 35–44 ☐ 45–54 ☐ 55–64 ☐ 65+ ☐

How many trips do you make a year?

Less than one ☐ One ☐ Two ☐ Three or more ☐

Are you a AAA member? Yes ☐ No ☐

Name of AAA club ______

About your trip...

When did you book? m m/ y y When did you travel? m m/ y y

How long did you stay? ______

Was it for business or leisure? ______

Did you buy any other travel guides for your trip? ☐ Yes ☐ No

If yes, which ones? ______

Thank you for taking the time to complete this questionnaire.

All information is for AAA internal use only and will NOT be distributed outside the organization to any third parties.